TATSUYA TANAKA

MINIATURE TRIP AROUND THE WORLD

NIPPAN IPS Co., Ltd.

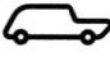
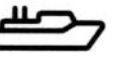

It's a Small World

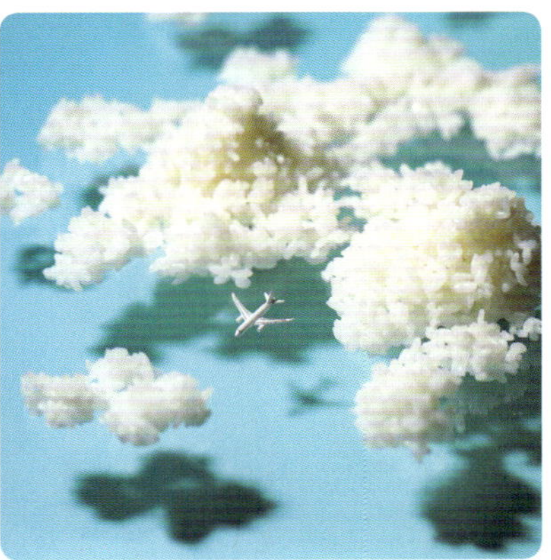

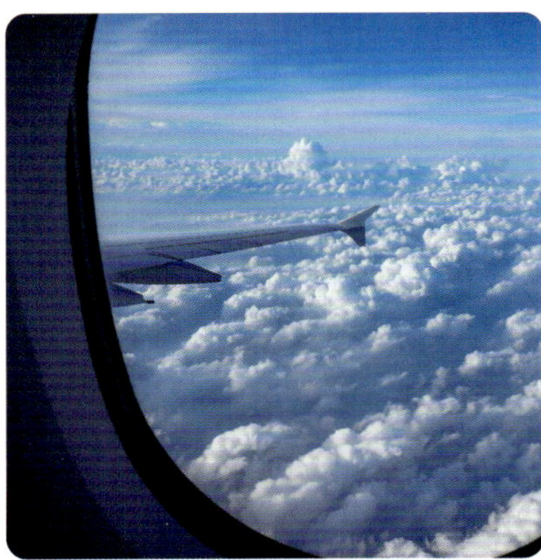

Have a rice trip!

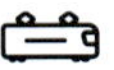

 Every day, for more than a decade, I've been sharing my work on the internet and people from all over the world have taken a look. My pieces use "mitate," they strive to liken one thing to another, so it's important that I seek out motifs that will be understood by everyone, regardless of their age, gender and nationality. With that in mind, when I travel abroad, rather than focus on unique cultural traits, I look for things we have in common, similarities in our toilets and toilet paper, the universal roundness of manholes, the flavor of McDonald's fries... Through my work, I have come to believe that if we can see our similarities and feel sympathy for one another, it will ultimately lead us to world peace. It's just like the words in that song, "It's a small world after all."
 Traveling in the small world in this book, I hope you will feel closer to the real world. And when you're done reading it, I urge you to travel abroad. It's a small world, so you should be able to go anywhere.

Tatsuya Tanaka

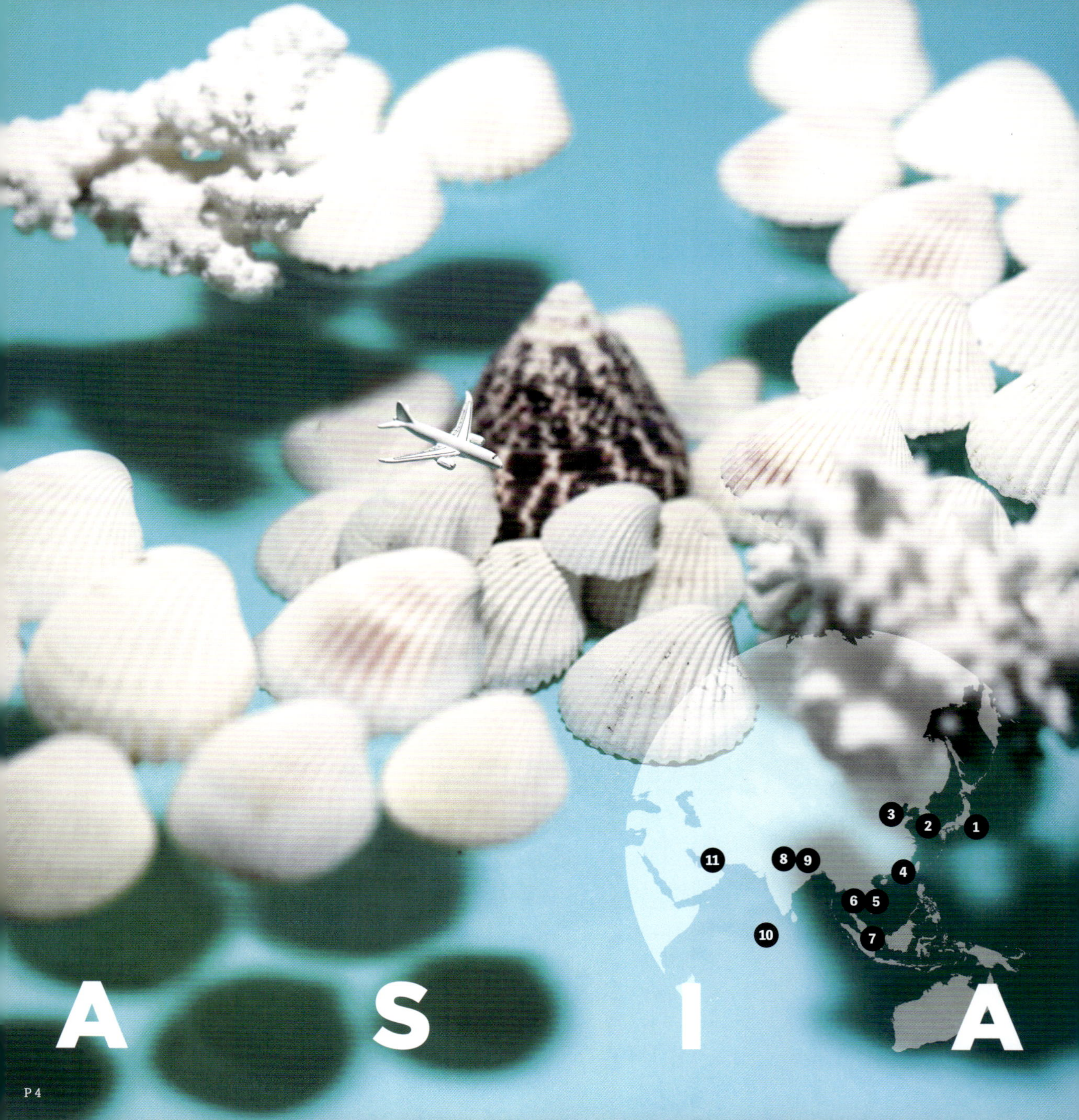

ASIA

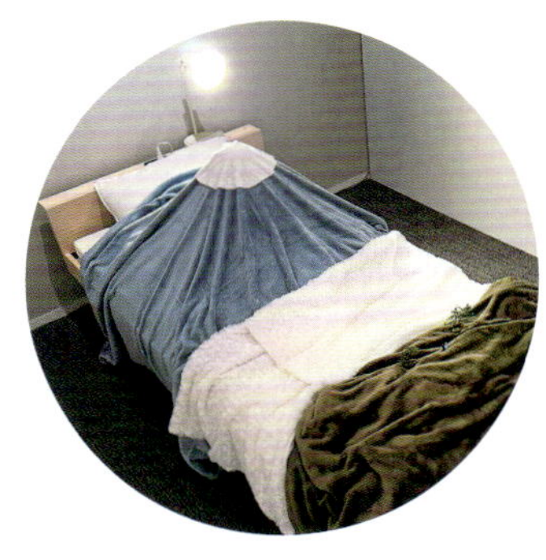

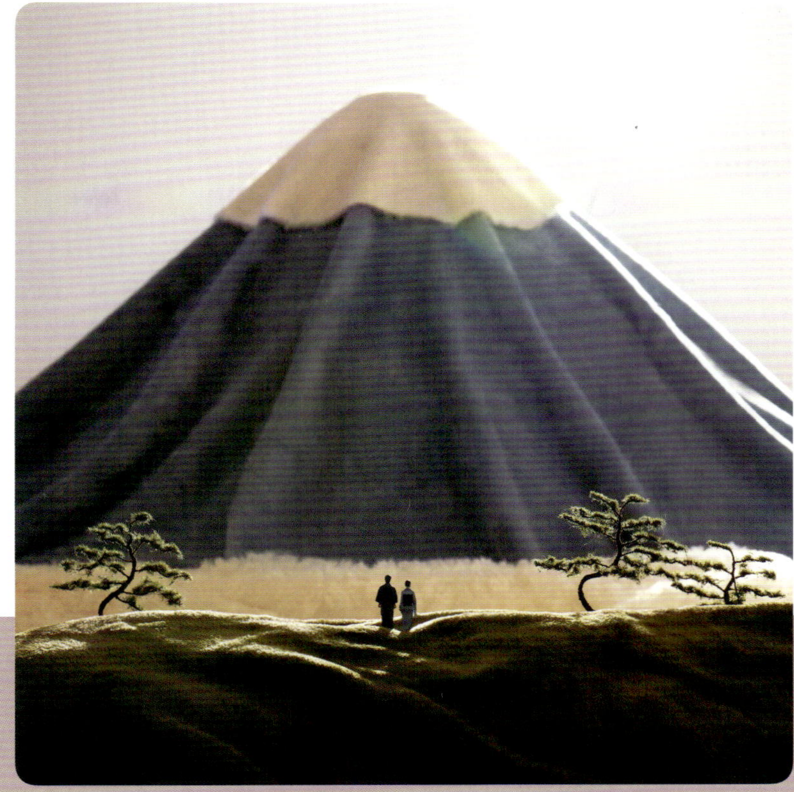

Finding Mount Fuji

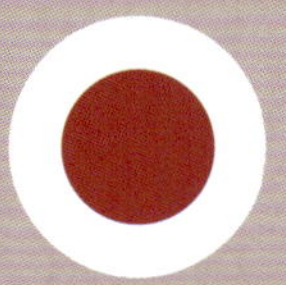

JAPAN

MT.FUJI

Returning from overseas, stranded in a hotel for a 3-day quarantine, Tanaka-san used bed sheets, towels and blankets to depict Mt. Fuji. A bedside light became the sun.

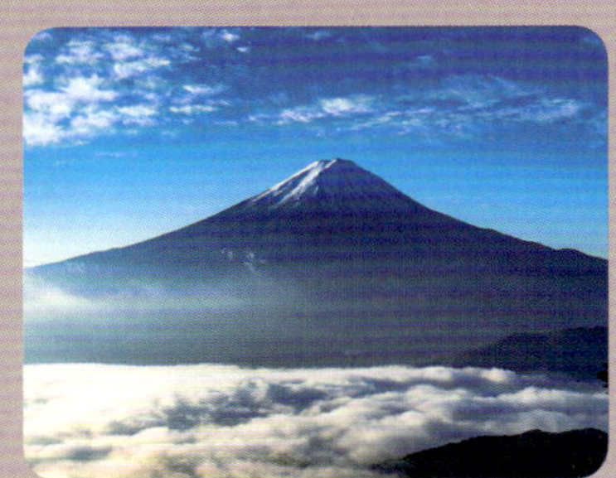

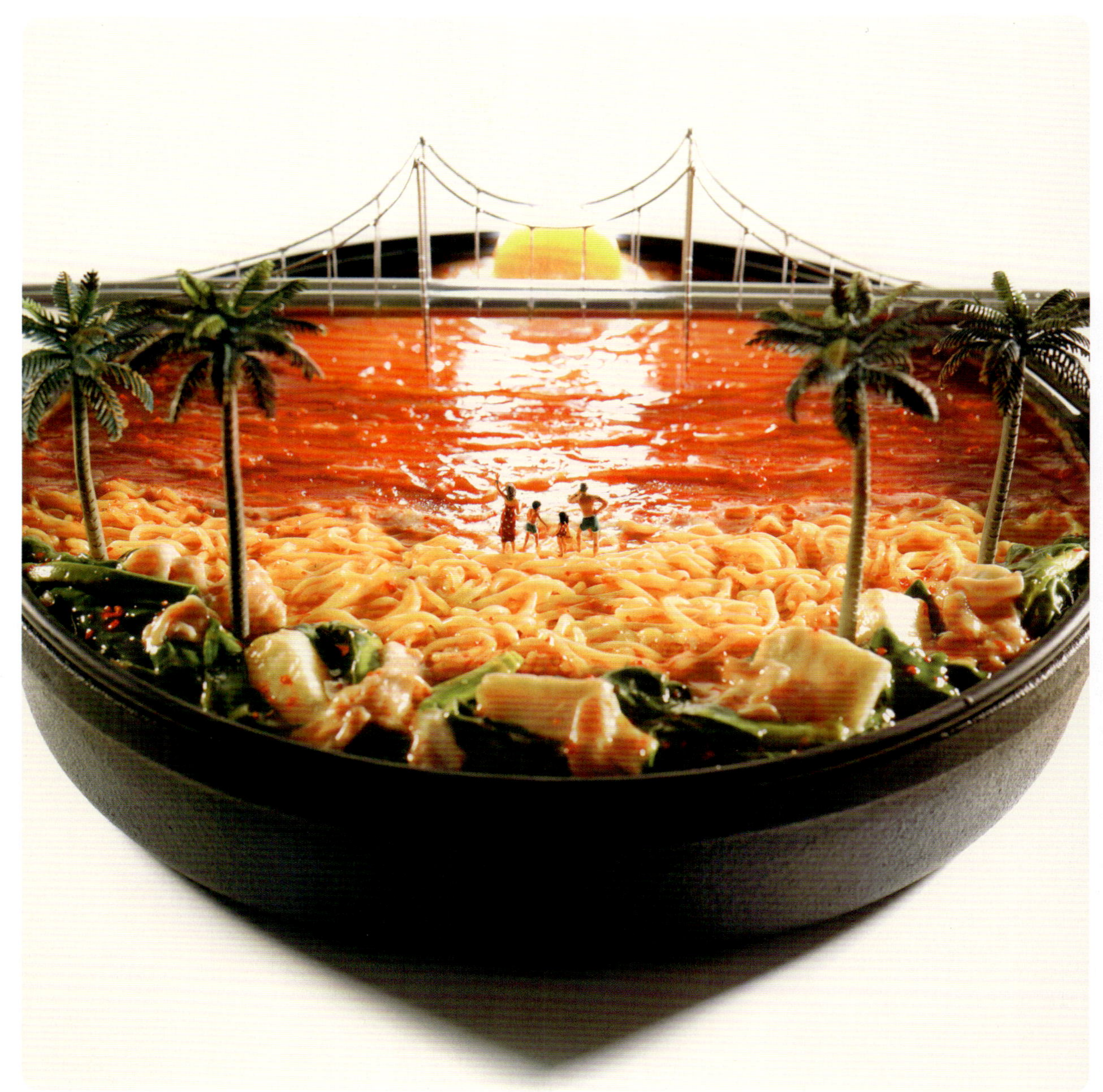

Gwangalli Beach

REPUBLIC OF KOREA

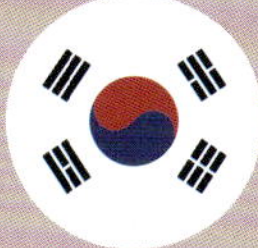

GWANGANDAEGYO BRIDGE

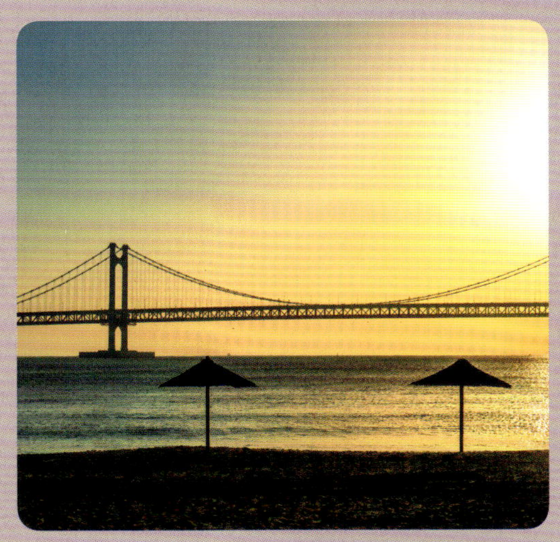

Also known as Diamond Bridge, this suspension bridge is more than 7 kilometers long which makes it the second longest in South Korea. Located in Busan, the bridge is best viewed from Gwangalli Beach at sunset or during nightly LED light shows that change seasonally. When the sun sets behind the bridge it looks like a big raw egg being added to a traditional Korean spicy hot pot dish. Silver metal Korean chopsticks and toothpicks become the bridge and the sun's last light turns the ocean into a spicy red soup. The noodles are Gwangalli Beach.

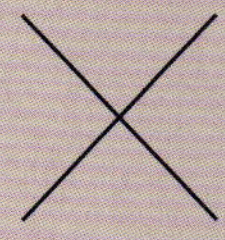

JJIGAE

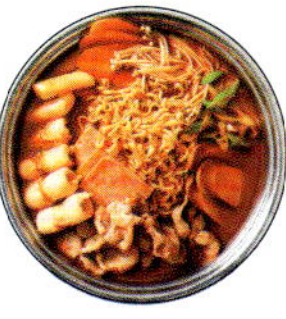

This spicy Korean hot pot usually has meat, seafood and vegetables and is flavored with red chili paste, soy bean paste and soy sauce. It is also popular in Japan where it is called chige nabe and often makes use of kimchi and pork belly for flavor.

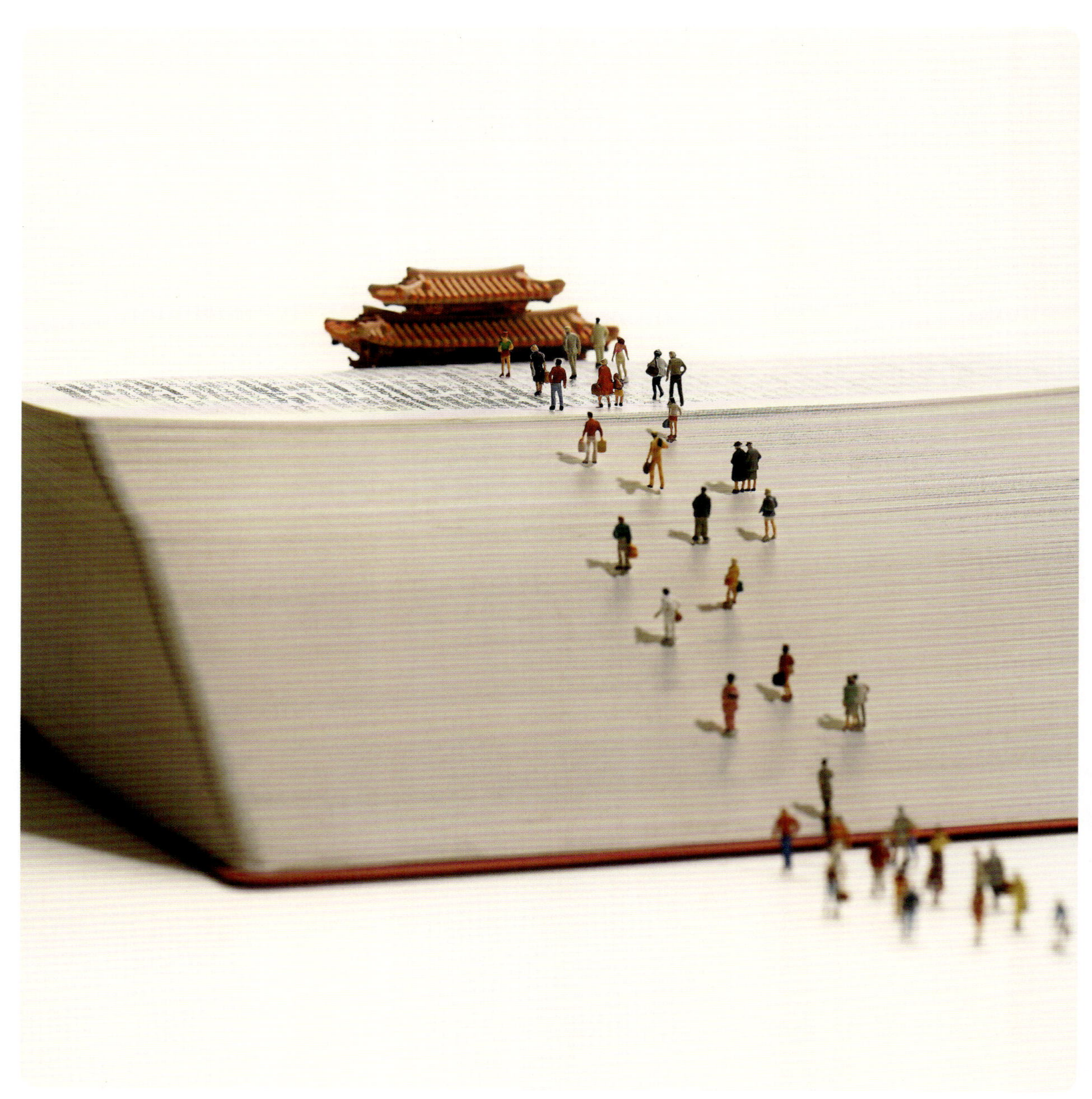

Stairway to History

PEOPLE'S REPUBLIC OF CHINA

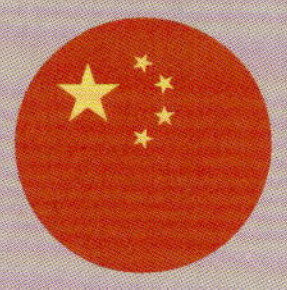

THE FORBIDDEN CITY

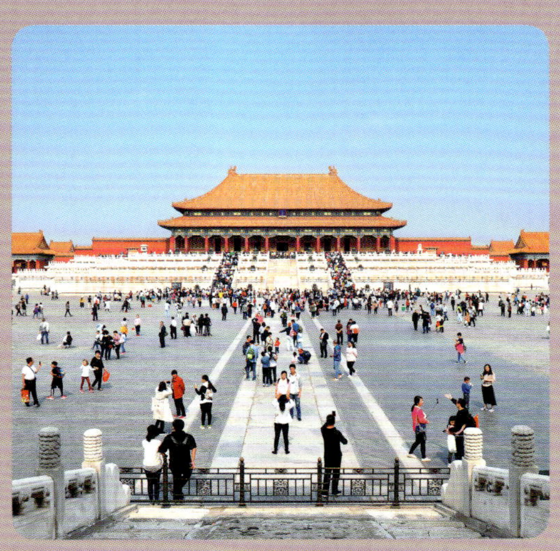

Built early in the 15th century, this immense palace compound located in Beijing was home to 24 of China's emperors over a period of more than 500 years. The complex has nearly 1000 buildings and is one of the best preserved wooden compounds in the world. Apparently about 1 million workers were needed to build it. Some of the largest stones used may have been pulled on icy roads from a quarry 70 kilometers from Beijing. The roof tiles were shaped such that they were difficult for a bird to land on so the city was forbidden to ordinary people and to birds.

DICTIONARY

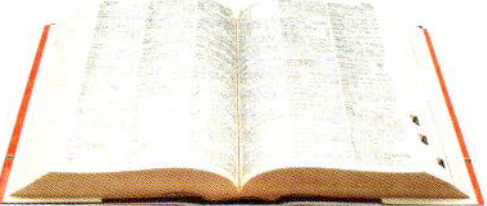

A dictionary, like an ancient palace, contains an accumulation of culture. Climbing the side of an open dictionary one finds a steep path into the past. Sometimes, along the way, we encounter even more than we can comprehend.

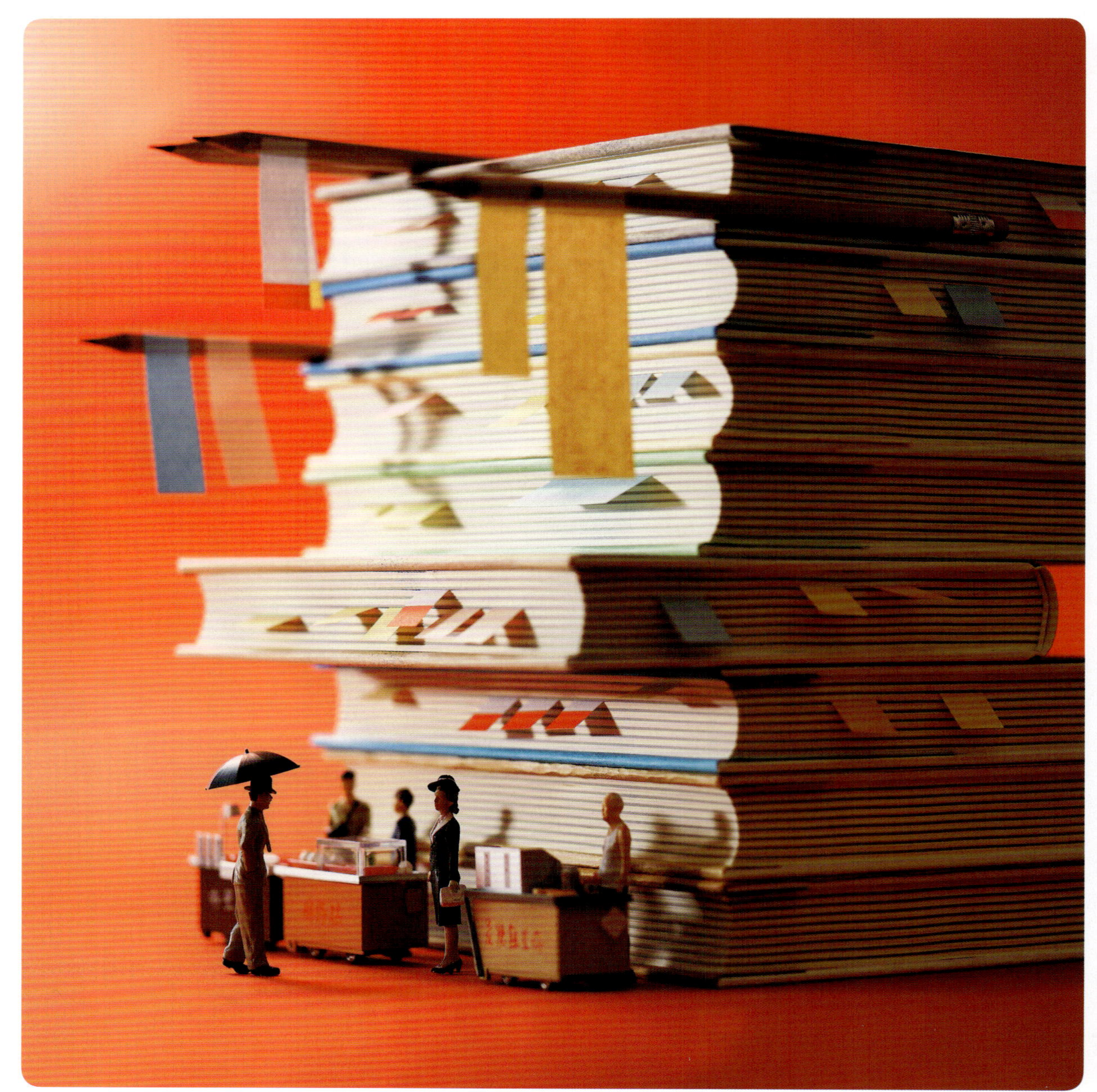

Hong Kong Night Scene

PEOPLE'S REPUBLIC OF CHINA

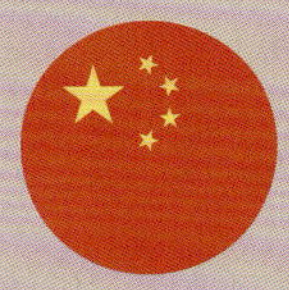

HONG KONG

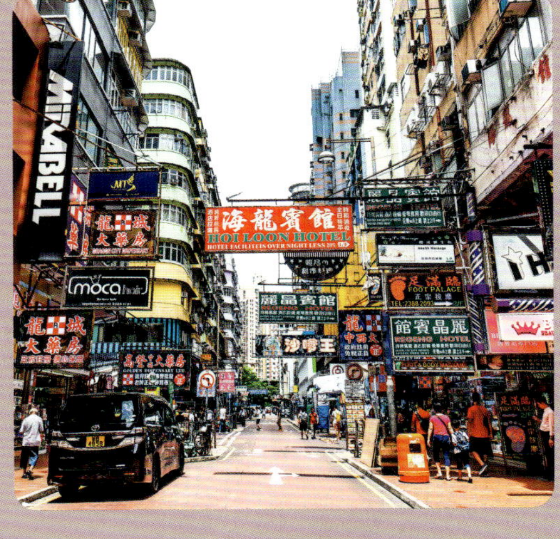

Buildings in Hong Kong come in all sorts of sizes and colors. They're often covered with bright signage and creatively bedecked with laundry, hence the colorful sticky notes. The people present in this scene reflect the international, cultural melting pot character of this city. The city's location and history are certainly in a large part responsible for this dynamism, and for the variety of dishes available in the food carts, food trucks and markets. The name Hong Kong means "fragrant harbor" and these foods certainly add to the city's fragrance.

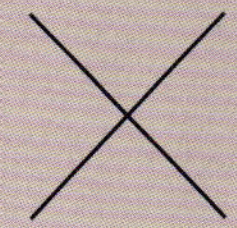

STICKY NOTES

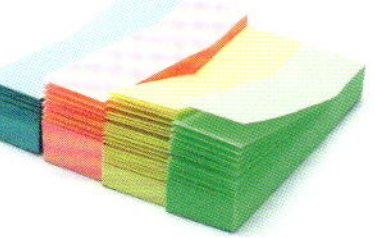

This low-adhesion technology was accidentally discovered in 1968 but sticky notes didn't go on sale until 1980. They were originally a canary yellow color because that was the color of the scrap paper that happened to be available in a nearby lab.

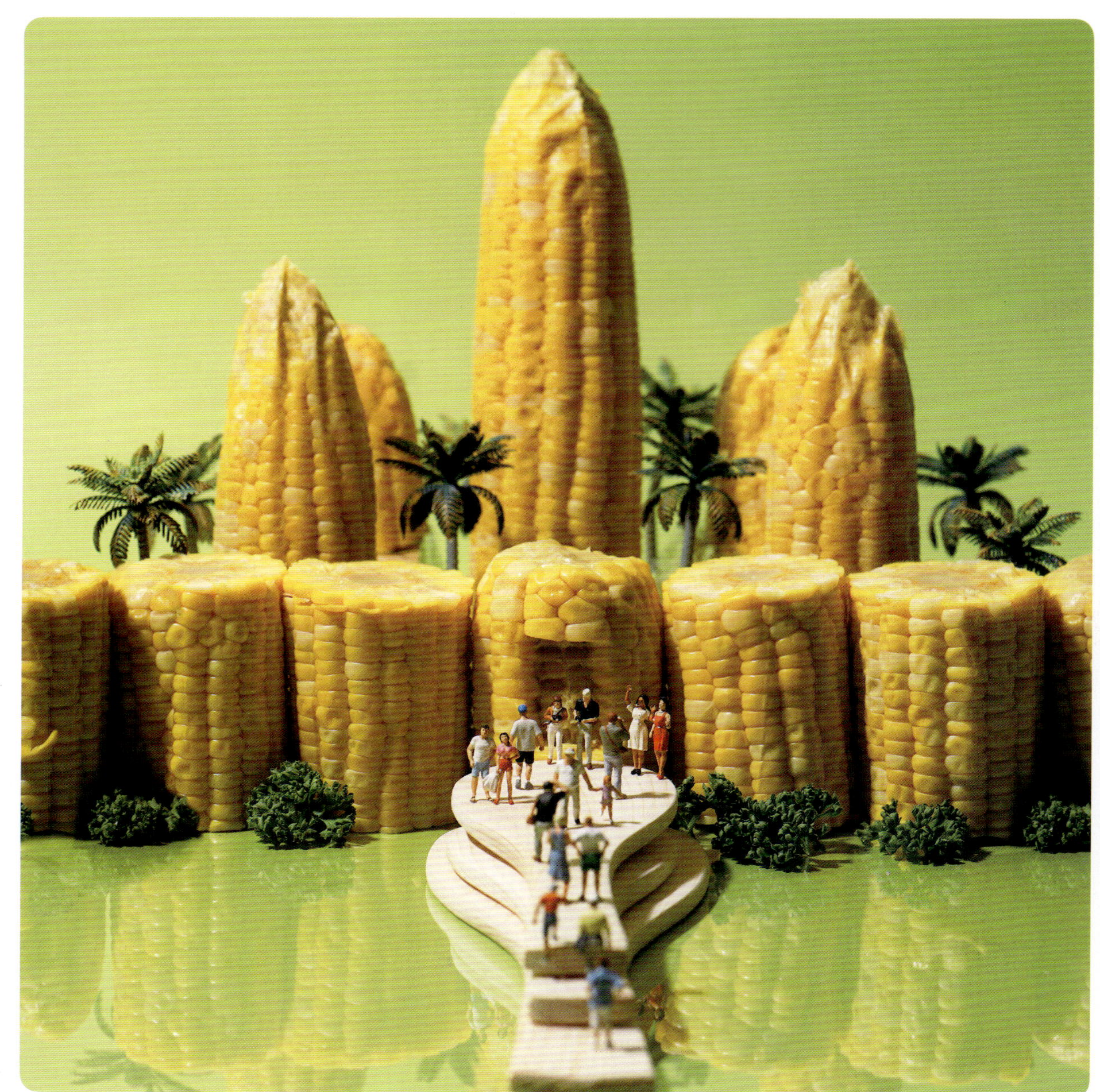

Angcorn Wat

CAMBODIA

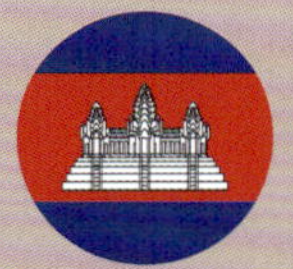

ANGKOR WAT

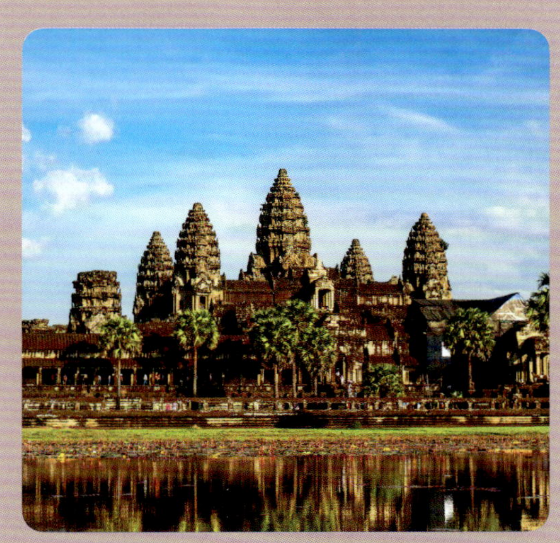

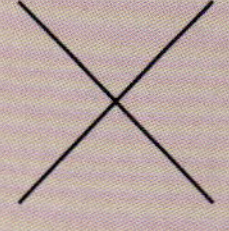

Apparently Angkor Wat is the largest religious monument on the planet. That's a lot of corn! Angkor Wat started out as a Hindu temple but eventually became a Buddhist temple. The shape of the temple is meant to resemble Mt. Meru, a five-peak mountain located at the center of the universe in Hindu mythology. Brahma, Vishnu and Shiva are thought to live there. Inscriptions carved in the rock suggest that it took 35 years, 6,000 elephants and 300,000 workers to build Angkor Wat. It was built in the first half of the 12th century, without any machinery of course.

CORN

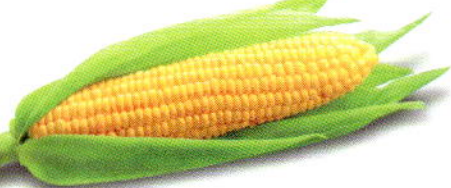

Angkor Wat has a foundation of immense sandstone rocks that were transported to the site on roads and canals. We can imagine that this was much more difficult and time consuming than lining up corn and adding a parsley garnish.

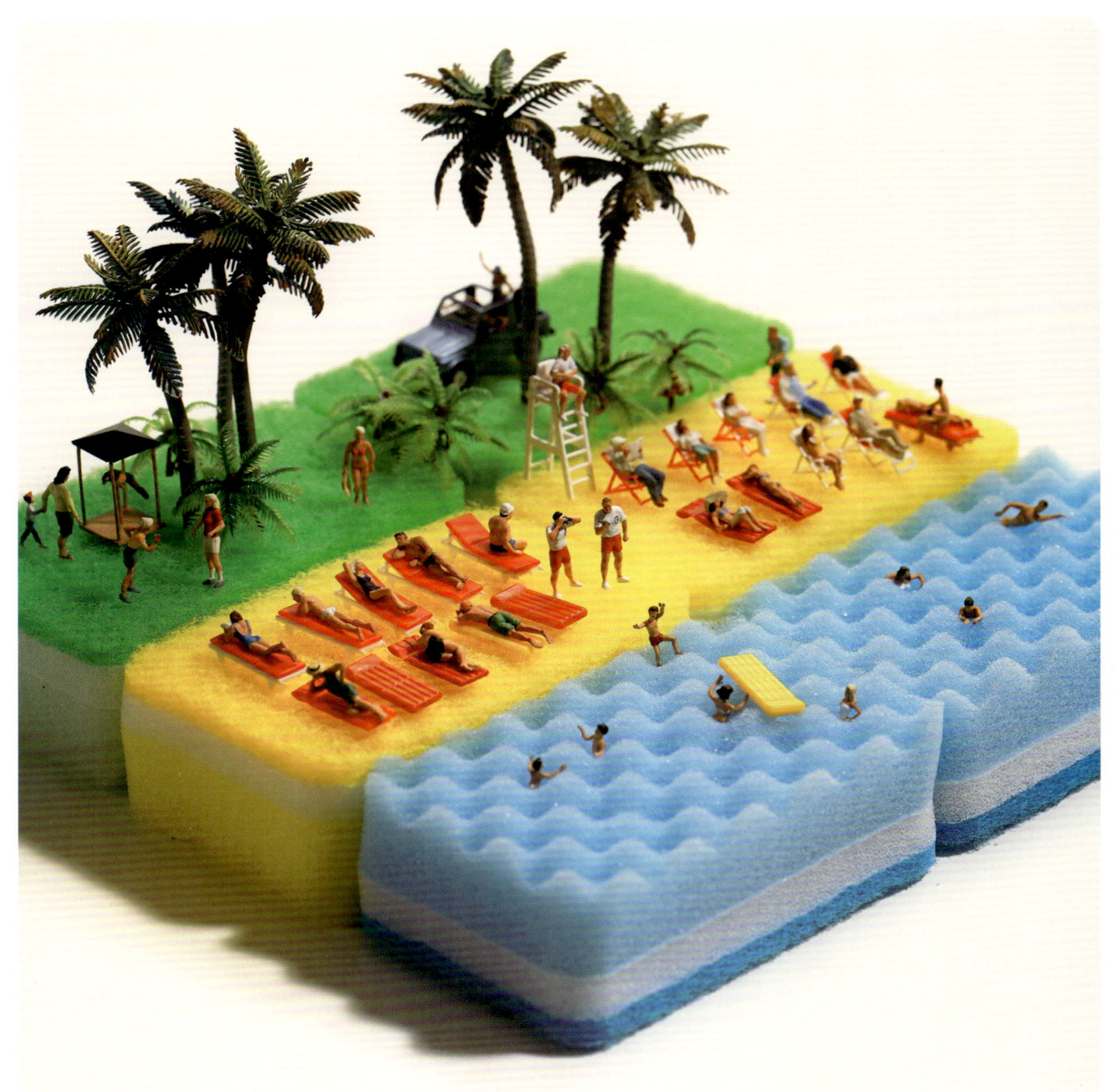

Soaking Up the Summer

THAILAND

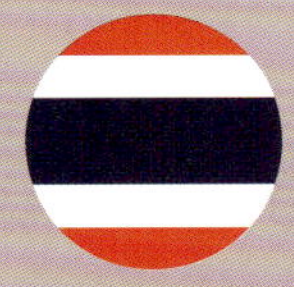

PATTAYA BEACH

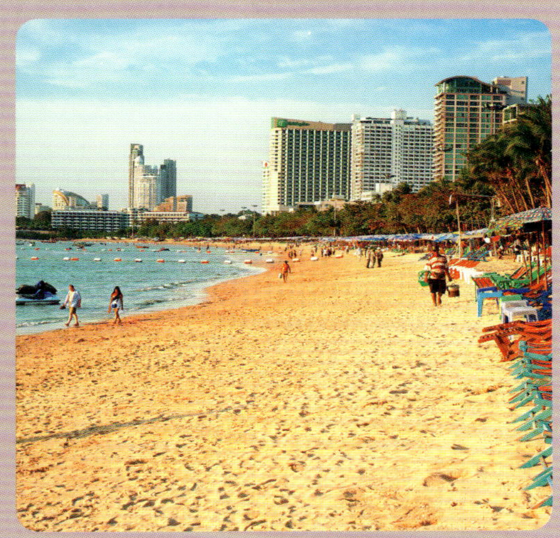

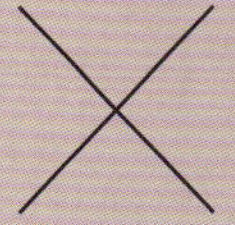

Looking out on a tranquil bay, Pattaya is a beach resort a couple of hours southeast of Bangkok. Once a small fishing village, it became a popular destination in the 1960s and the rest is history. Apparently the beach is 15 kilometers long and the town that borders it has become fairly sizeable. In addition to Thai food, there are lots of other restaurants offering cuisine from all over the world to choose from. And there are a number of islands that are easily accessible by boat from Pattaya. Some are quite small but certainly larger than a sponge.

SPONGES

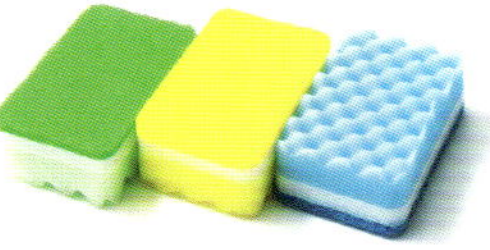

These kitchen sponges were purchased in the Japanese equivalent of a dime store where pretty much everything costs 100 yen, or a dollar. Two packs of sponges suggest a 2-dollar investment. Hiring 30 extras probably costs a lot more.

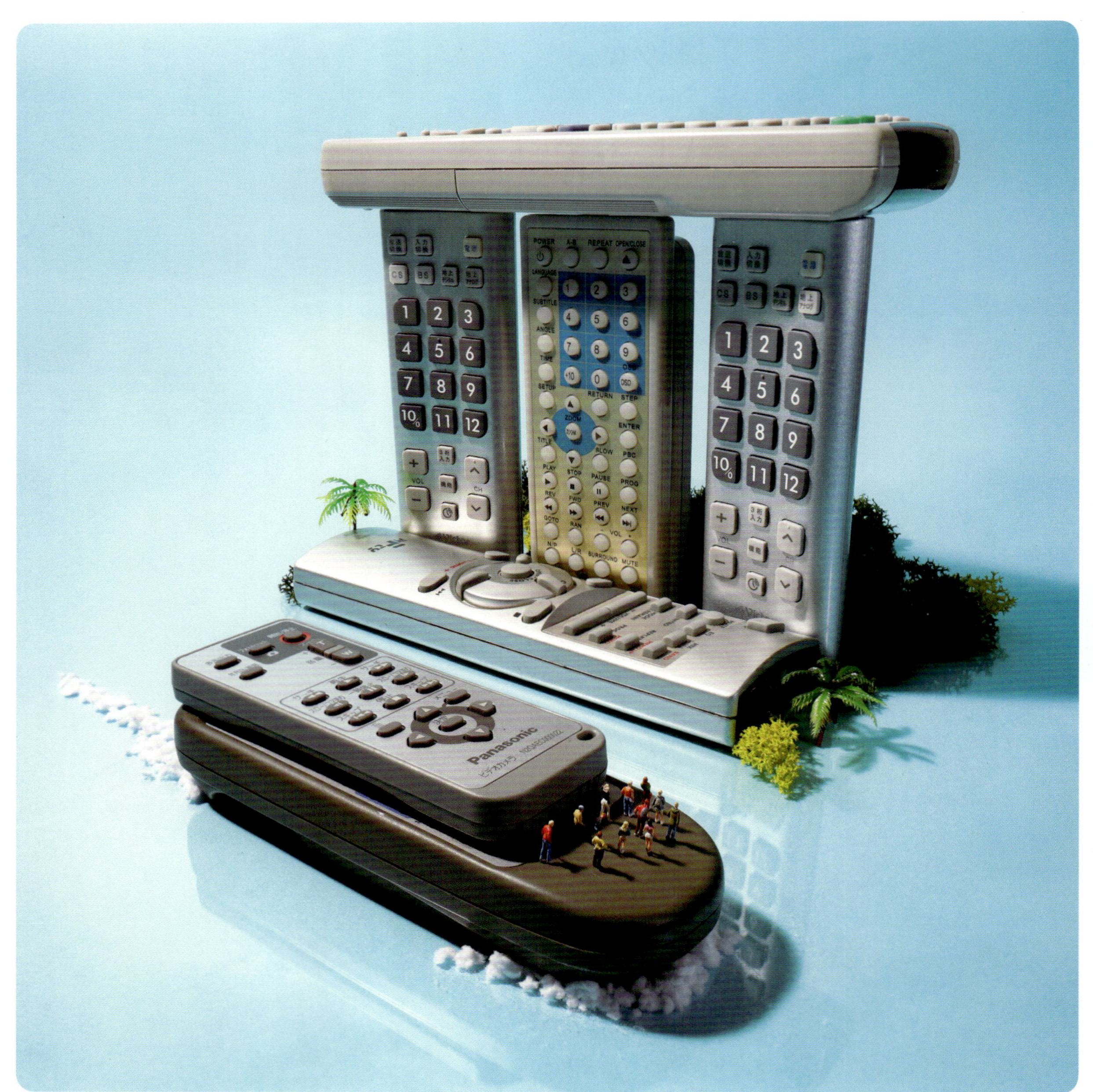

Remote Bay Sands

SINGAPORE

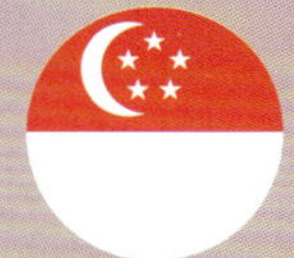

MARINA BAY SANDS

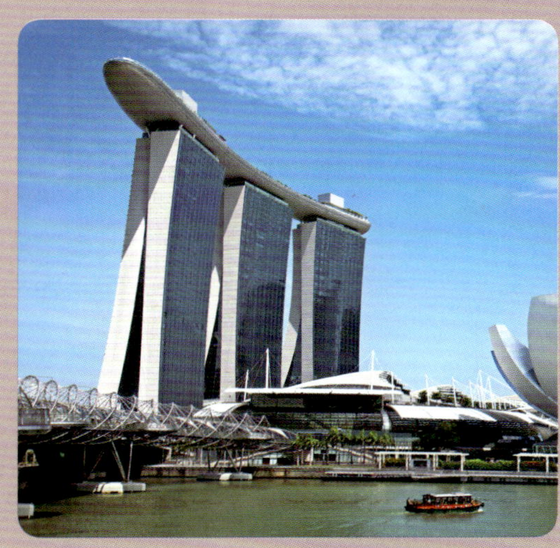

This extravagant complex cost a whopping $8 billion Singapore dollars to build! That sounds like a lot of money! It's certainly a lot of money to bet on a new casino and a hotel with 2500 rooms, but it seems to be paying off. Apparently business is booming and the building has become one of the most famous landmarks in the world. One big attention getter is the infinity pool way up on the top floor. Guests get to swim in it and visitors get to gawk at it. And there's talk of adding a fourth tower. Let's hope Tanaka-san has another remote controller.

REMOTE CONTROLER

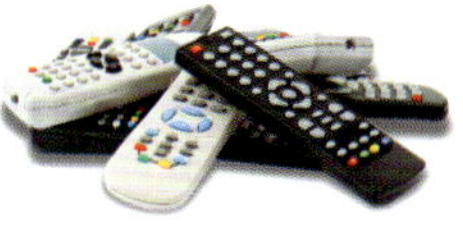

Tanaka-san has used remote controls in the past to depict buildings but wanted to do something more dynamic when he came upon Marina Bay Sands as a subject. He found boat-like remotes to depict a boat and to adorn the top of Marina Bay Sands.

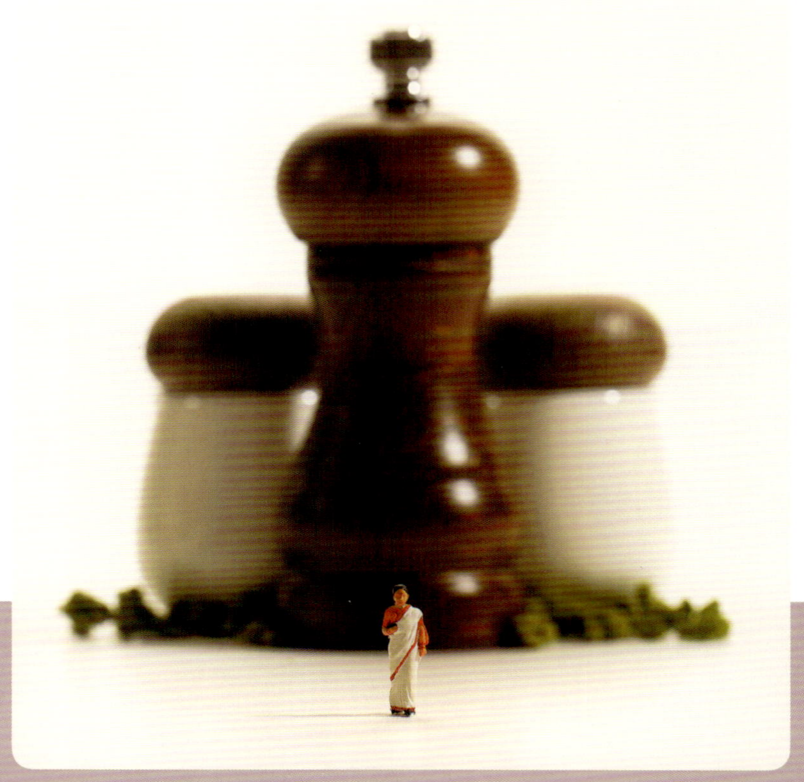

Taj Mahal

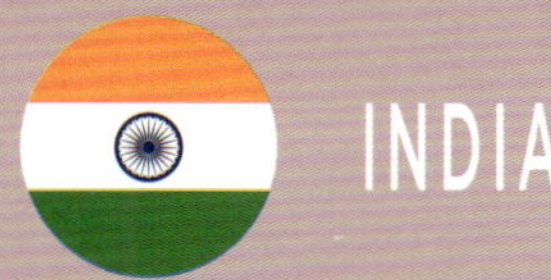

INDIA

TAJ MAHAL MAUSOLEUM

Salt shakers and a pepper mill express the balanced grandeur of Taj Mahal, a monument to a Mughal emperor's love for his wife who died while giving birth to their 14th child.

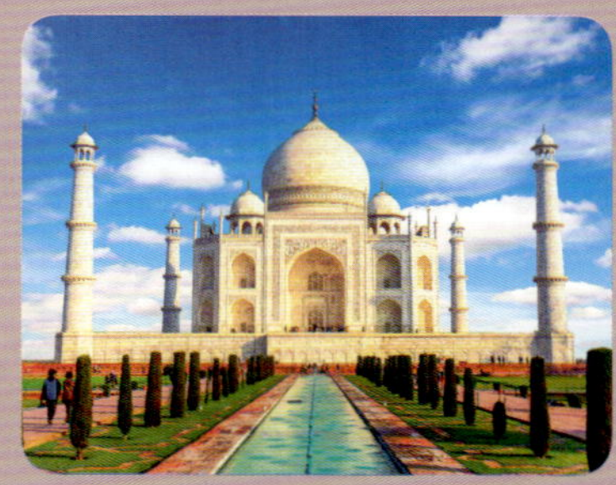

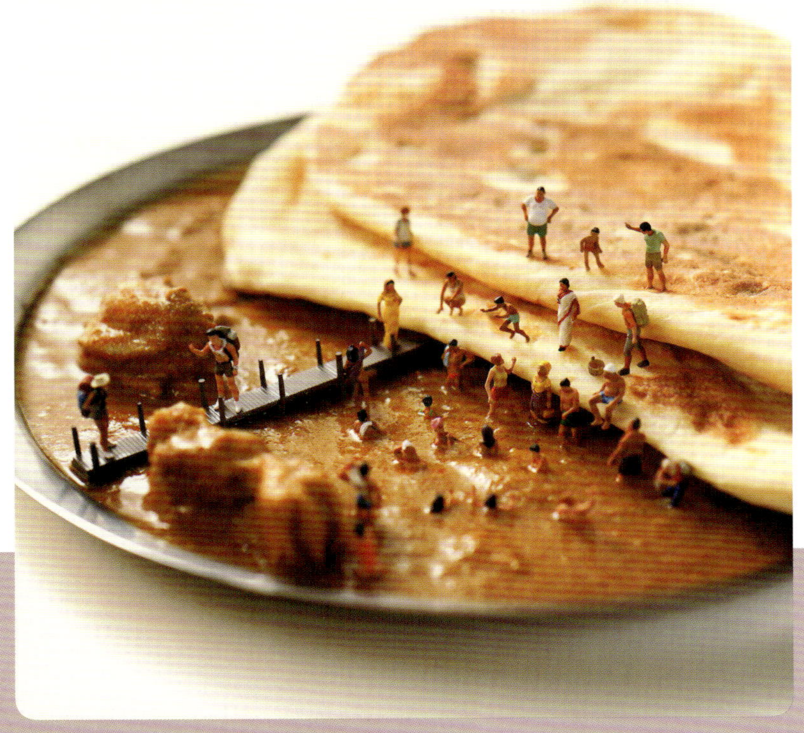

Ganges River

GANGES RIVER

Curry, naan bread and the Ganges occupy central roles in Indian life. Here, naan becomes a stone embankment along a curry Ganges River. This is the ultimate soul food!

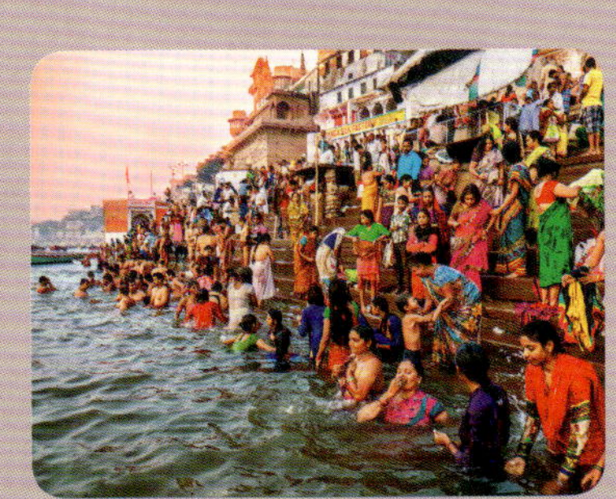

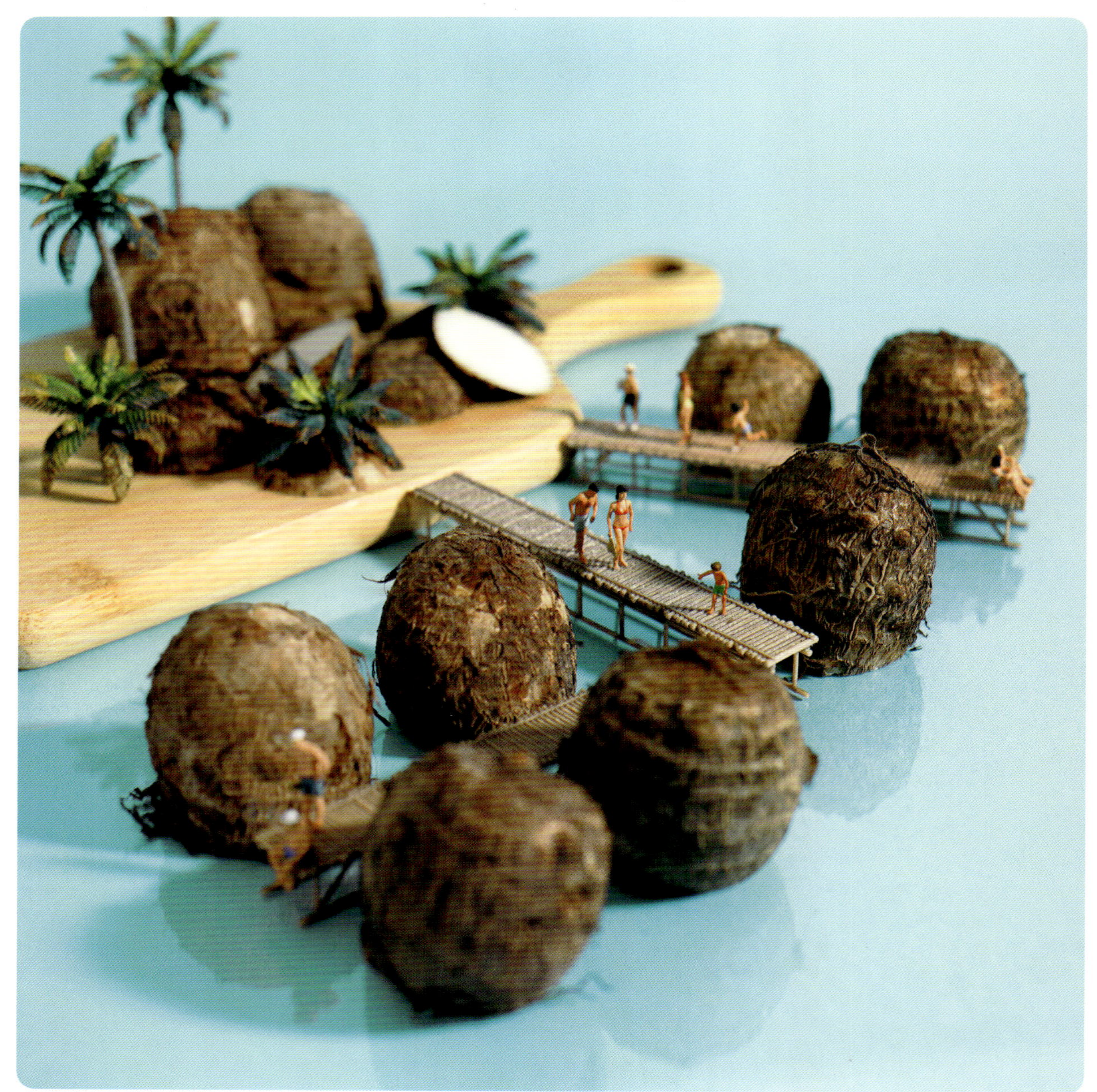

Overwater Bungalows

MALDIVES

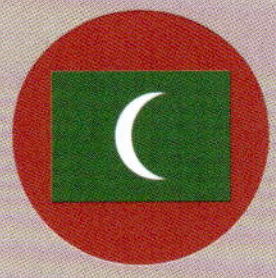

NORTH MALÉ ATOLL

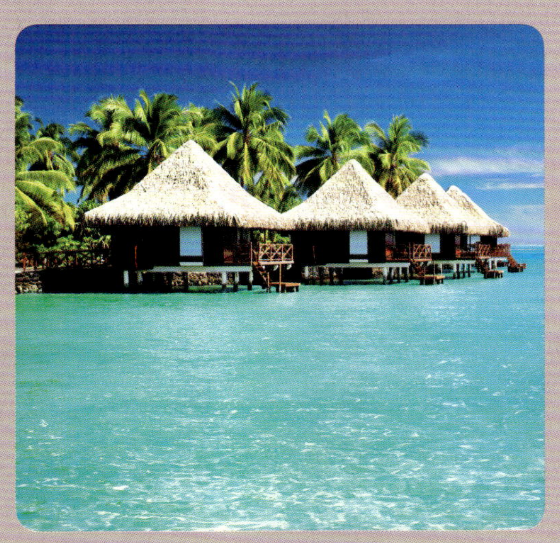

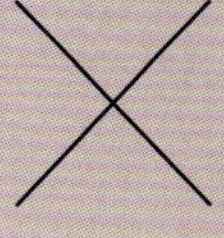

There are more than 1000 coral islands in the Maldives and a total of 26 atolls. The atolls are made up of coral reefs and sand bars. With an average elevation of only 2 meters, this is the world's flattest country. A long time ago, people here gathered and traded huge amounts of cowry shells that were a form of international currency. Fishing is an important livelihood and more recently tourism has become a vital source of income as well. The state religion is Islam, the coconut palm is the national tree, and the overwater bungalows are quite popular.

TARO

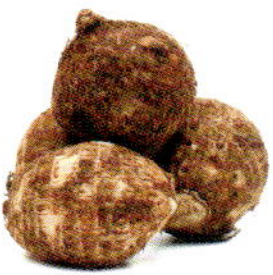

This piece was made with real taros. Being round, taros have a tendency to roll off the cutting board hence their placement in the ocean where they became floating villas. A big fan of taros, Tanaka-san apparently ate them after the shoot.

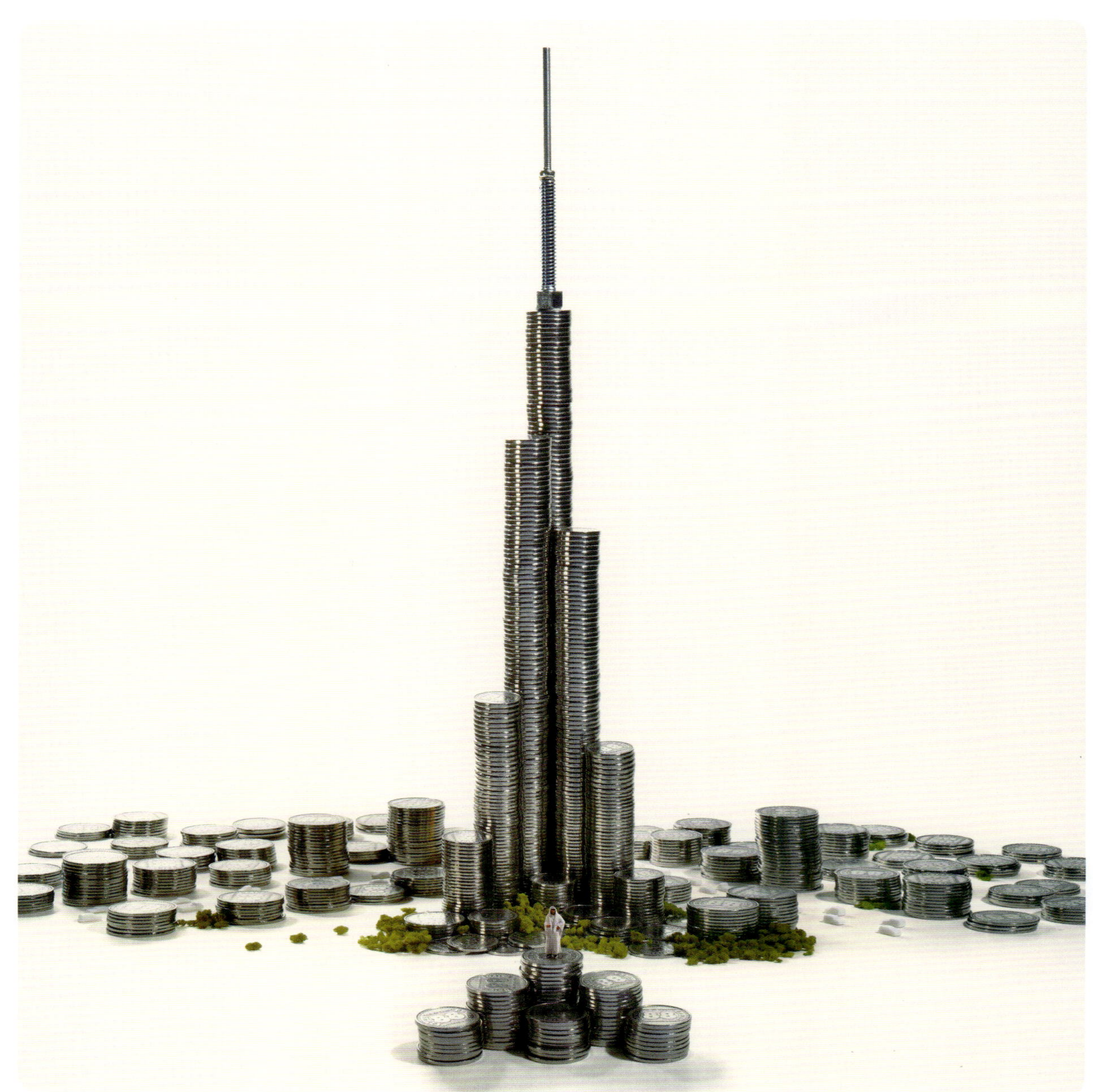

Burj Khalifa

UNITED ARAB EMIRATES

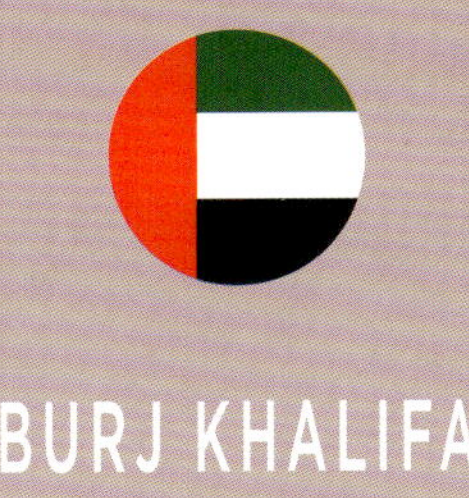

BURJ KHALIFA

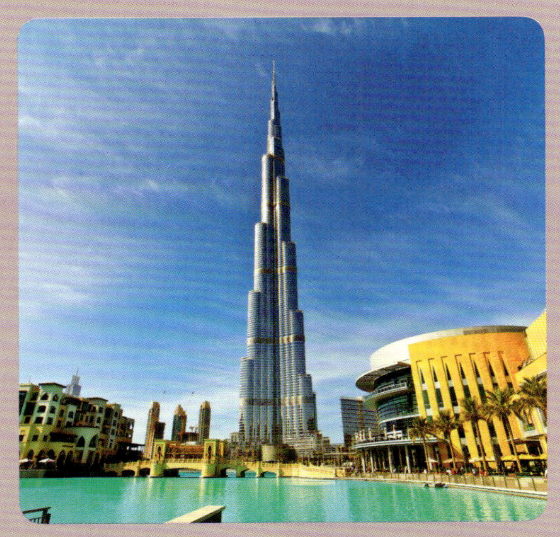

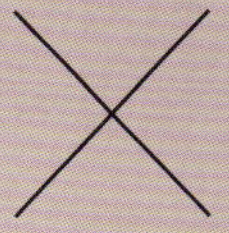

This is the tallest building in the world. It's more than 800 meters tall, making it almost three times the height of the Eiffel Tower. That's kind of difficult to imagine. It has 163 floors, 30,000 residents, and 9 hotels! Apparently downtown Dubai has thrived since the completion of this building in 2010, although the building itself hasn't been very profitable. It is environmentally friendly however, insofar as huge amounts of water used in the building are recycled into the cooling system, used to irrigate the surrounding grounds and to feed the Dubai Fountain.

COINS

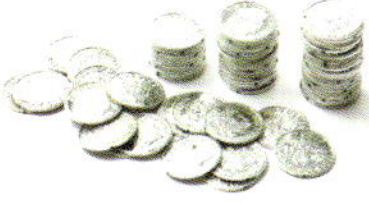

Here, the accumulation of wealth – in the form of coins – has led literally to the accummulation of floors in the world's tallest building. Ironically, with rising metal prices worldwide, some coins in circulation cost more to make than they are worth.

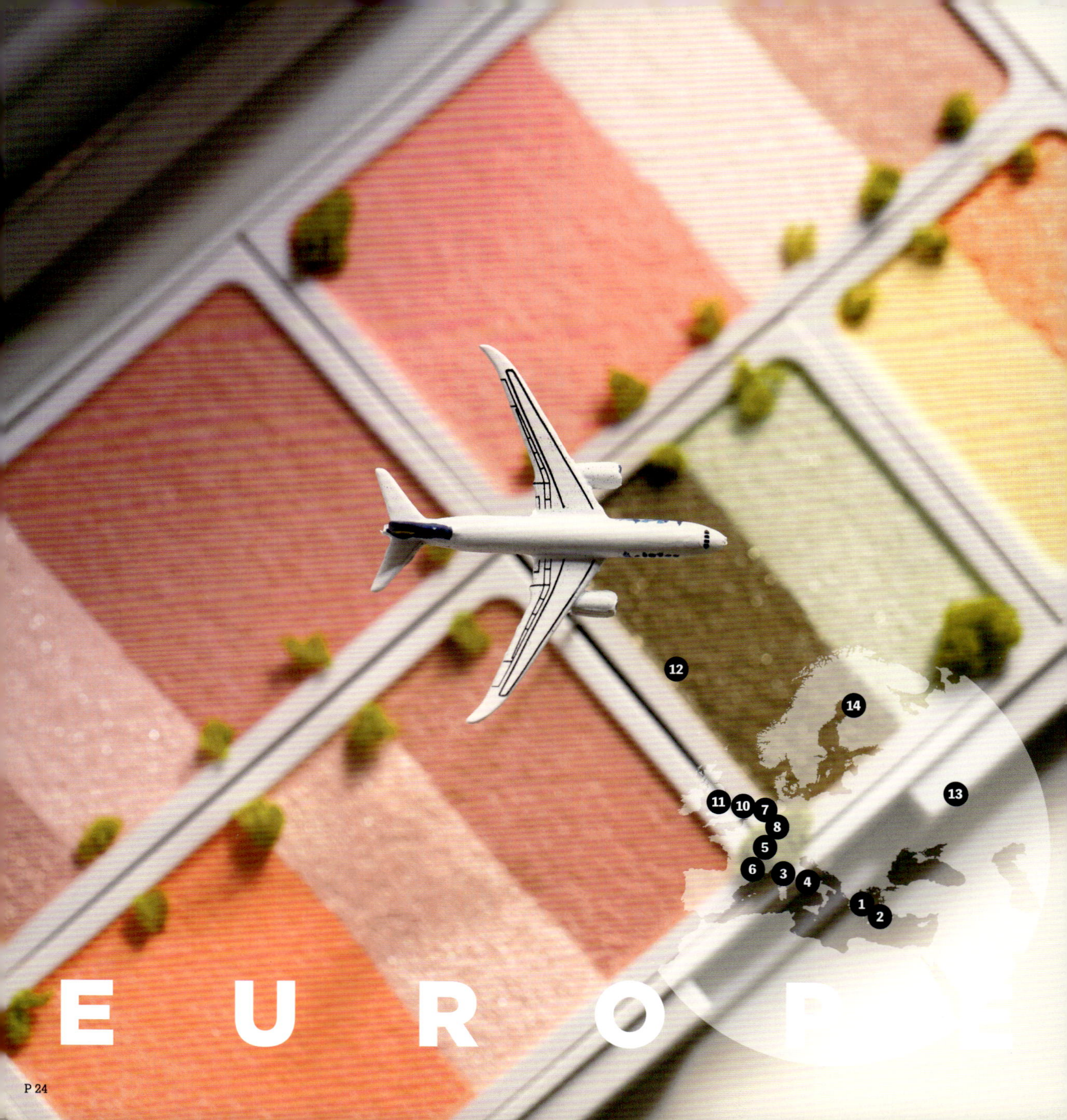
12
14
13
11 10 7
8
5
6 3 4
1 2
E U R O P

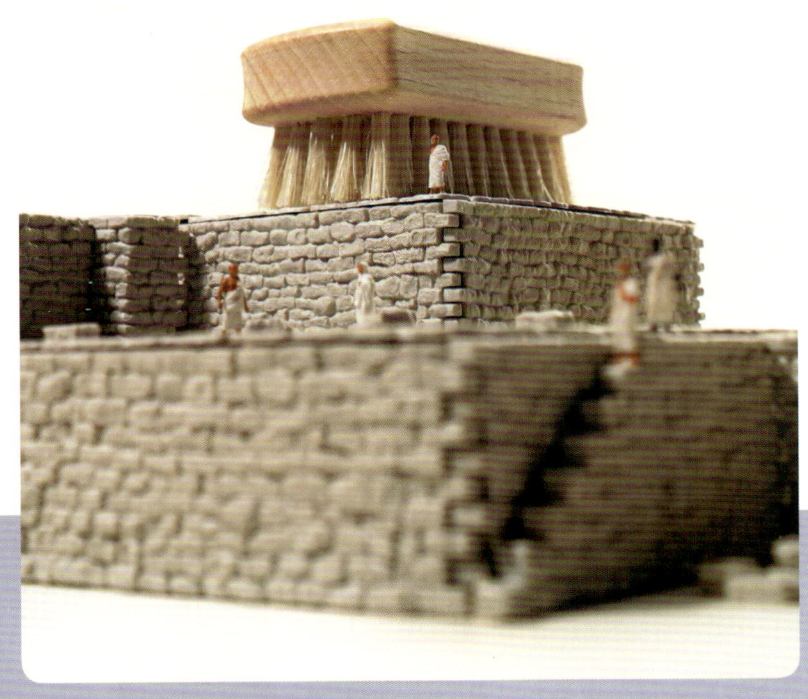

Parthenon

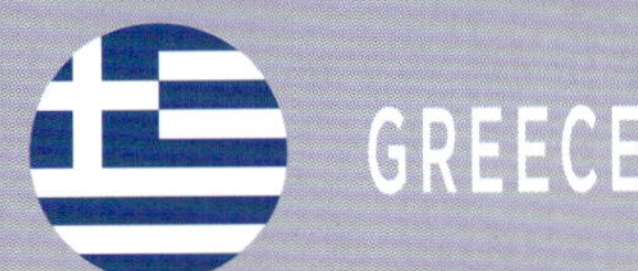

GREECE

PARTHENON

With people dressed in tunics and a large rock foundation, a shoe shine brush becomes the Parthenon, one of Greece's most popular destinations. The Doric columns are 10.4 meters tall.

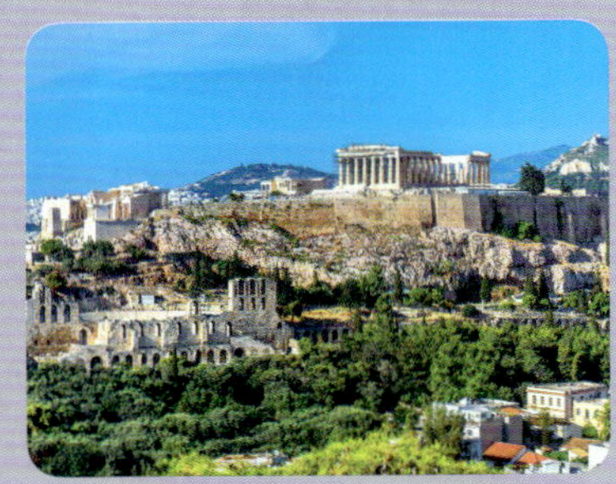

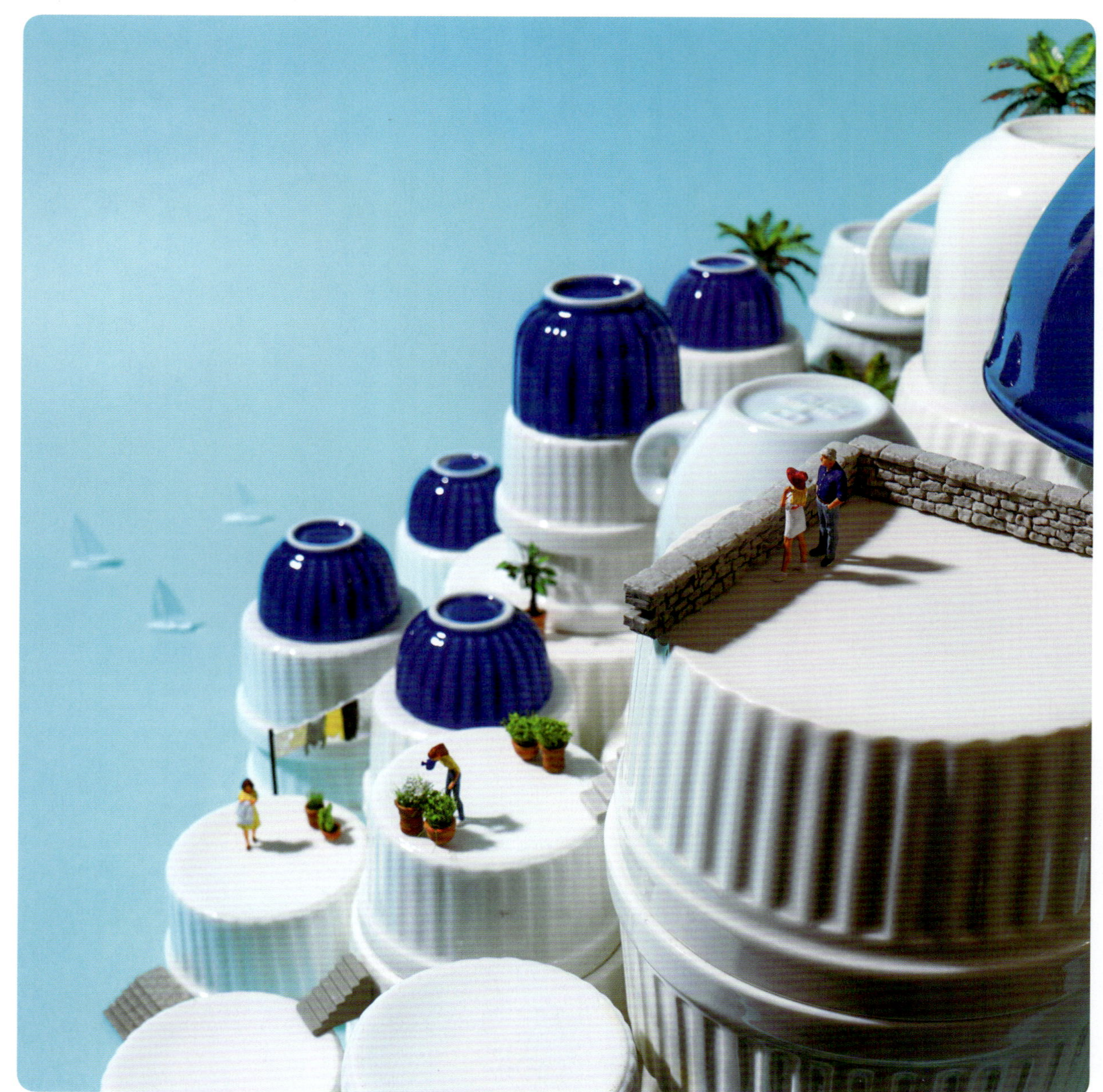

Santorini

GREECE

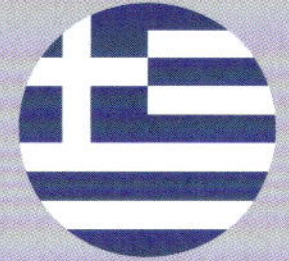

SANTORINI

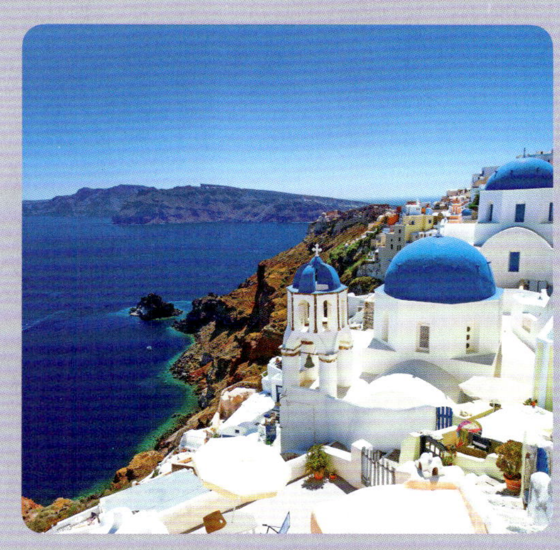

Tanaka-san makes use of especially tiny boats to give a sense of depth and distance when depicting the massive, deep crater at Santorini. He uses soufflé dishes, coffee cups and tiny blue bowls from his own kitchen cupboard to create this scene. Although there is very little rainfall on Santorini, grapes are ingeniously grown here, their vines curled into wreaths that capture nocturnal moisture. Apparently this is also the only inhabited caldera in the world. That may not impress Tanaka-san though, because he lives quite close to an active volcano!

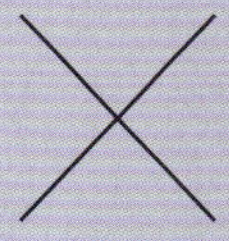

SOUFFLE DISH

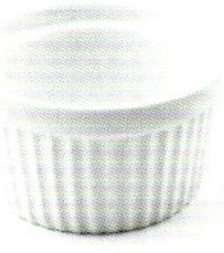

Porcelain soufflé dishes are ideal for cooking and eating souffles, crème brulee and the like. Flipped over, they're also a natural when depicting stuccoed houses and white towers in persistently sun-bleached locations.

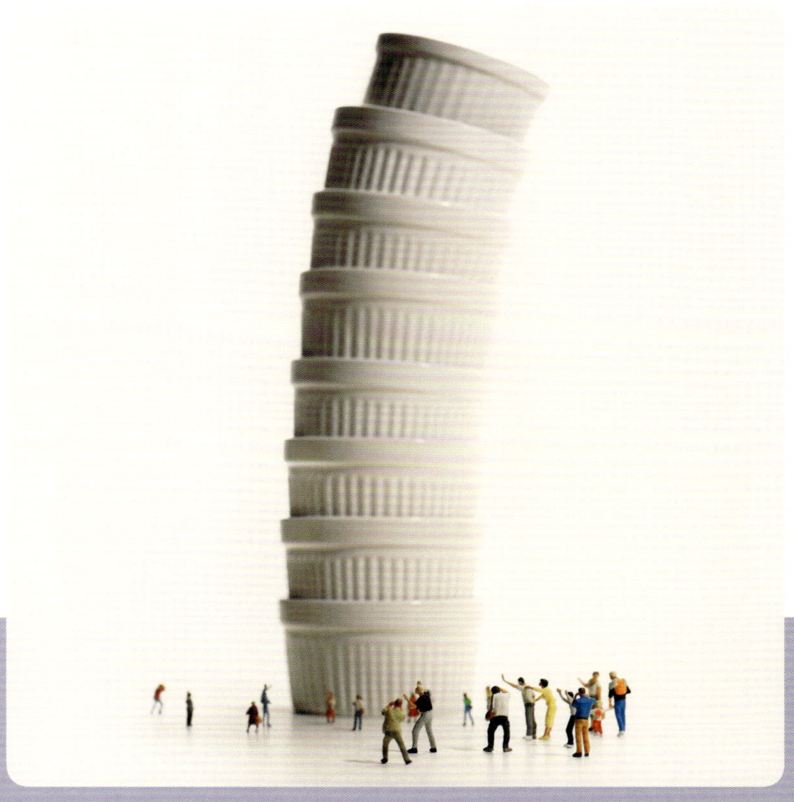

World Heritage Site in the Back of My Cupboard

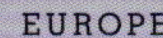 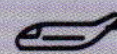

ITALY

LEANING TOWER OF PISA

When you stack too many soufflé dishes, you get the leaning tower effect. And yet there's something about the tower in Pisa that defies gravity in a way that doesn't quite work at home.

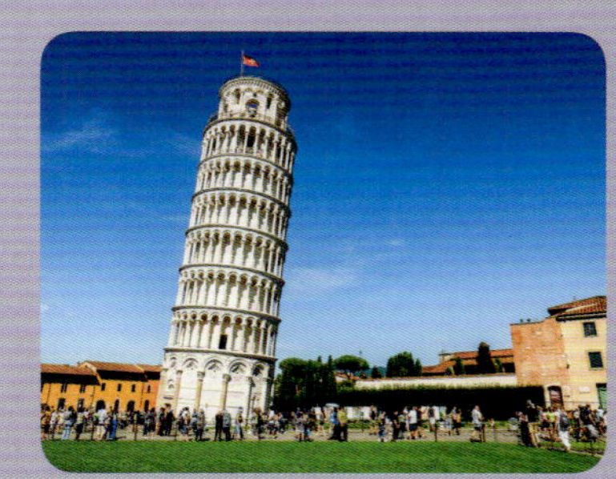

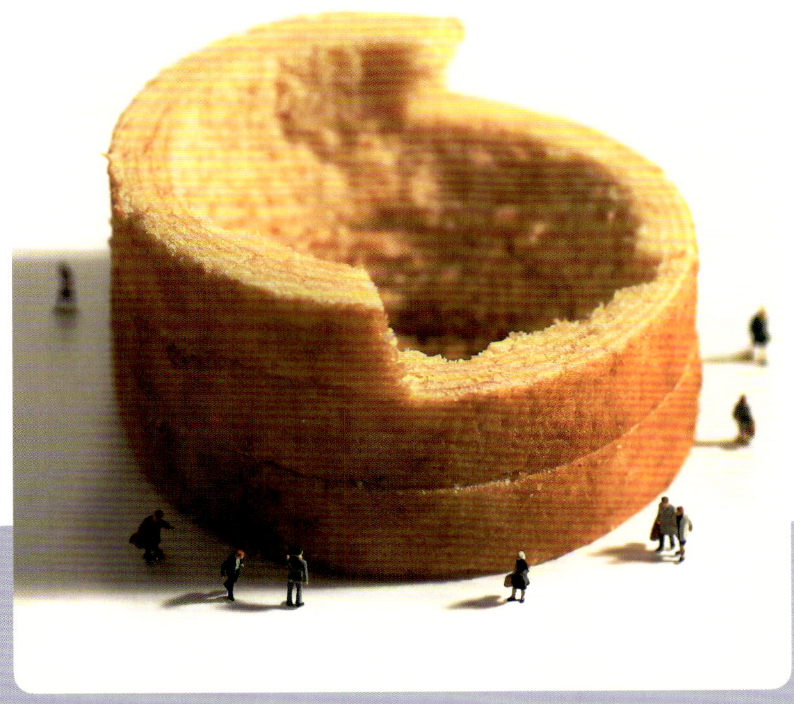

Colosseum

COLOSSEUM

Tanaka-san's children like to eat the soft, middle area in sliced bread and – in this case – roll cake. Without its creamy center, this cake came to resemble the colosseum in Rome.

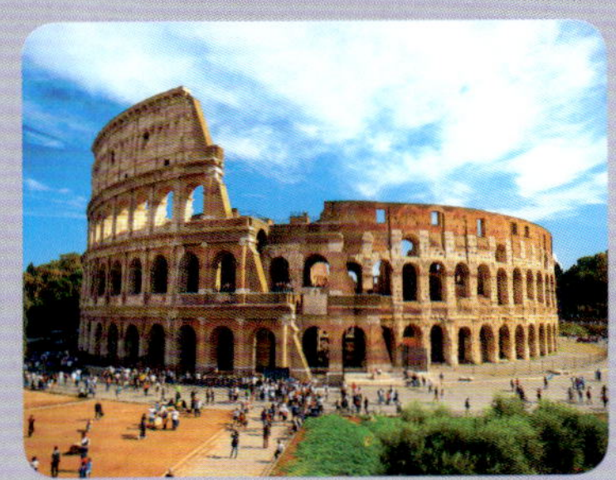

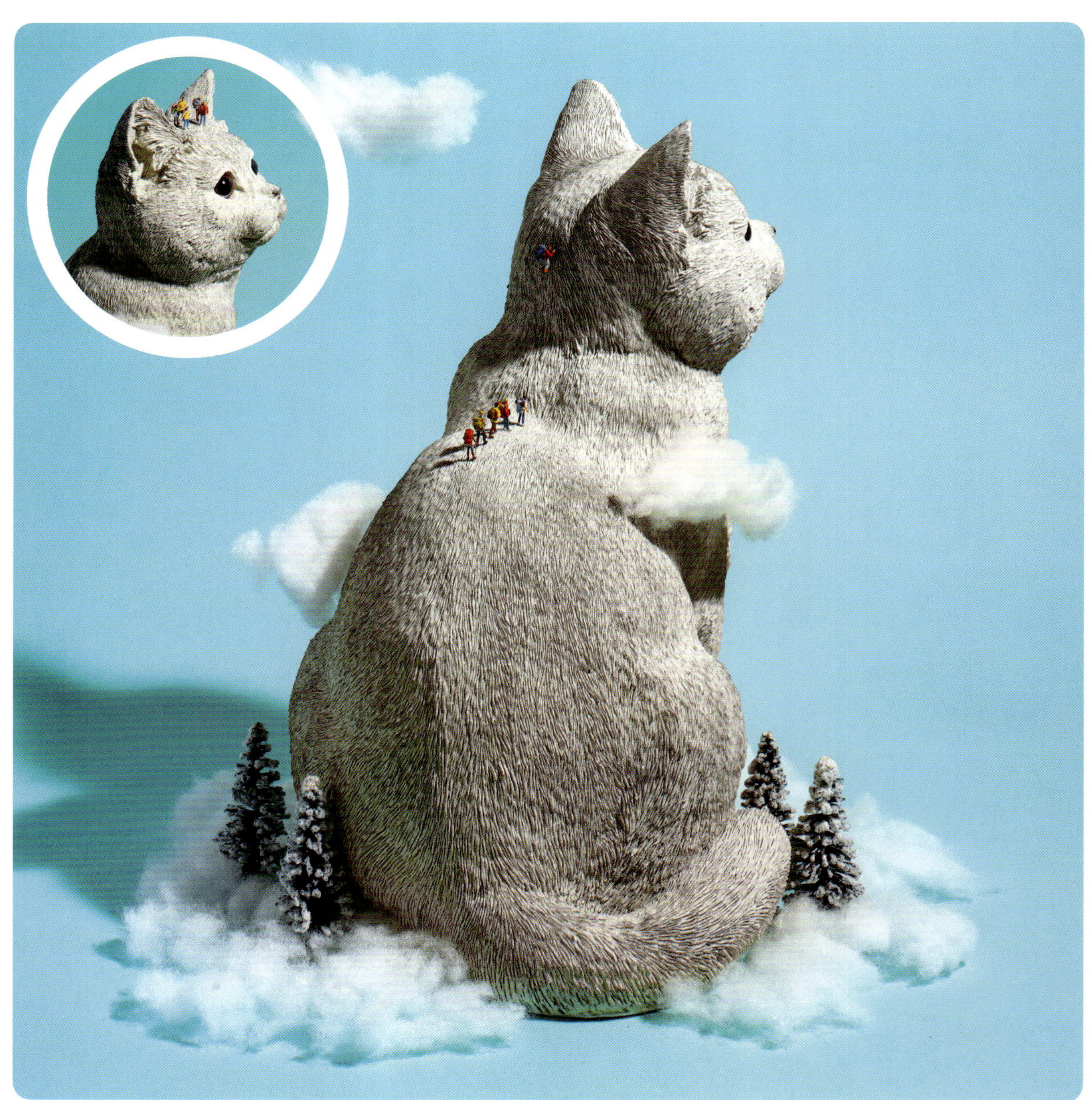

Frozen Cat Mountain

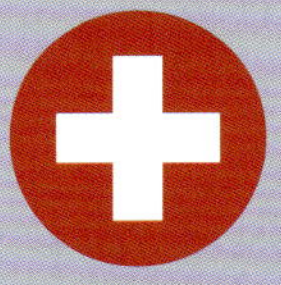

MATTERHORN

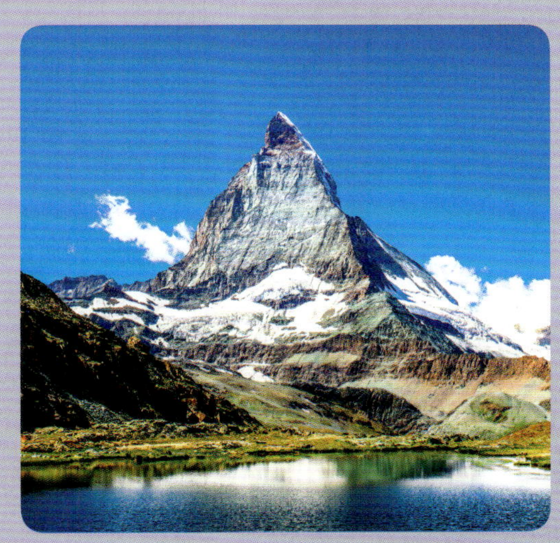

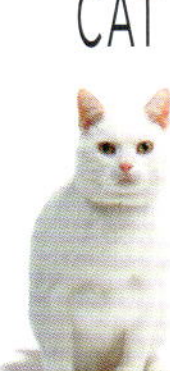

The 12th highest summit in the Alps, the Matterhorn is located on the border of Switzerland and Italy. Being quite photogenic, it is one of the best-known mountains in Europe. If you're looking for a way to remember the name of this mountain, perhaps you could think of it as a giant HORN made out of very hard MATTER. In fact, "Matterhorn" is German for "peak in the meadows." The first ascent by a man was made on July 14, 1865. The first woman to climb the Matterhorn was wearing a long flannel skirt when she reached the top on July 22, 1871.

CAT

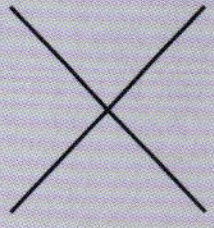

One can begin to appreciate the range of Tanaka-san's imagination when a white cat becomes a snow-covered mountain. Of course some mountains are more catlike than others. The Matterhorn appears to have only one ear.

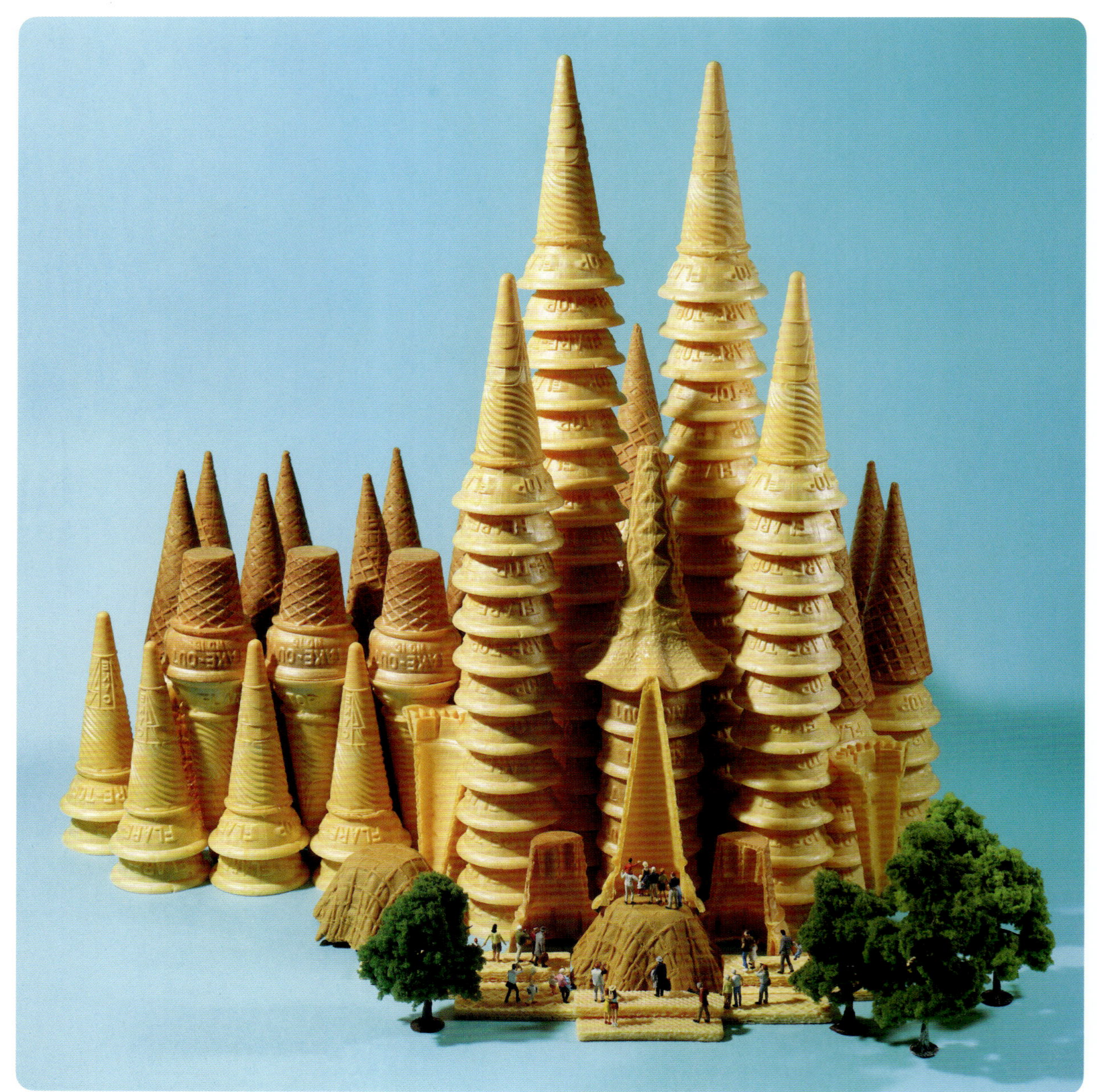

Sagrada Familia

SPAIN

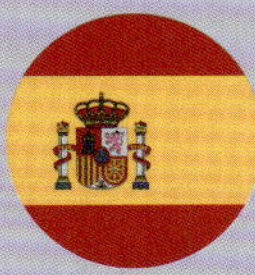

SAGRADA FAMILIA

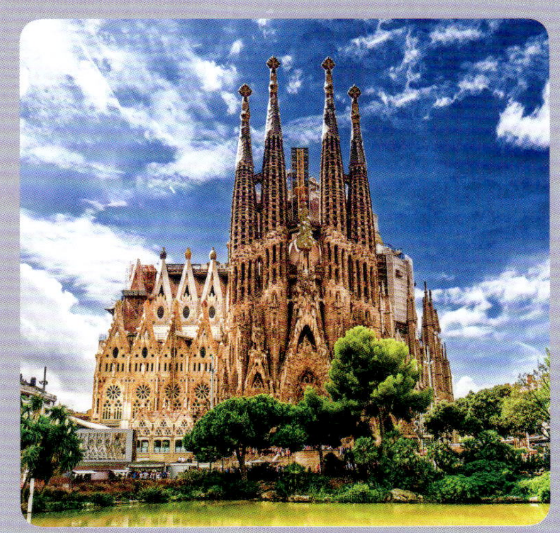

This glorious, organic structure designed by Antoni Gaudi and located in Barcelona, is probably best known for being under construction for more than 100 years. Actually, construction started in 1882. The work is paid for by visitors and the public which accounts for how long it is taking to build. The basilica is formally known as the Expiatory Temple of the Sacred Family. When completed it will have three facades – Nativity, Passion and Glory - and 18 spires. There are only 8 spires now so one gets a sense that this may take a bit more time.

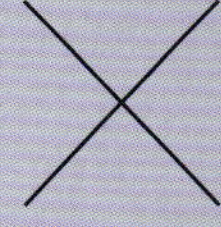

CONE

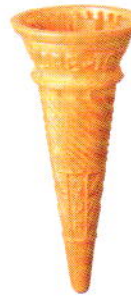

Edible ice cream cones have a shape and texture that resemble the delightfully animate design of Sagrada Familia. Tanaka-san uses lighter colored wafer cones in the front and darker sugar cones in the back to show variation in color.

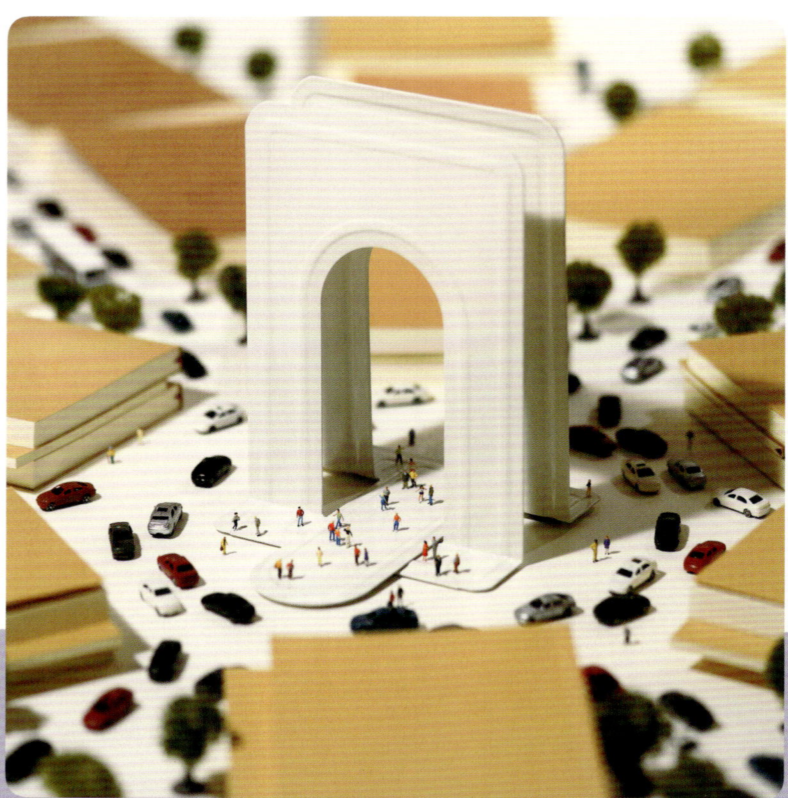

Triumphal Arch

FRANCE

ETOILE ARC DE TRIOMPHE

While a red bookend might become the Golden Gate Bridge, a white bookend may find itself in the middle of Paris, surrounded by book buildings, speeding cars and goggling tourists.

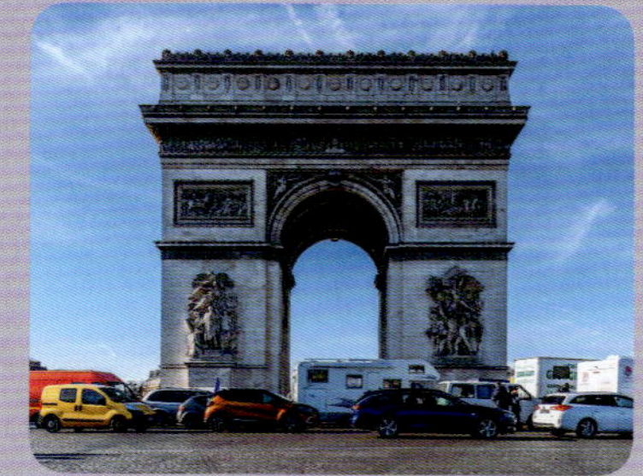

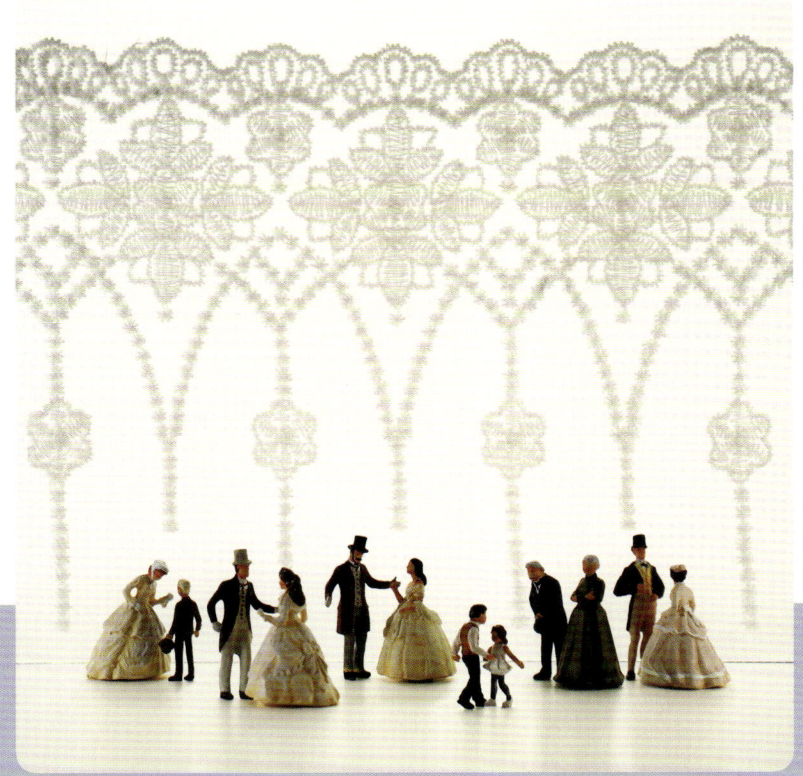

Lace Palace

VERSAILLES PALACE HALL OF MIRRORS

Here the Hall of Mirrors – 357 in all – in the Palace of Versailles reflects the same silk elegance found in the dresses the women are wearing. And guest are reminded of the royalty's vast wealth.

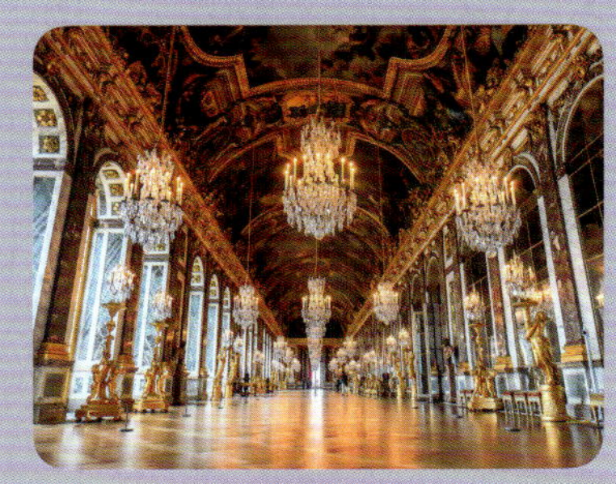

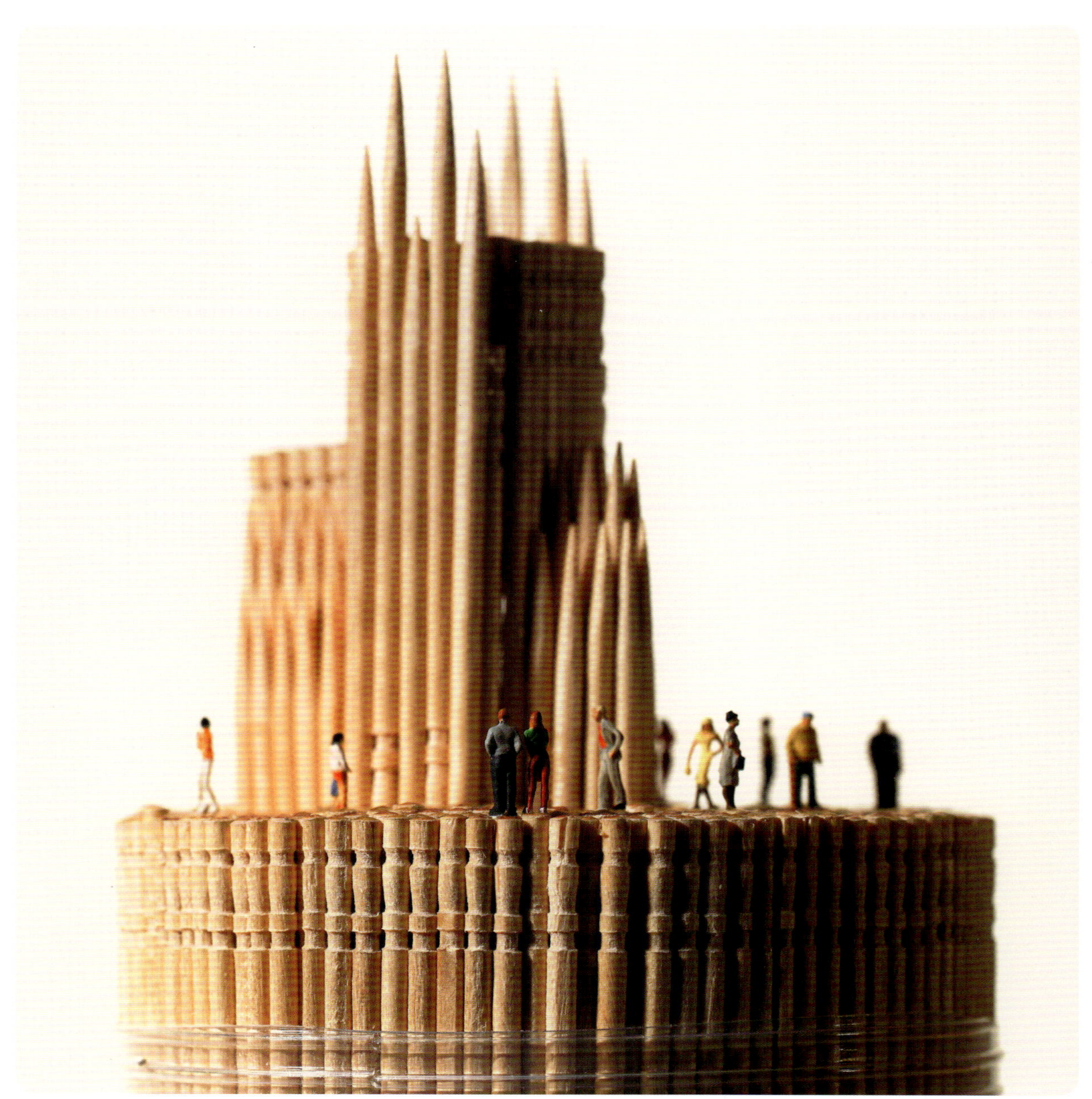

Cologne Cathedral

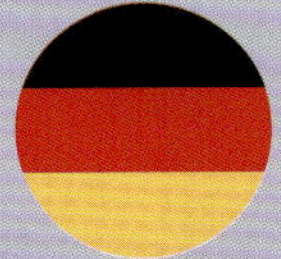

COLOGNE CATHEDRAL

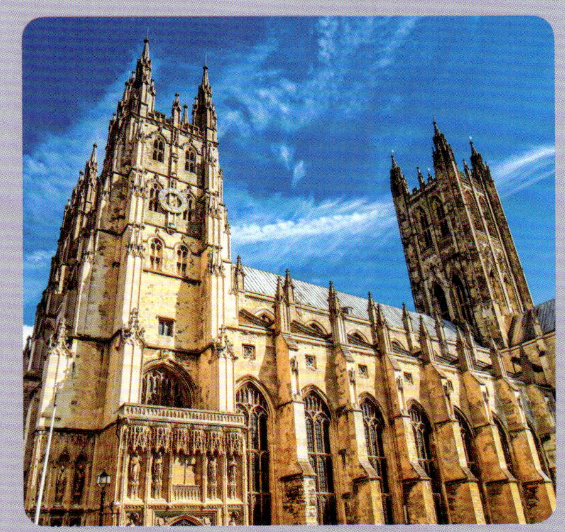

Welcome to the Cologne Cathedral, another of Tanaka-san's kitchen drawer world heritage sites. Apparently this Gothic masterpiece was originally built to store the relics of the Three Magi who visited Jesus in Bethlehem, shortly after his birth.Their remains were brought to Cologne in 1164 and construction of the cathedral began in 1248. One wonders where they kept them. Setting a nice precedent for Sagrada Familia, the cathedral apparently took 600 years to build. It boasts the world's largest church façade and the largest freely swinging church bell.

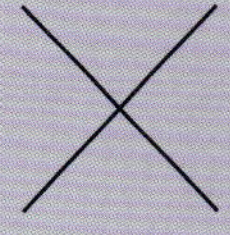

TOOTHPICKS

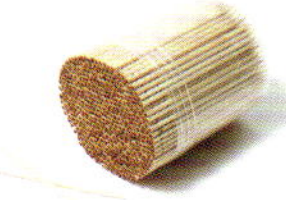

Tanaka-san enjoys using Japanese toothpicks in his work. Pointed at one end, they often have grooves at the other, flat, end. These grooves lend them an architectural quality, the appearance that wood or stone has been elegantly carved.

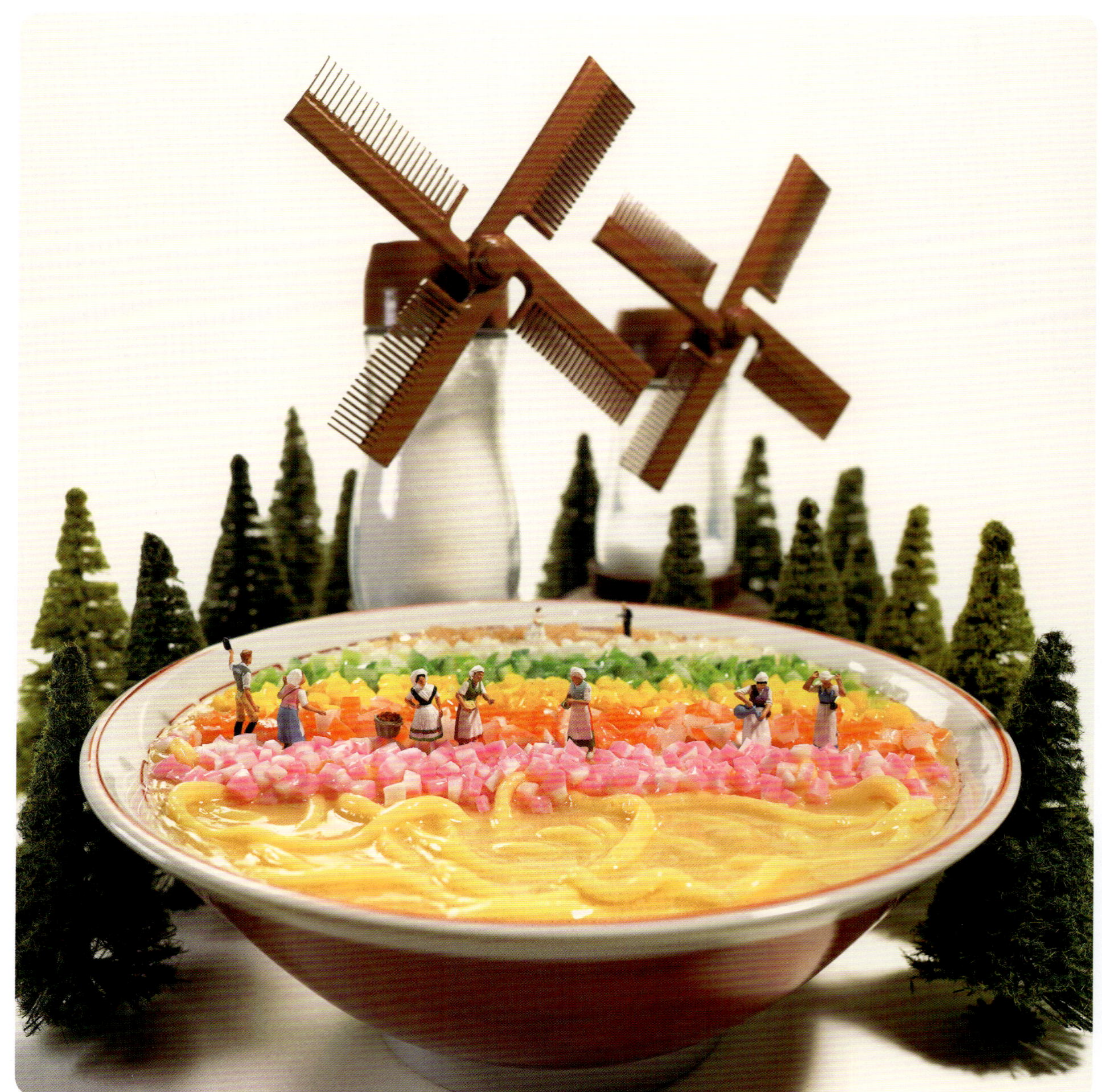

Dutch Noodles

NETHERLANDS

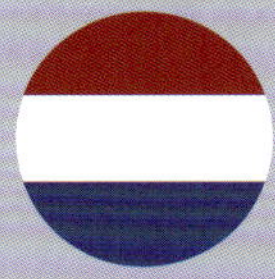

KEUKENHOF GARDENS

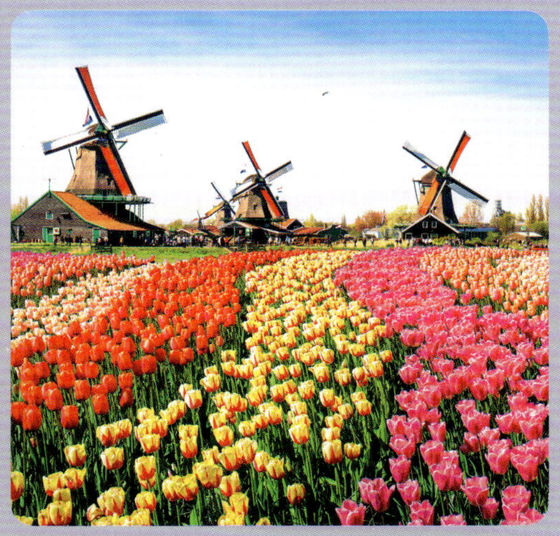

Literally meaning "kitchen garden," the Keukenhof Gardens started out as an English landscape garden in 1857. Then, in 1949, a bunch of Dutch bulb growers collaborated to plant spring bulbs. In the years since, the gardens have become a mecca for flower lovers. More than 7 million tulips, lilies and other bulbs are donated annually by bulb growers and planted by hand over a period of three months. They're timed to bloom when the garden is open for 8 weeks in the spring. In the end, the bulbs are dug up and many are fed to local livestock.

NAGASAKI CHAMPON

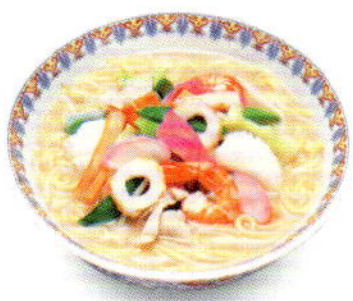

The Dutch enjoyed trade relations in Nagasaki when Japan was closed to the outside world. That's why there's a Dutch theme park near Nagasaki and Tanaka-san has taken champon noodles, a popular dish in Nagasaki, and given them a Dutch twist.

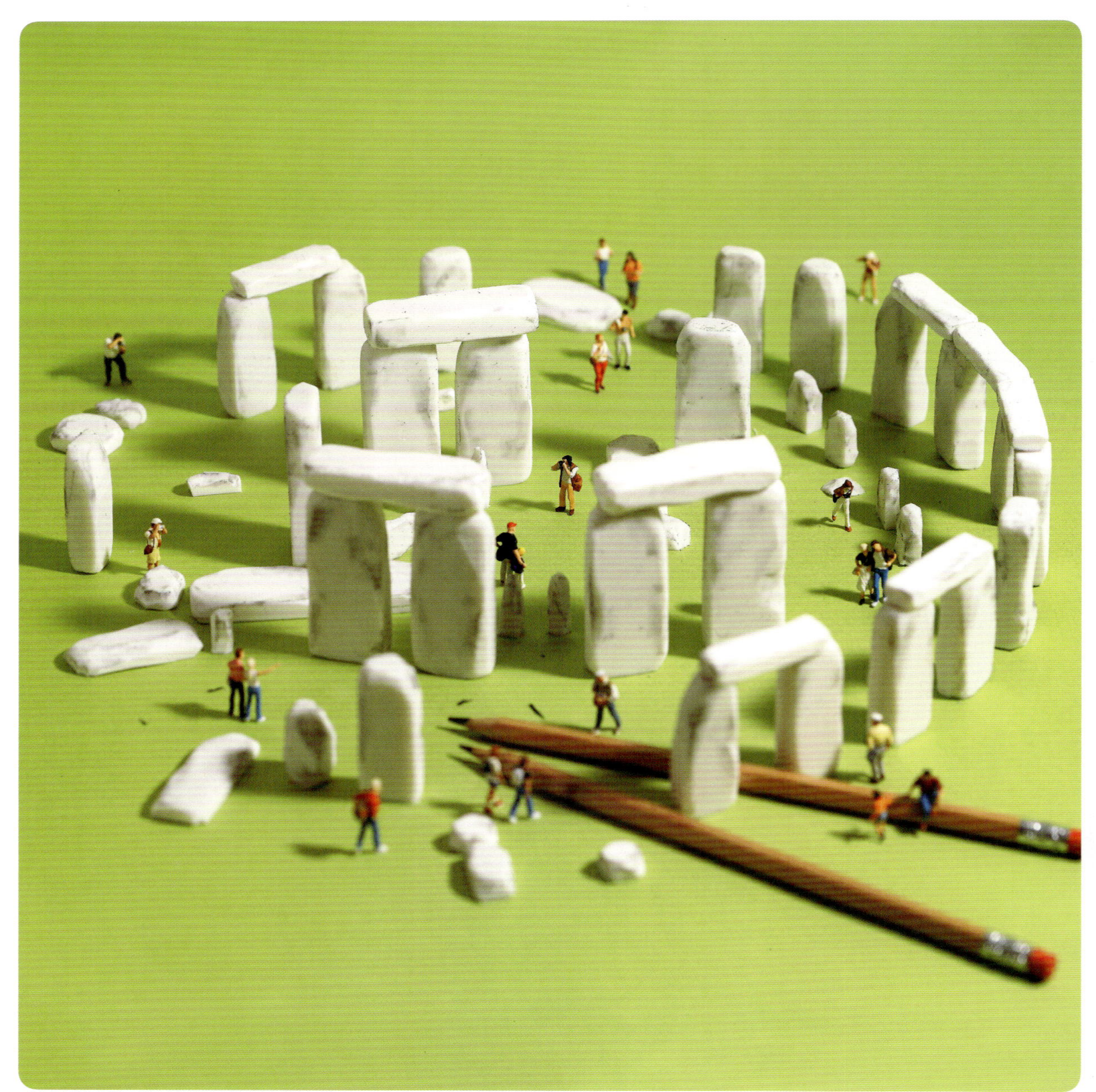

Eraserhenge

GREAT BRITAIN

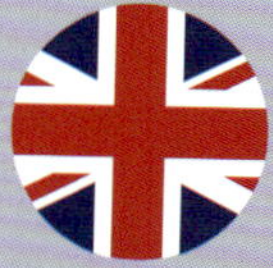

STONEHENGE

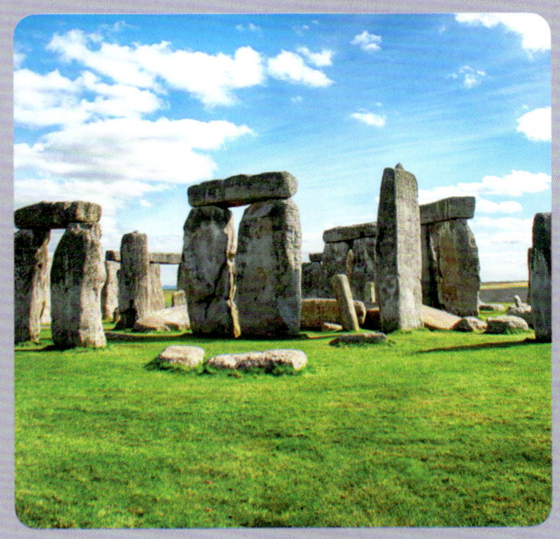

Like the Forbidden City in China and Angkor Wat in Cambodia, this is another not entirely understood example of people long ago moving very large stones over a fairly great distance, and, in this case, standing them up. The Stonehenge site is about 5000 years old although many of the stones may have been brought 1000 years later. Given the placement of the stones in relation to the sun it is thought that Stonehenge may have been a calendar of sorts. Here, Tanaka-san has added pencils to make it easier to understand that the massive white stones are actually erasers.

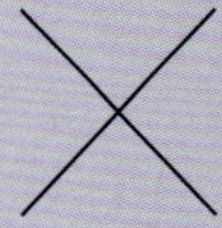

ERASER

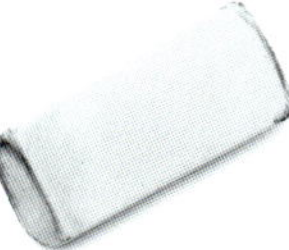

Aged by the elements, the ruins at Stonehenge are much like partially used erasers. Without due care, like erasers, they may eventually disappear. It could be said that a desk drawer full of partially used erasers is an archaeological site as well.

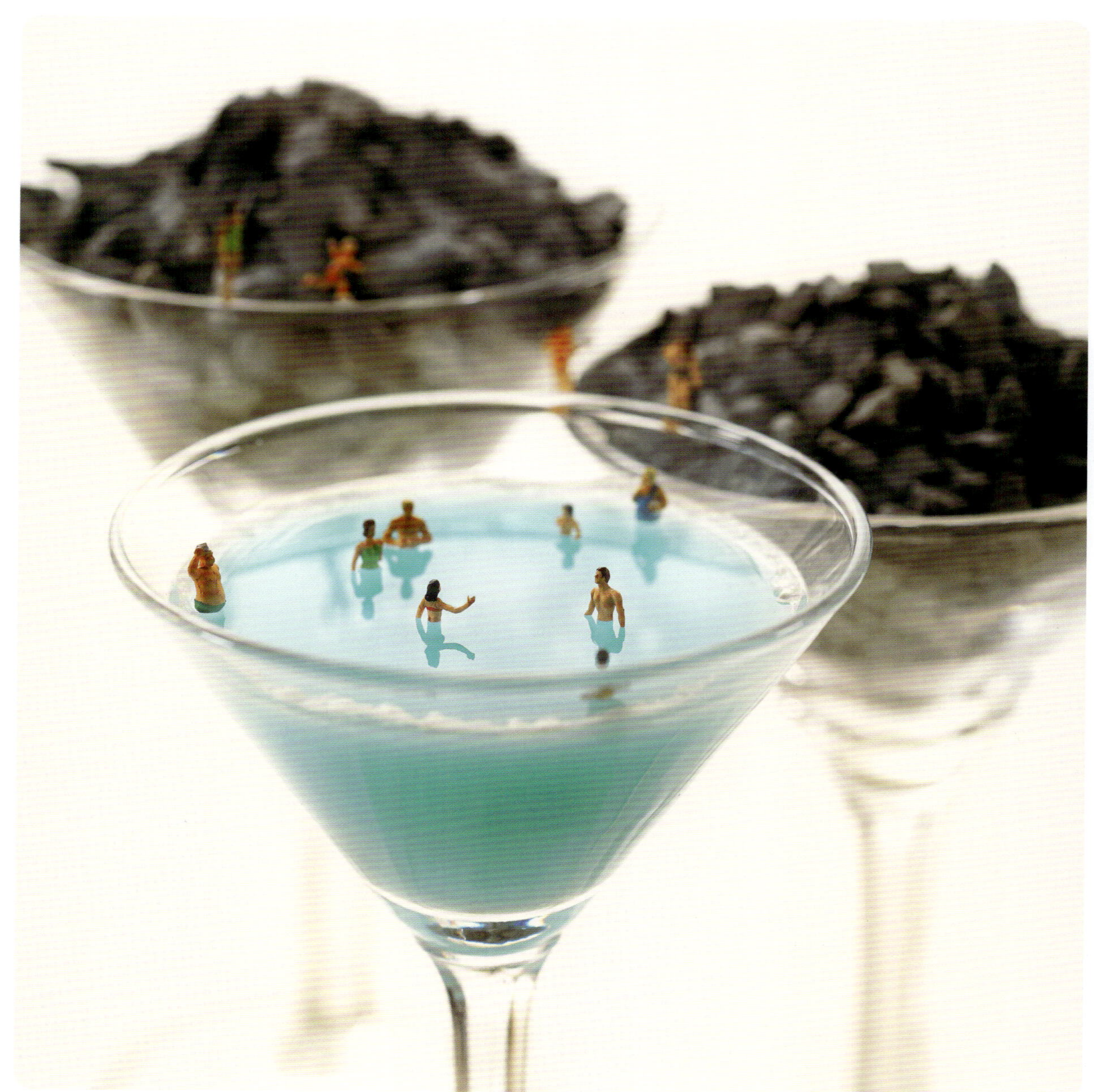

Blue Lagoon

ICELAND

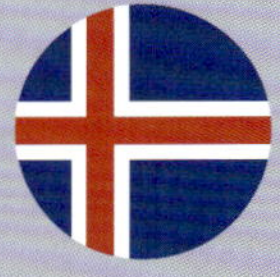

BLUE LAGOON

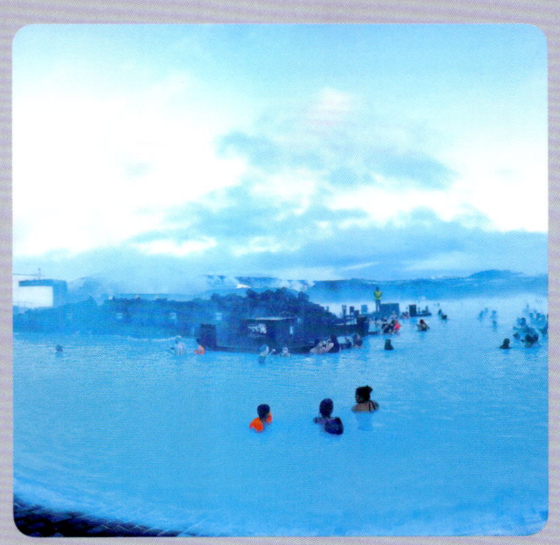

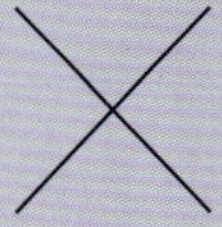

Located in southwest Iceland, the Blue Lagoon has become a popular tourist destination. The spa's warm water comes from a geothermal power plant nearby and has a high concentration of silica which makes it blue. The soft white mud that's at the bottom of the lagoon is apparently good for your skin. You might feel a bit faint if you stay in the bath for too long, much as you would if you were to drink too much alcohol so either should probably be practiced in moderation. That said, the Blue Lagoon is an ideal temperature for a long soak.

COCKTAILS

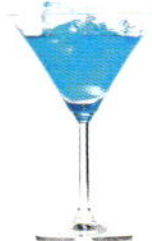

Cocktails have been around for a couple of hundred years. There's actually a Blue Lagoon martini made with Curaçao liqueur, vodka and lemon. It doesn't seem to be related to the skin-friendly spa in Iceland although they do have an in water bar.

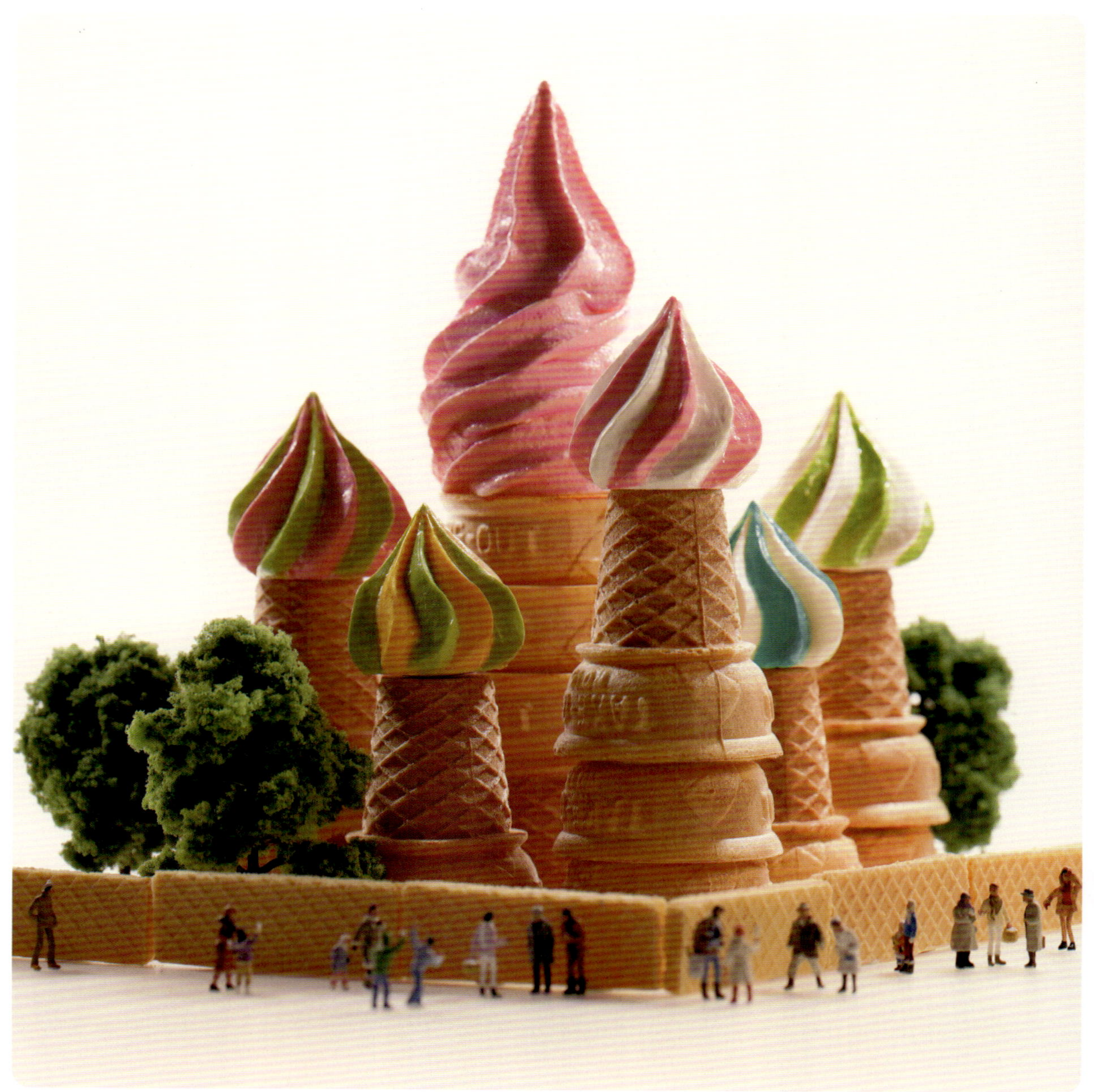

Russian Fantasy

RUSSIA

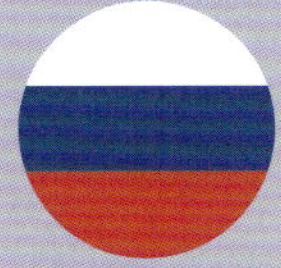

ST. BASIL'S CATHEDRAL

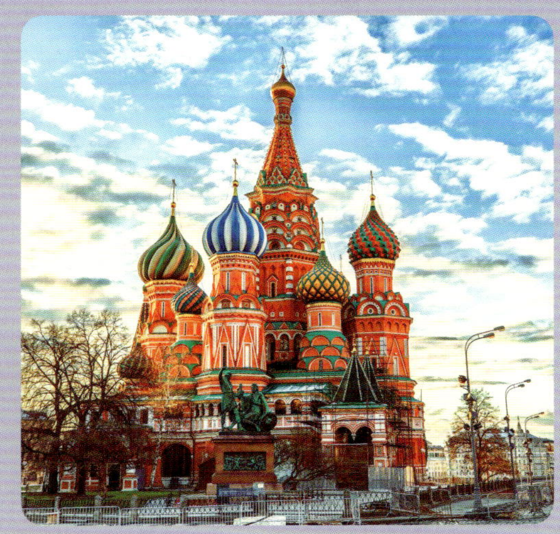

Located in the Red Square in Moscow, this cathedral with its nine domes is remarkably playful and upbeat for a structure built in the 16th century on the orders of a guy called "Ivan the Terrible." Ivan was apparently "terrible" in the sense that he "inspired terror" in those around him. The cathedral was originally painted white - to match the white stone of the nearby Kremlin - and had gold domes, the color of caramel ice cream. It wasn't until the 17th century that the cathedral was painted the brilliant, fantasy land colors it remains to this day.

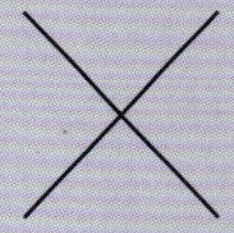

SOFT SERVE ICE CREAM

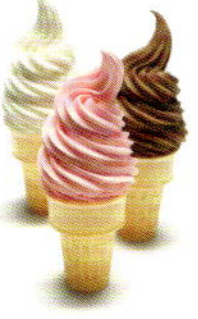

In its colder regions, Russia is so cold that ice cream will not easily melt. In Moscow, temperatures average -3°C to -9°C in the winter but have reached a record low of -42°C. That low, your ice cream would probably be as hard as a rock.

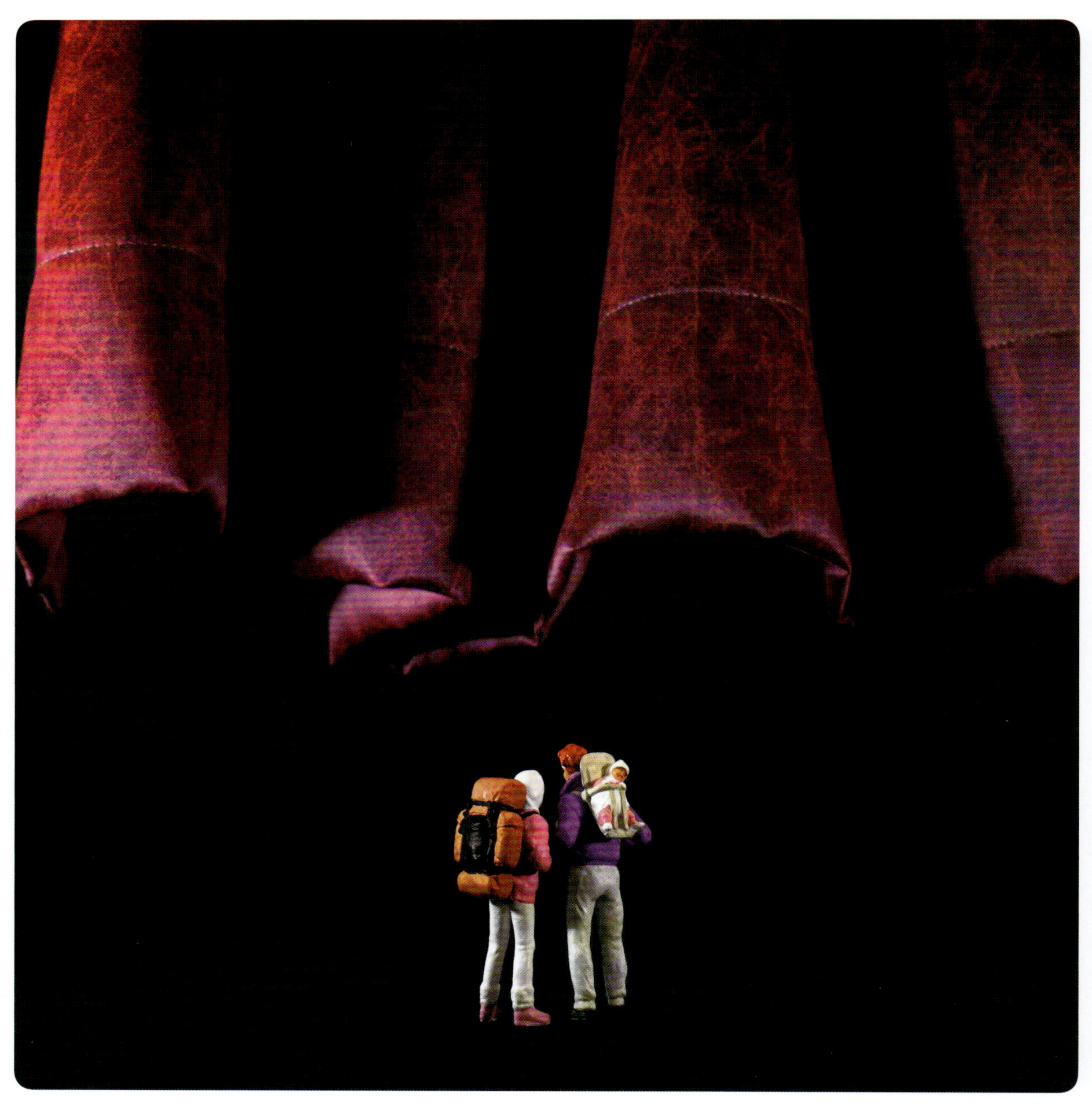

Aurora Curtainalis

FINLAND

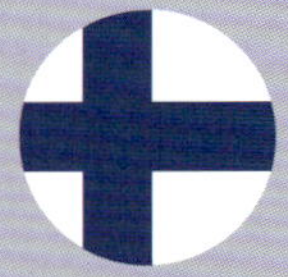

SAARISELKÄ

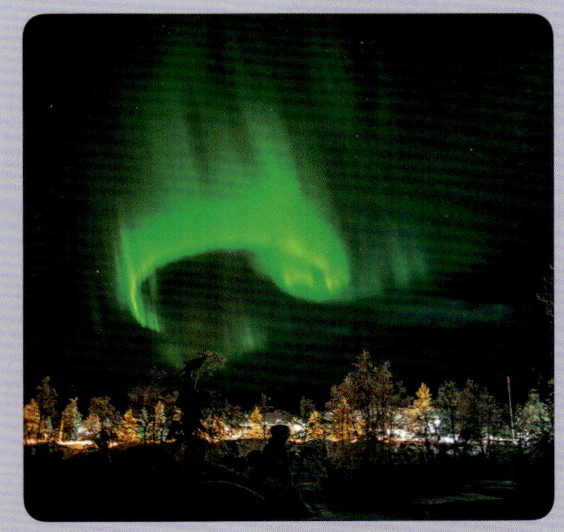

You have to travel pretty far north to get to Saariselkä. In fact, at 260 kilometers above the Arctic Circle, it's often advertised as the northernmost holiday resort in the world. Sounds pretty warm! The Lapland village of Saariselkä has a population of only about 350 people. While there, you can enjoy skiing, hiking and spas, and learn about Sámi culture and reindeer husbandry. There's also a good chance you'll be able to see the Northern Lights either from the warmth of a glass igloo or, more exposed to the elements, out under the night sky.

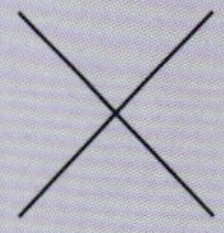

CURTAIN

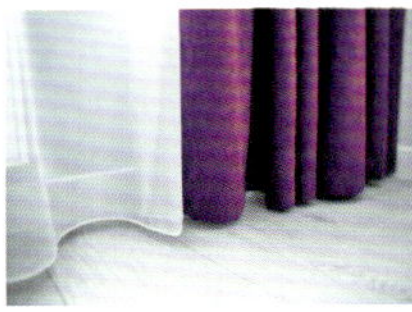

Viewed from below, a curtain of the right color and texture looks like the northern lights which have the appearance of a curtain undulating in the heavens. Tanaka-san must get pretty far down on the floor to make these discoveries.

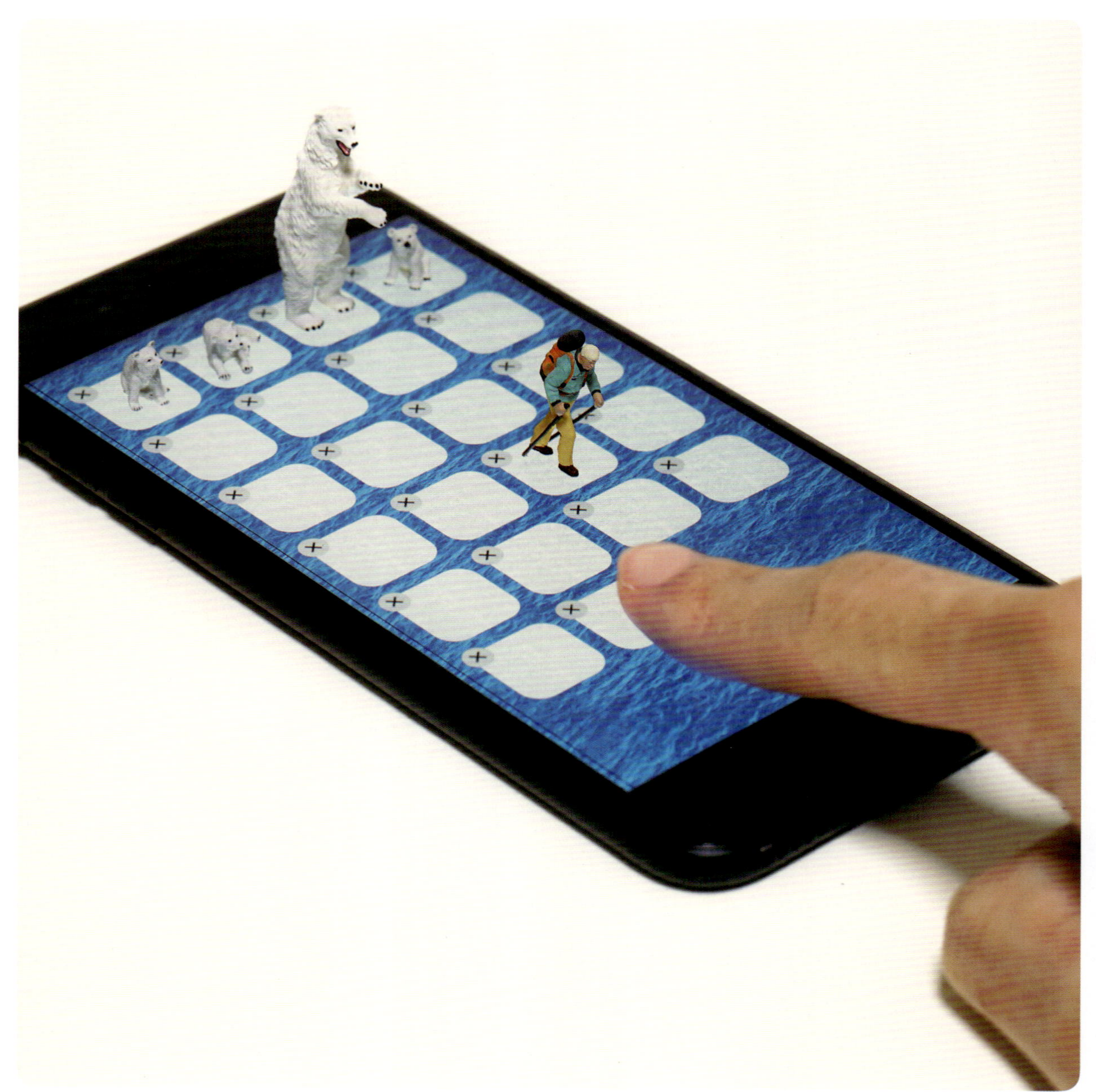

Freeze Frame

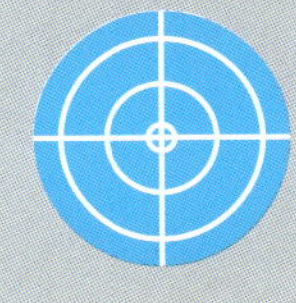

THE ARCTIC

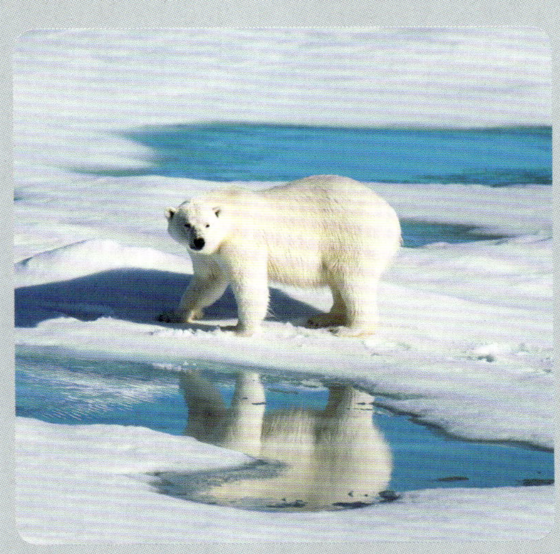

While we enjoy economic growth and technological innovation, these developments may ultimately lead to our own demise. Like applications being deleted on a smartphone, humans may be among the first to go, even before other species. Here, Tanaka-san is appealing to us not to turn our backs on other species such as polar bears.About 10% of the world's fresh water is frozen in the Arctic. This ice helps to stabilize the Earth's climate as a whole but, unfortunately, arctic ice is receding as the Earth warms. And this means that the polar bears' natural habitat is shrinking.

SMARTPHONE

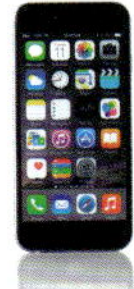

The smartphone is a revolutionary technological achievement that has made a remarkable number of other devices virtually obsolete. Cameras, watches, landline phones, compasses, alarm clocks, calculators, GPS devices, maps, TVs, payphones...

GREAT BRITAIN

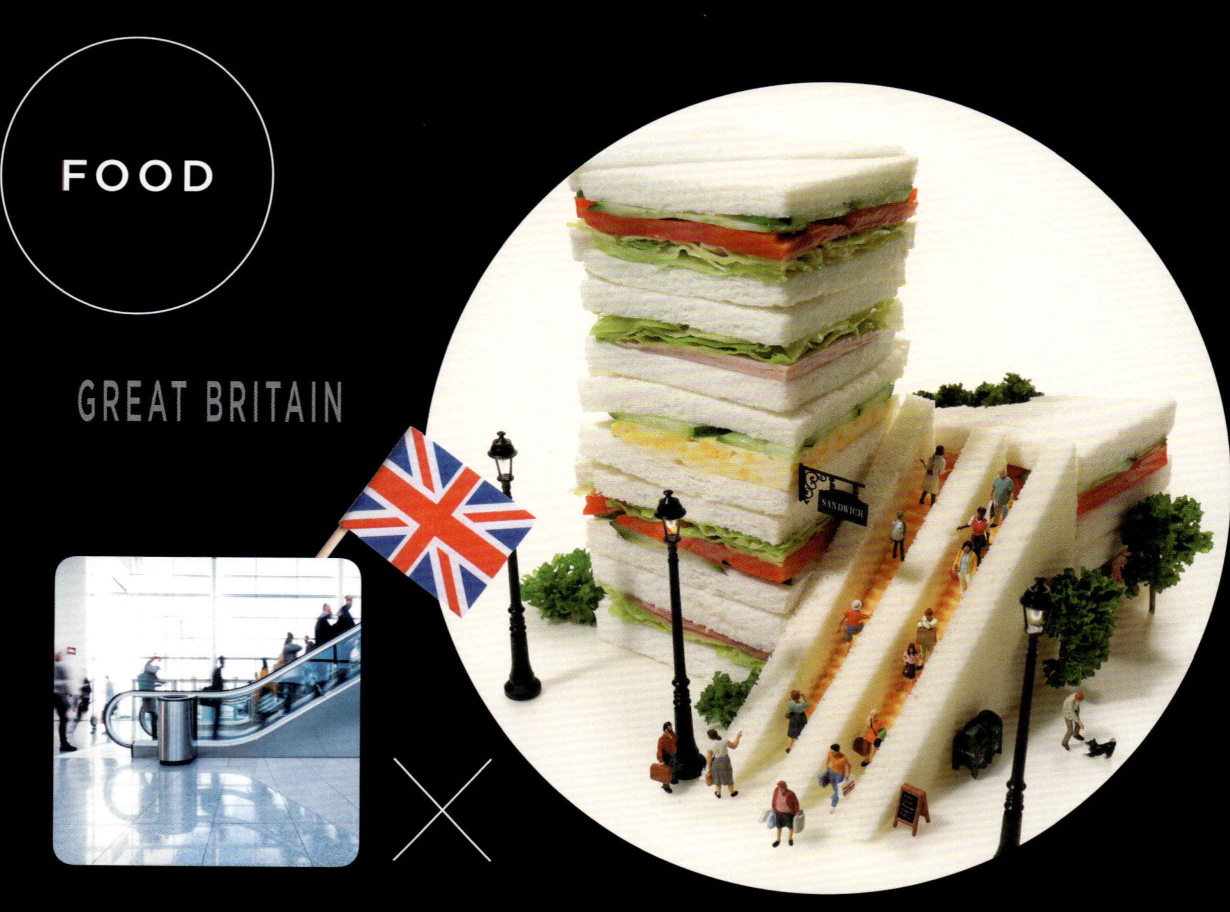

Sandwich Mall

ESCALATOR ✕ SANDWICH

Tanaka-san often enjoys a sandwich in the morning with a cup of coffee. First he made buildings with sandwiches, but here he has added a sandwich escalator with jagged cheese stairs.

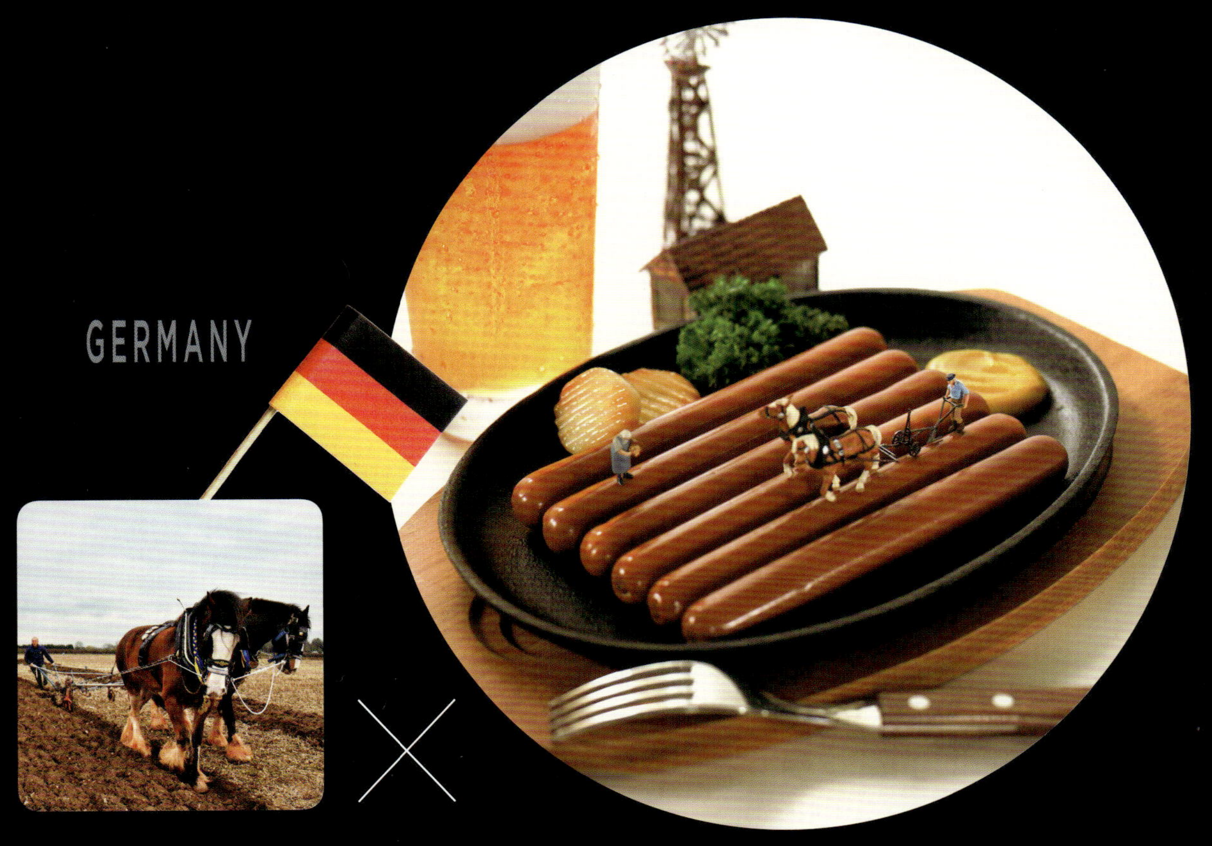

HORSE PLOW × SAUSAGE & BEER

Lined up together, sausages start to look like the furrows in a field and amber evening sunlight reminds us of the glass of beer we might enjoy after a hard day's work. I wonder what the horses will eat.

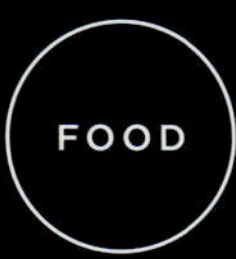

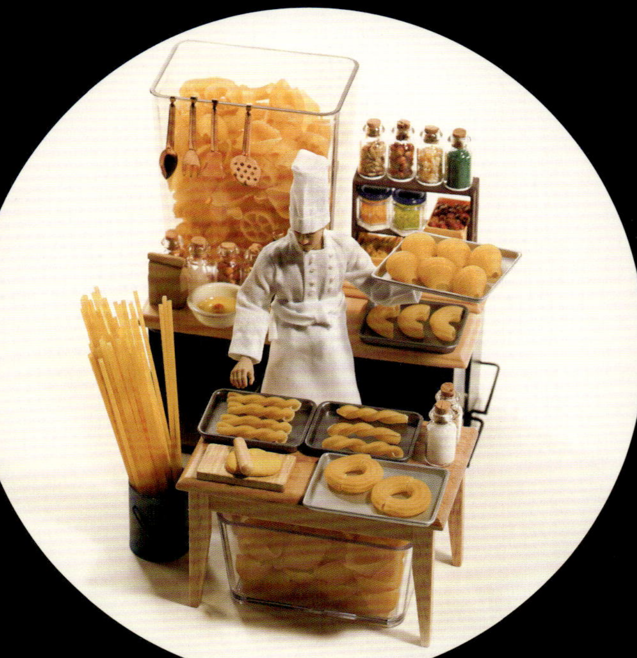

Pasta Bakery

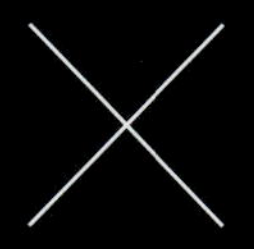

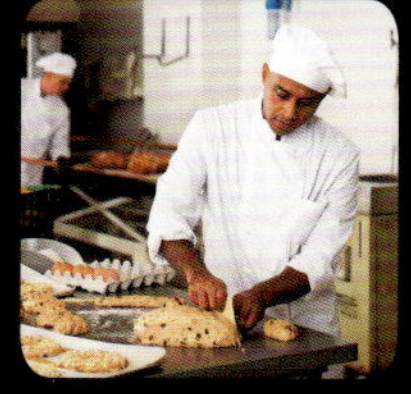

BAKER

Like bread, pasta comes in a wide variety of shapes, so many that it's difficult to remember their names.

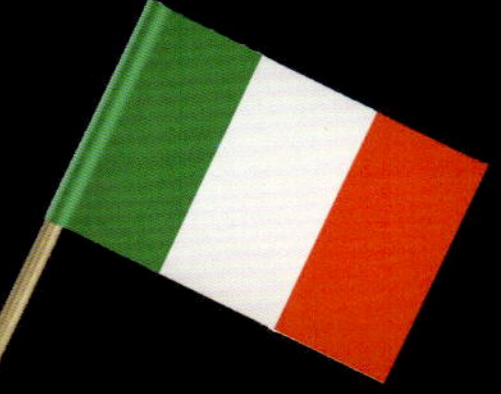

ITALY

PASTA

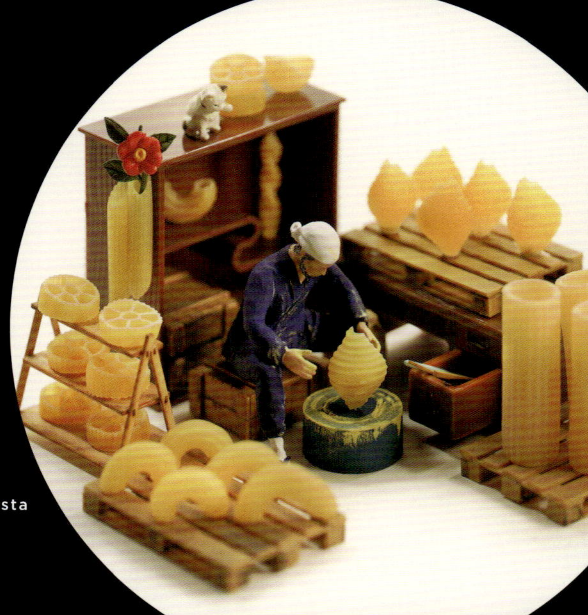

How to Make Pasta

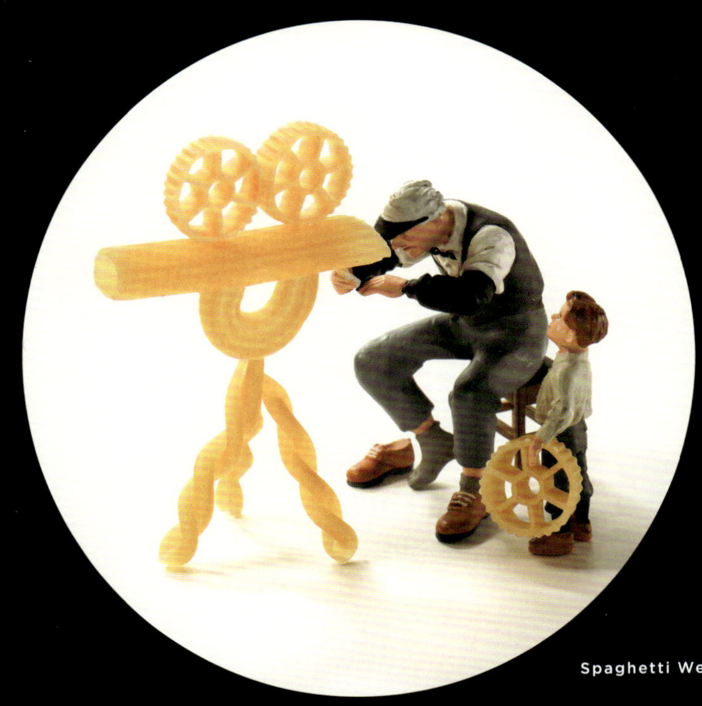

Spaghetti Western

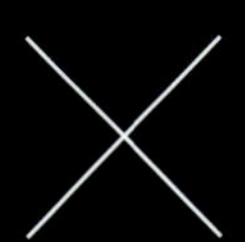

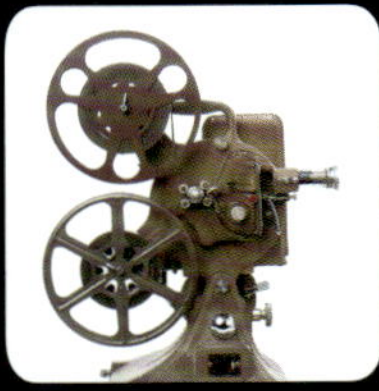

PROJECTOR

A boy looks on, holding a rotelle cinema film roll, while the operator looks through a piece of rigatoni.

POTTERY

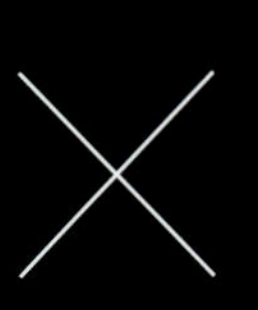

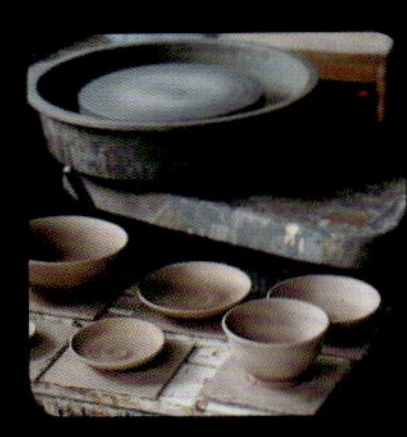

A potter shapes a piece of shell pasta. Pasta has a long shelf life, making it an ideal material for Tanaka-san to use.

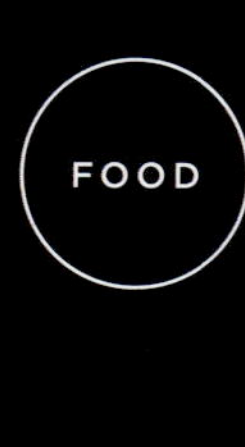

BELGIUM

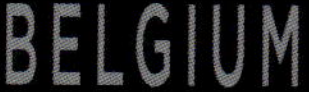

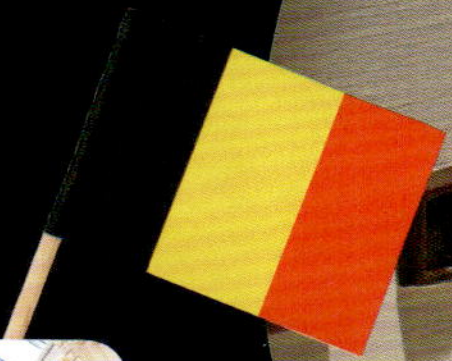

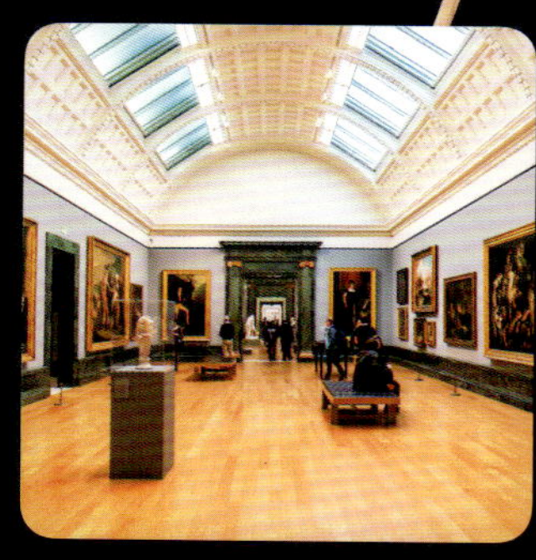

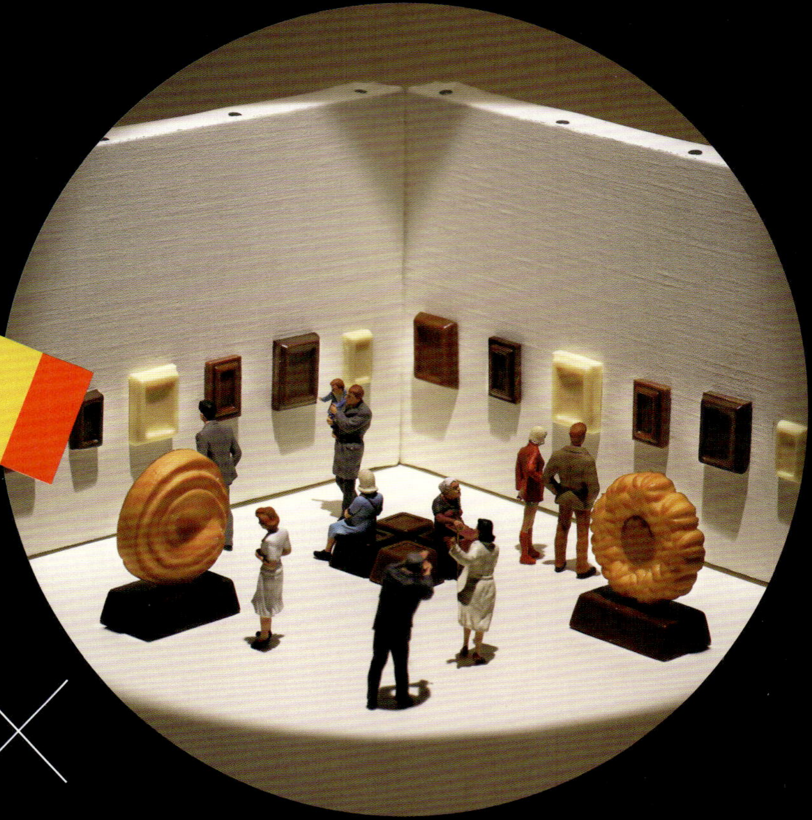

GALLERY

×

Choco-llection

CHOCOLATE

On the white canvas walls of an art gallery, chocolate squares look a lot like framed paintings. With a simple chocolate base, a cookie takes on the aura of modern art.

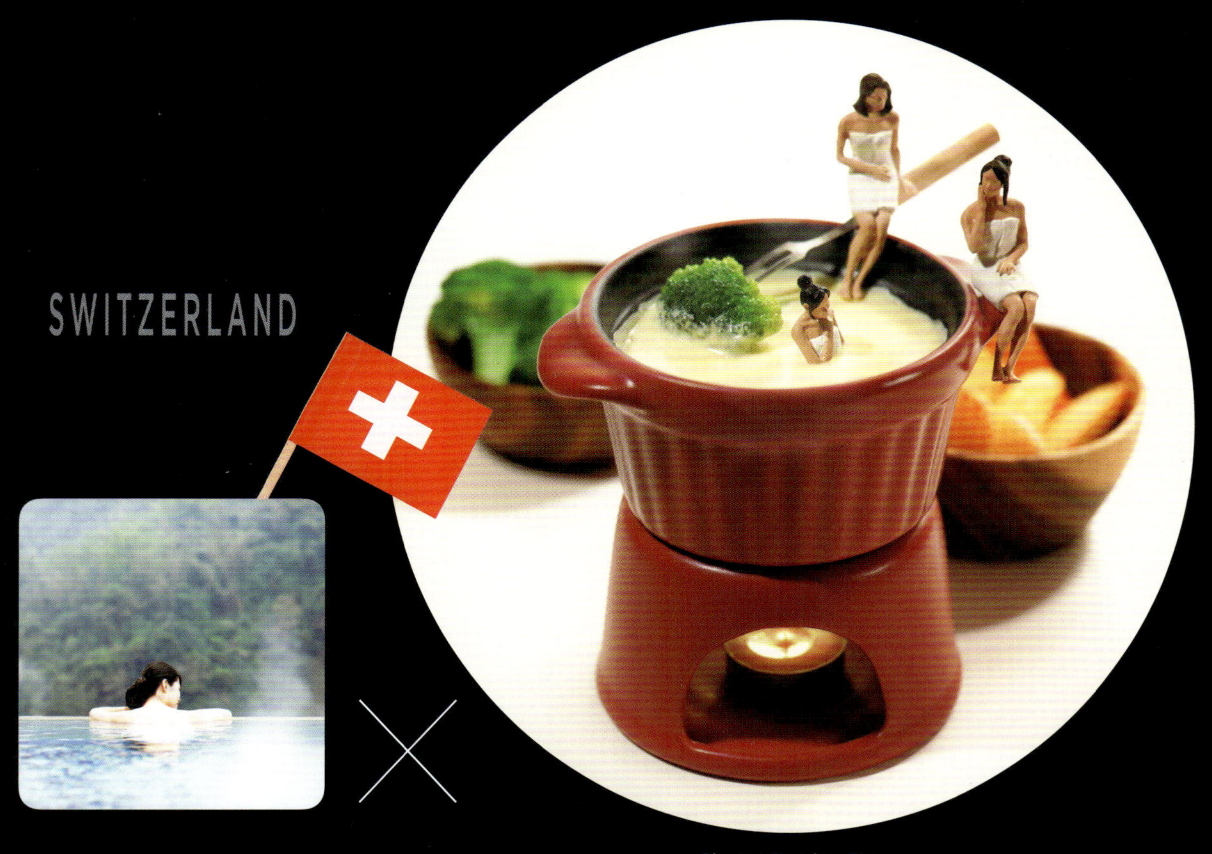

Cheese Fondue Spa

In our health boom world, there are all kinds of baths and skin packs and the like. Here we have a cheese fondue bath that makes your skin lucent and soft. And makes you hungry!

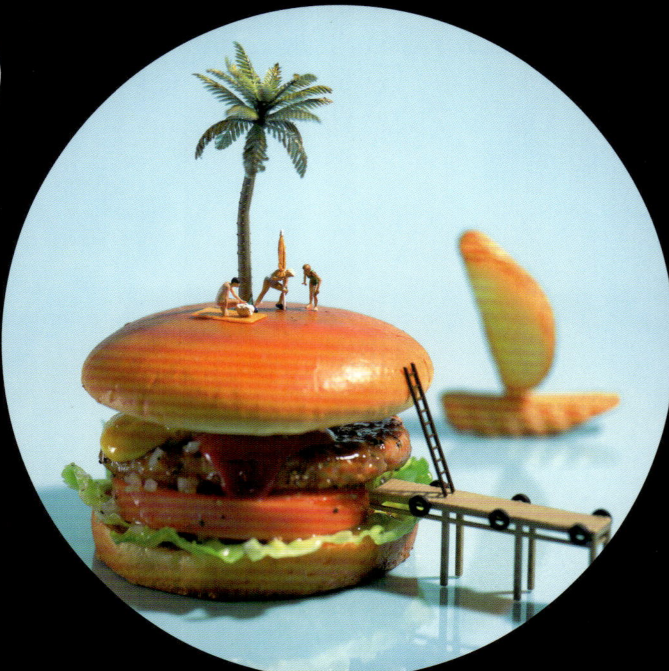

Picnic Burger

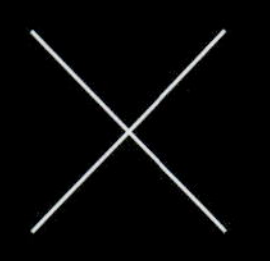

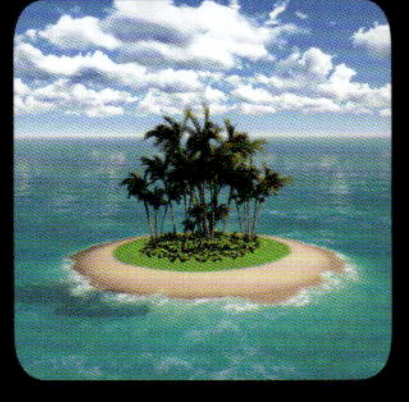

ISLAND

In the world of burger islands, the fatter the burger the better the view. Just hope the sharks aren't hungry.

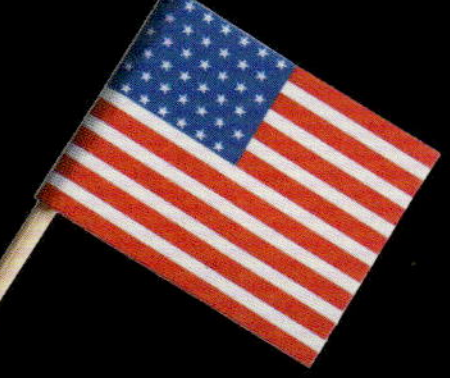

HAMBURGER

UNITED STATES OF AMERICA

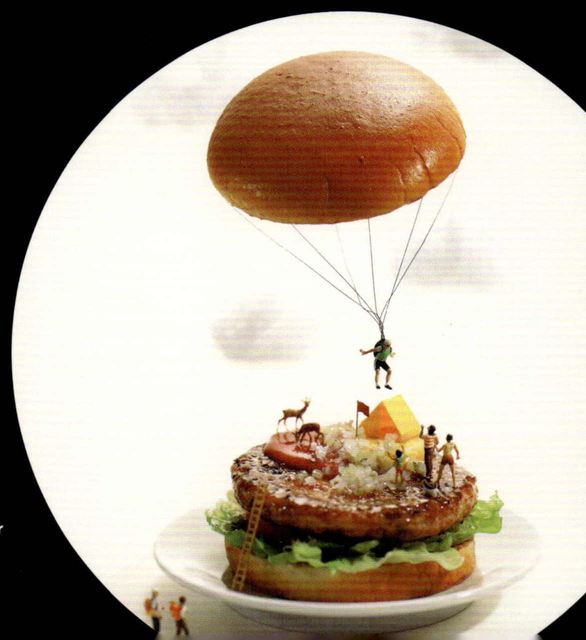

Parachute Burger

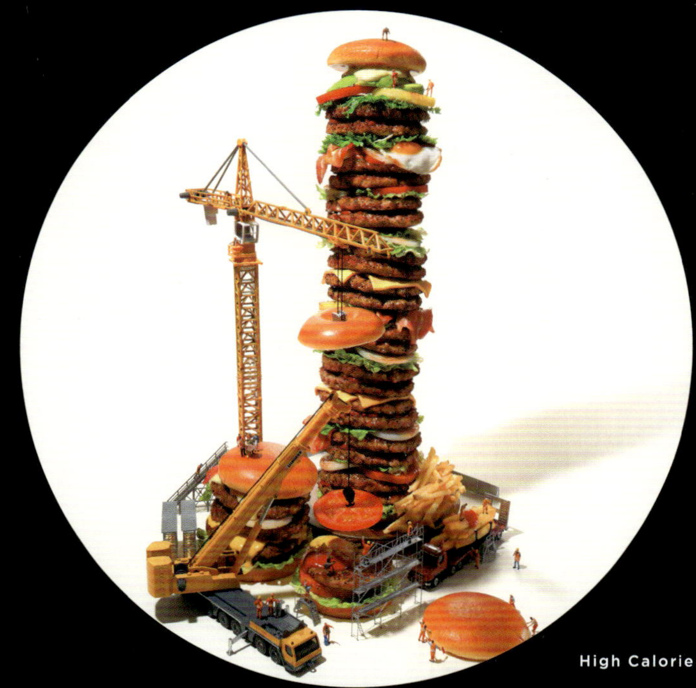

High Calorie Construction

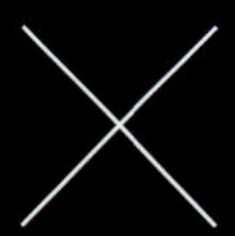

×

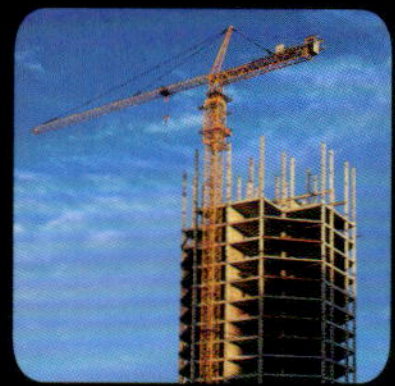

BUILDING

This is an extreme version of building your own burger. And it's quite a difficult climb to the upper floors.

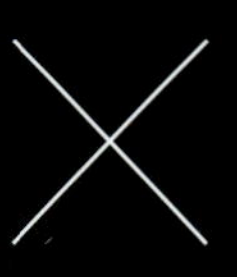

×

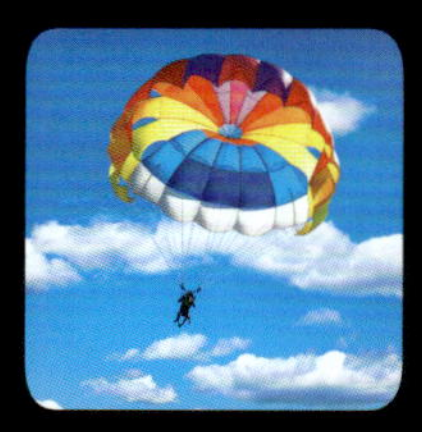

PARACHUTE

Tanaka-san likes working with hamburgers because they are easy to assemble and take apart.

JAPAN

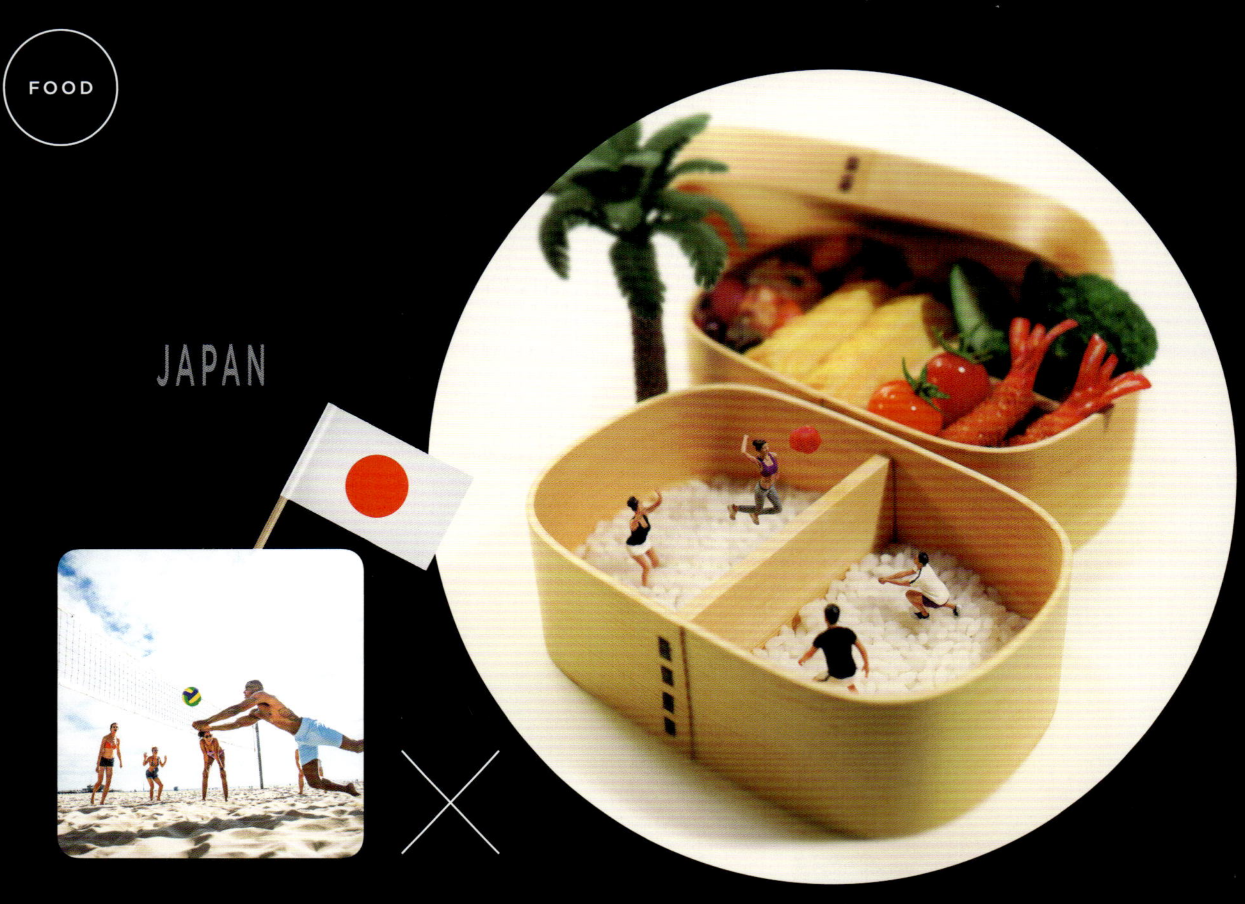
Beach Volleyball

BEACH VOLLEYBALL × BENTO

Here, rice is a beach and the umeboshi – pickled plum – is the volleyball. While the umeboshi adds color to the bento's design, it also helps preserve the rice when a bento is eaten on a warm day.

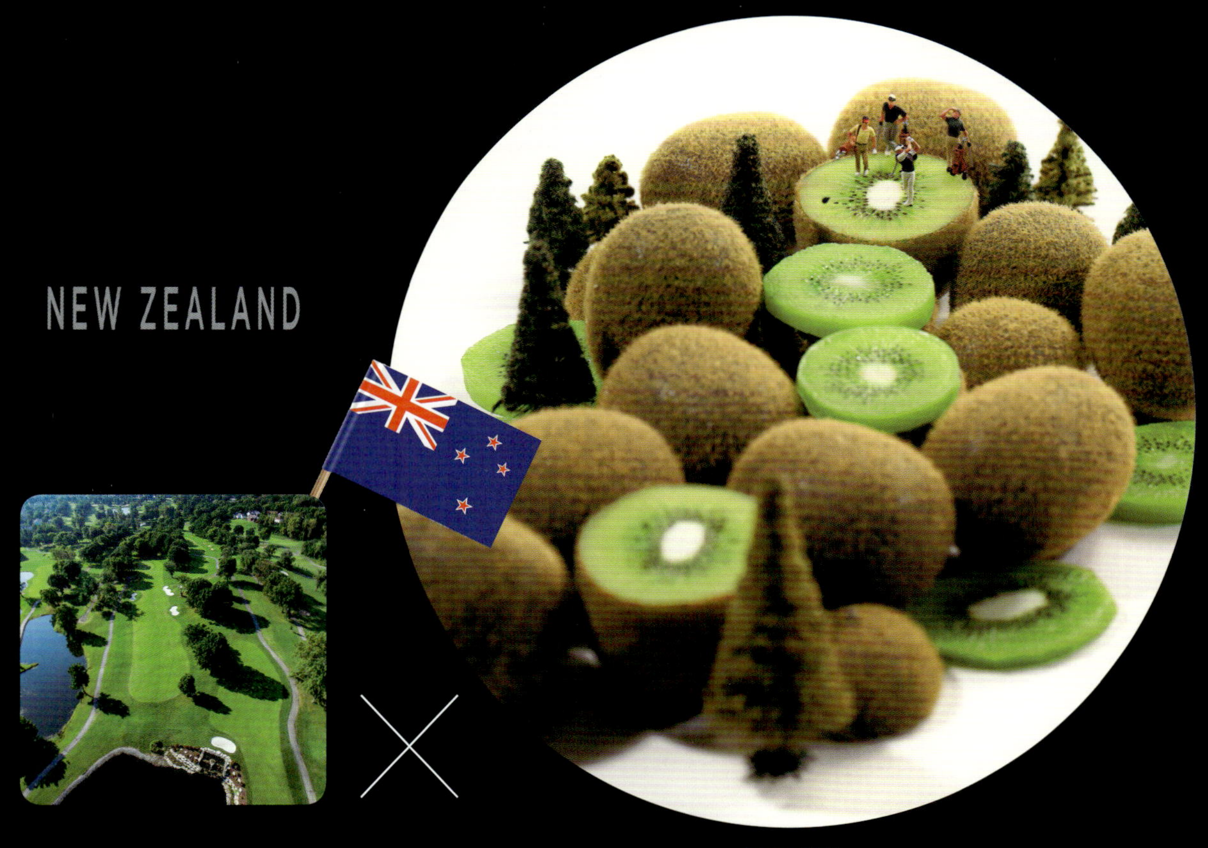

Green Kiwi

GOLF COURSE × KIWI FRUIT

Kiwi fruit looks like a fairway and a green. Its white centers are sand bunkers. The uncut kiwi fruit is the rough you really don't want to hit into. You miss that and you're really down under.

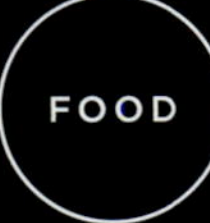

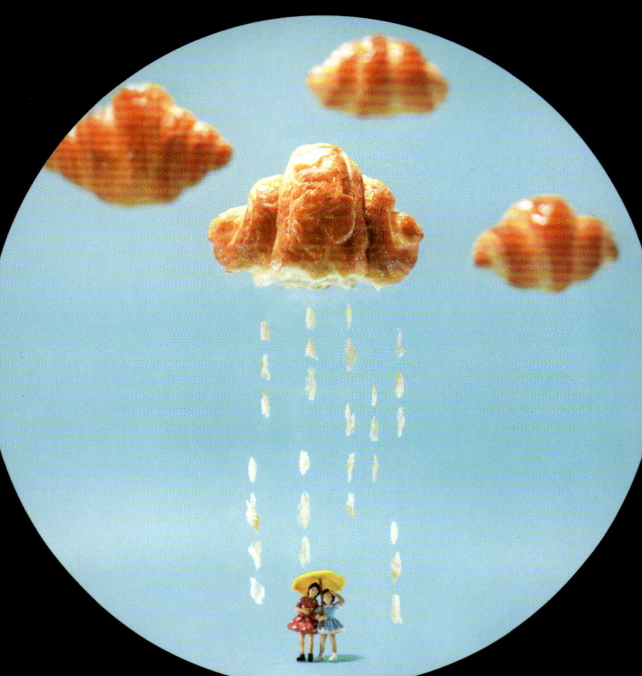

Bread Rain

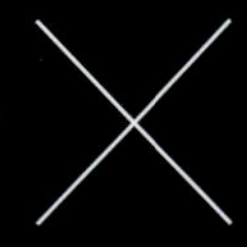

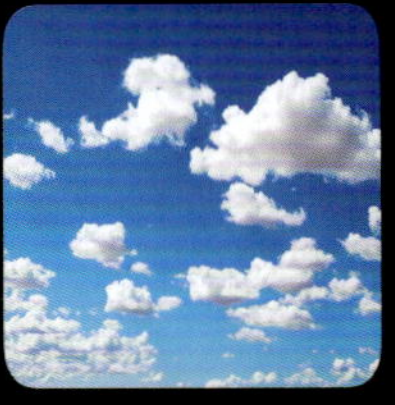

CLOUD

Just another cloudy day in France with a little bread rain precipitation. It's good they have an umbrella!

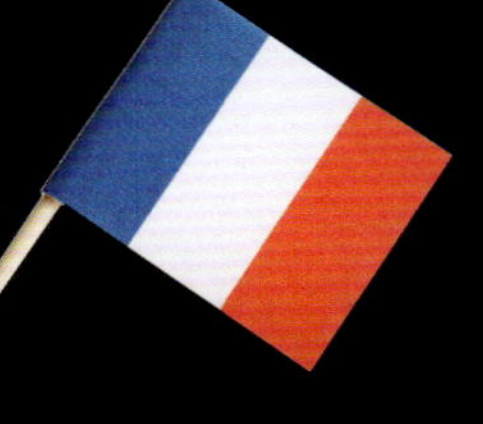

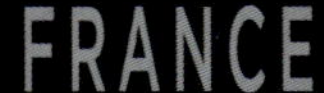

FRANCE

CROISSANT

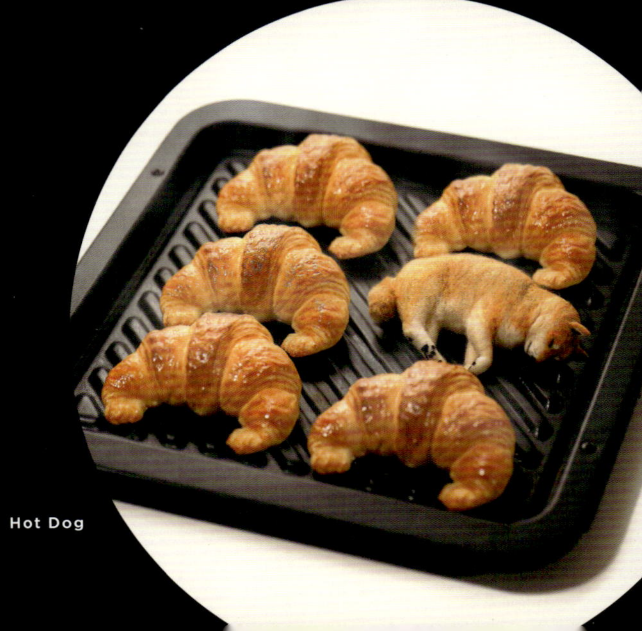

Hot Dog

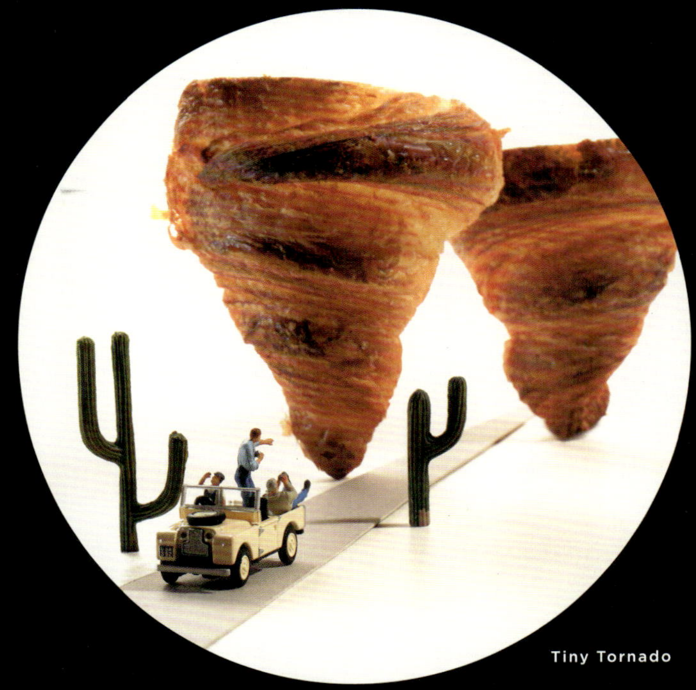

Tiny Tornado

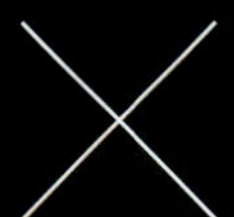

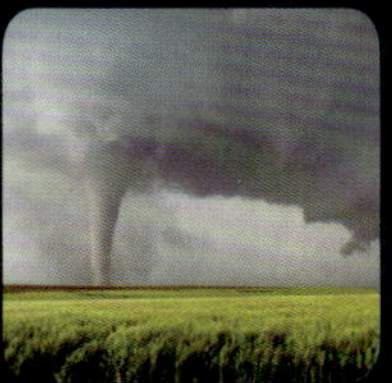

TORNADO

Cut in half and stood on its end, a croissant becomes a whirling tornado that kicks up a lot of dirt.

SHIBA INU

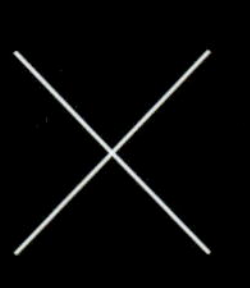

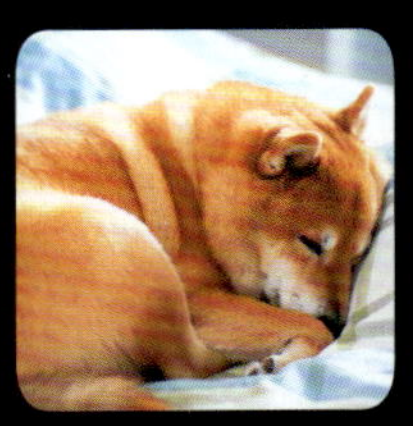

This Japanese hunting dog resembles a croissant when it sleeps on a baking pan. This is not to be tried at home!

PEOPLE'S REPUBLIC OF CHINA

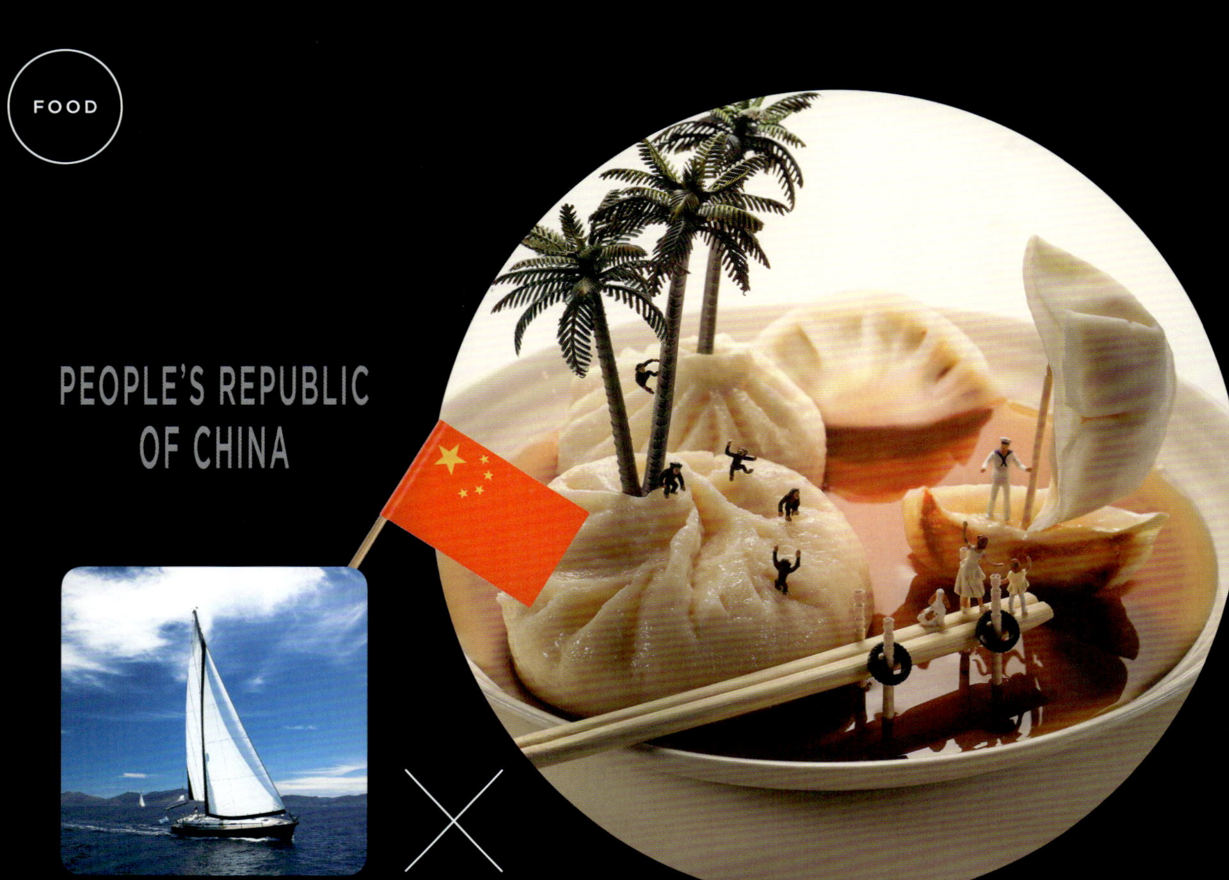

Dumpling Islands

YACHT ✕ DUMPLING SUM

Tanaka-san eats a lot of gyoza and dumplings so he has a number of pieces that make use of them. Here, all eyes – monkeys included - are on the gyoza sailboat.

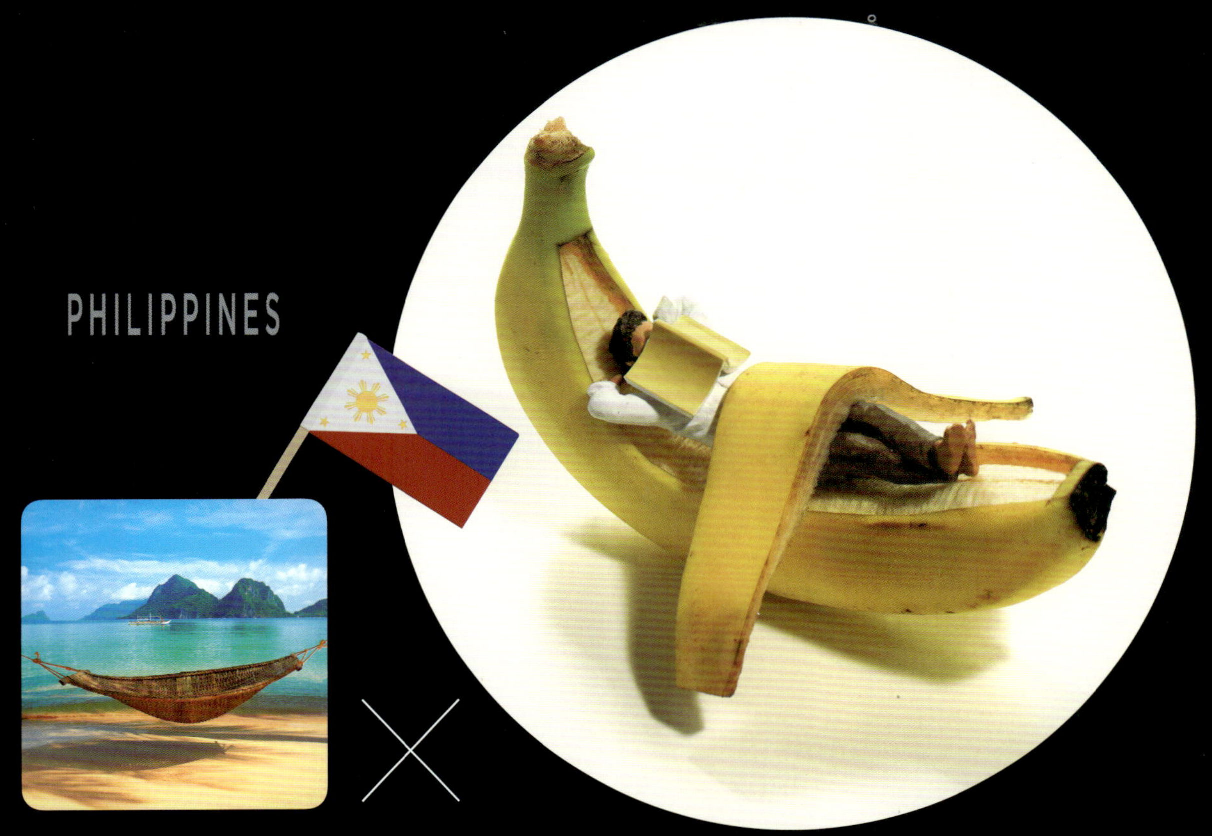

How to sleep on a banana.

Tanaka-san's son suggested that bananas look like beds so he used this idea to make a banana's hammock, in keeping with the banana's curved shape. And he added a banana blanket.

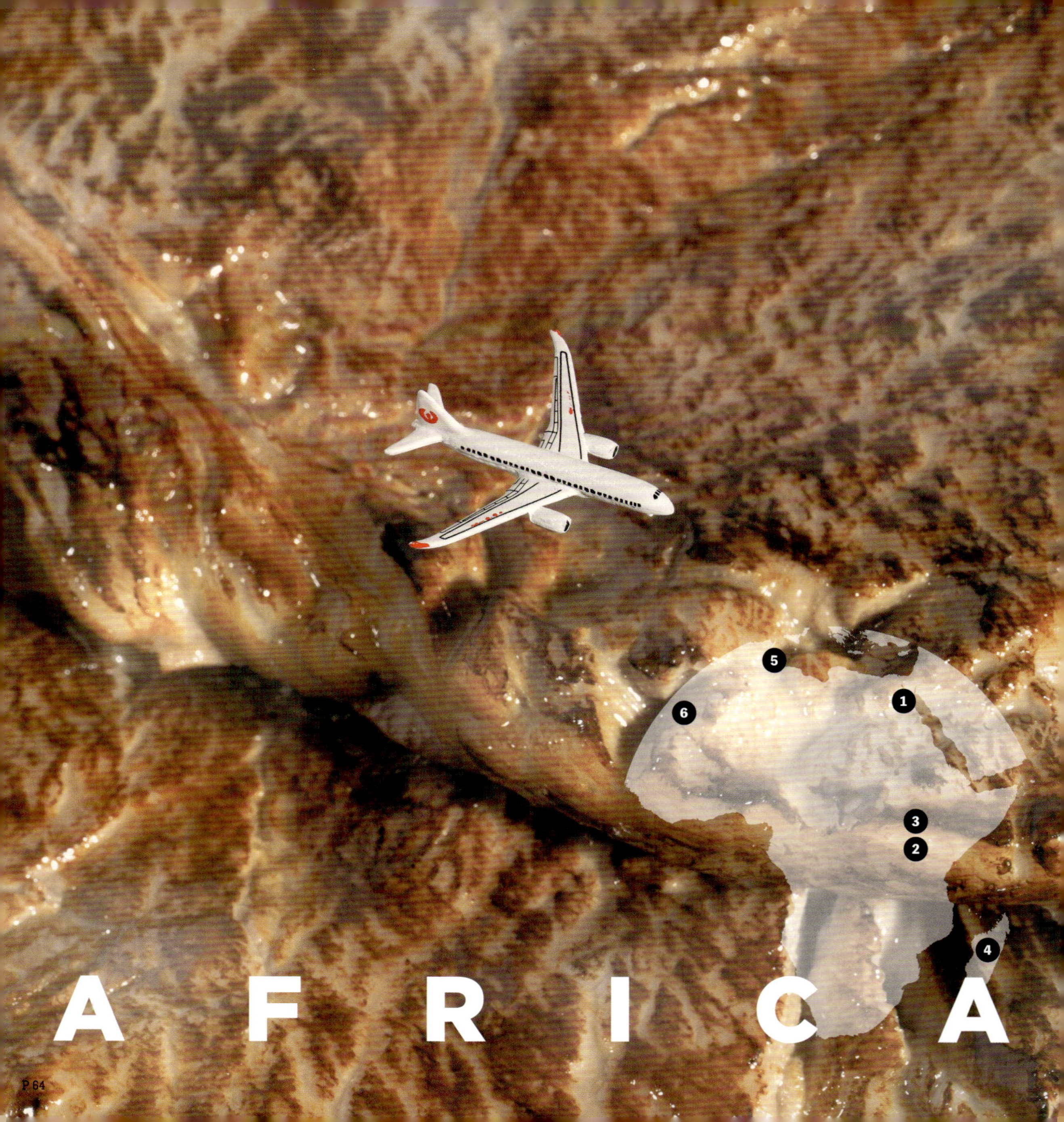

5
6
1
3
2
4
AFRICA

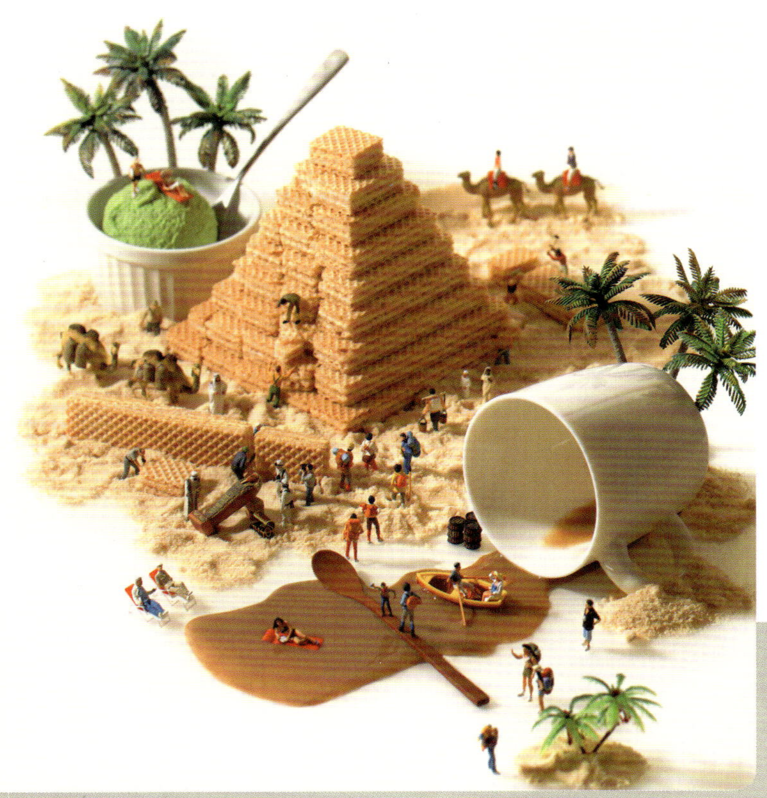
Egyptian Sugar High

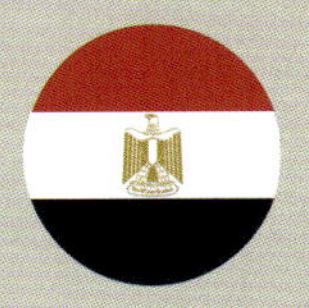

EGYPT

PYRAMID

A sweet oasis. The desert sands are brown sugar, a luxury traded widely in the past. Wafers are piled high to create a pyramid and spilled milk coffee is a nearby river, perhaps the Nile.

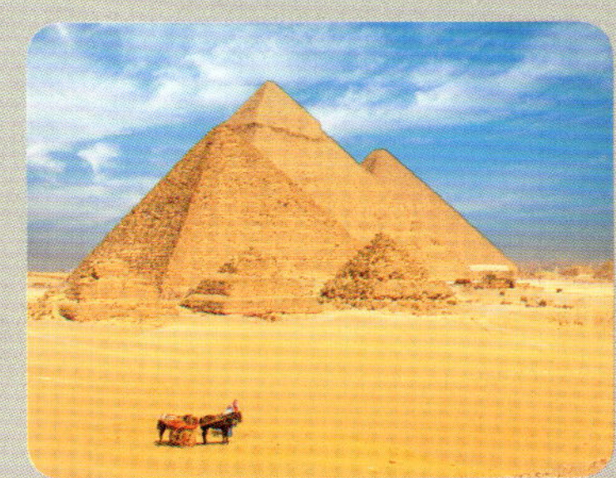

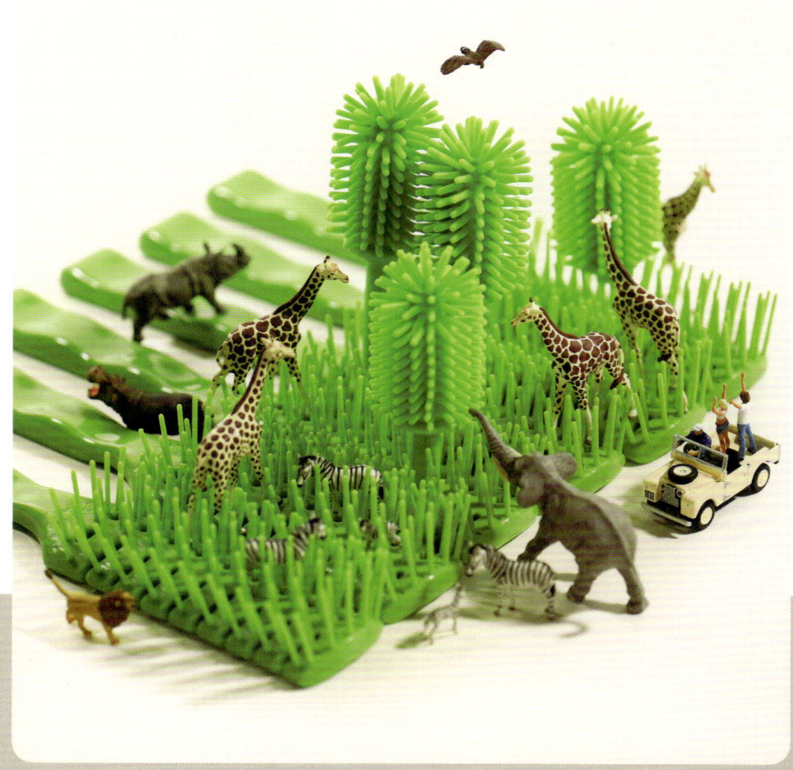

A clean environment?

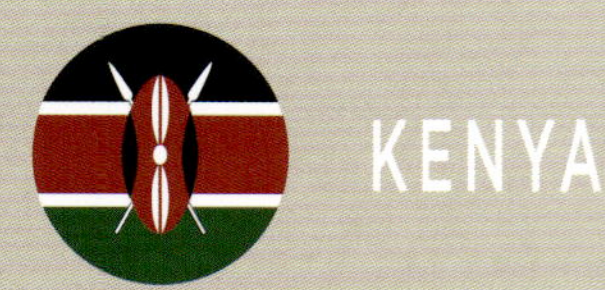

KENYA

NAIROBI NATIONAL PARK

In Tanaka-san's piece, tourists enjoy a safari in what first appears to be a lush natural environment when, in fact, it's a plastic world with no nourishment to offer these wild animals.

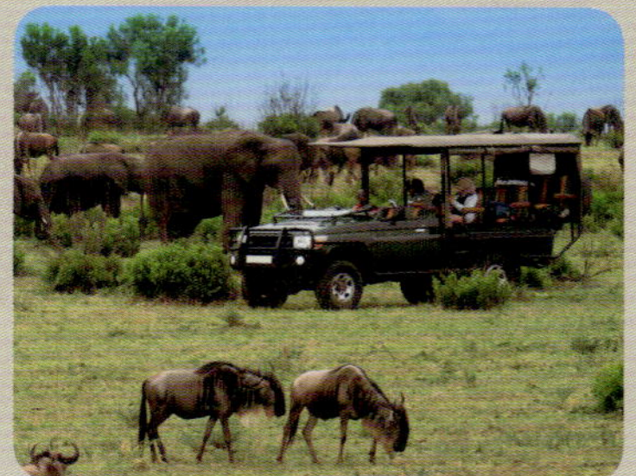

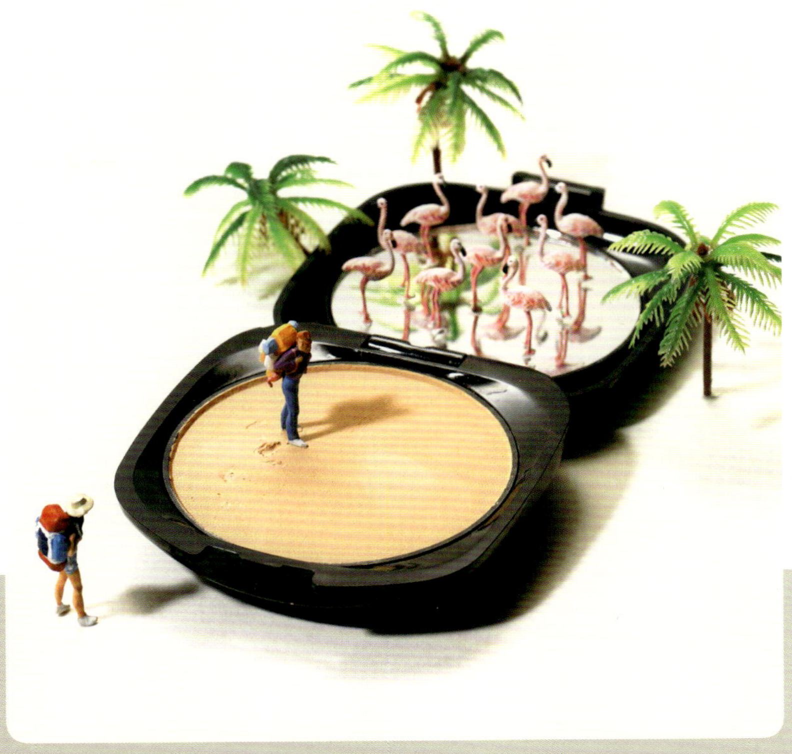

Mirror-mingo

LAKE NAKURU

Flamingos are reflected on a compact mirror and powder foundation is fine desert sand. With rising water levels, the flamingo population at Lake Nakuru has declined.

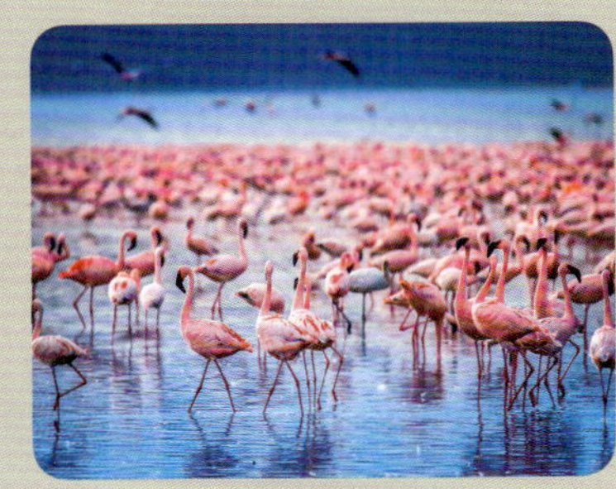

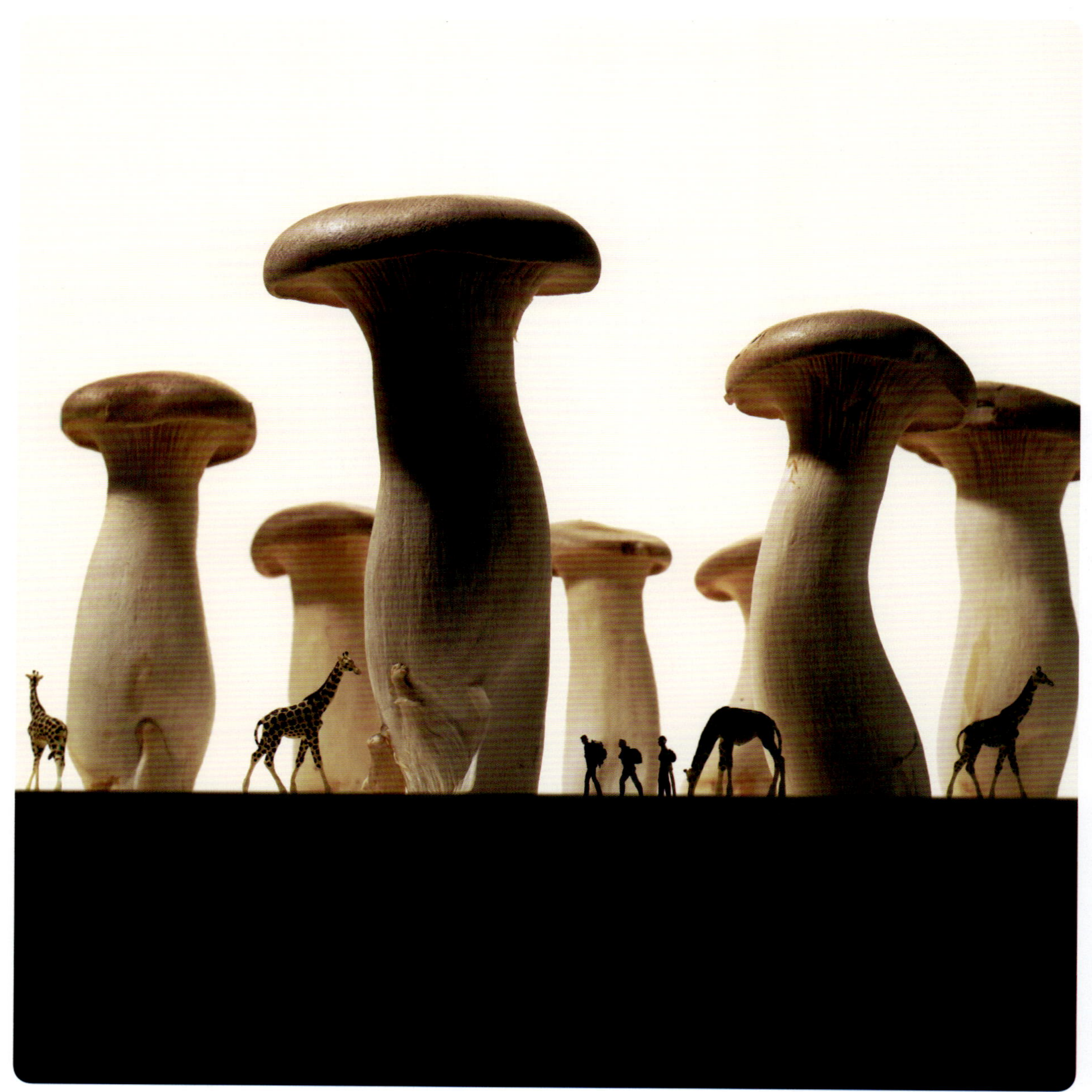

Baobab Safari

MADAGASCAR

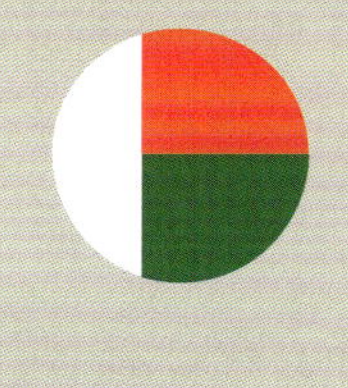

MORONDAVA

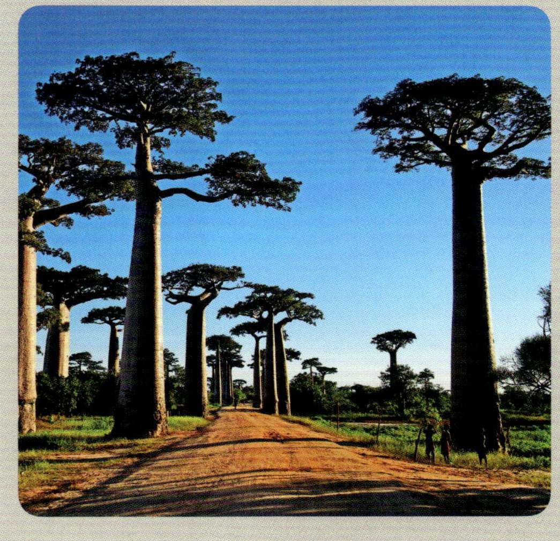

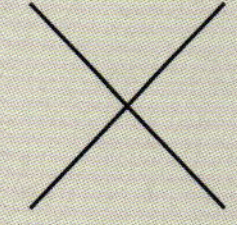

Near Morondava, on the coast of West Madagascar, one finds the Avenue of the Baobabs and the Kirindy Forest Reserve, which has the greatest density of primates in the world and a large number of baobab trees as well. The largest variety of baobab, the Adansonia Grandidieri, reaches heights of 30 meters and has a trunk that is 3 meters around. Locally these trees are called "Renala" which means "Mother of the Forest." Baobabs are photogenic at sunset, sunrise and at night, under the stars. Oh and they look good in the middle of the day too!

KING OYSTER MUSHROOM

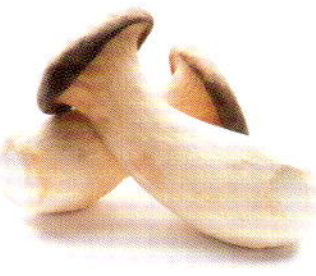

Seen from this angle, king oyster mushrooms resemble giant baobab trees standing proud in the African savannah. The people and animals that walk among them give us a sense of their size. Some trees may live for more than 1000 years!

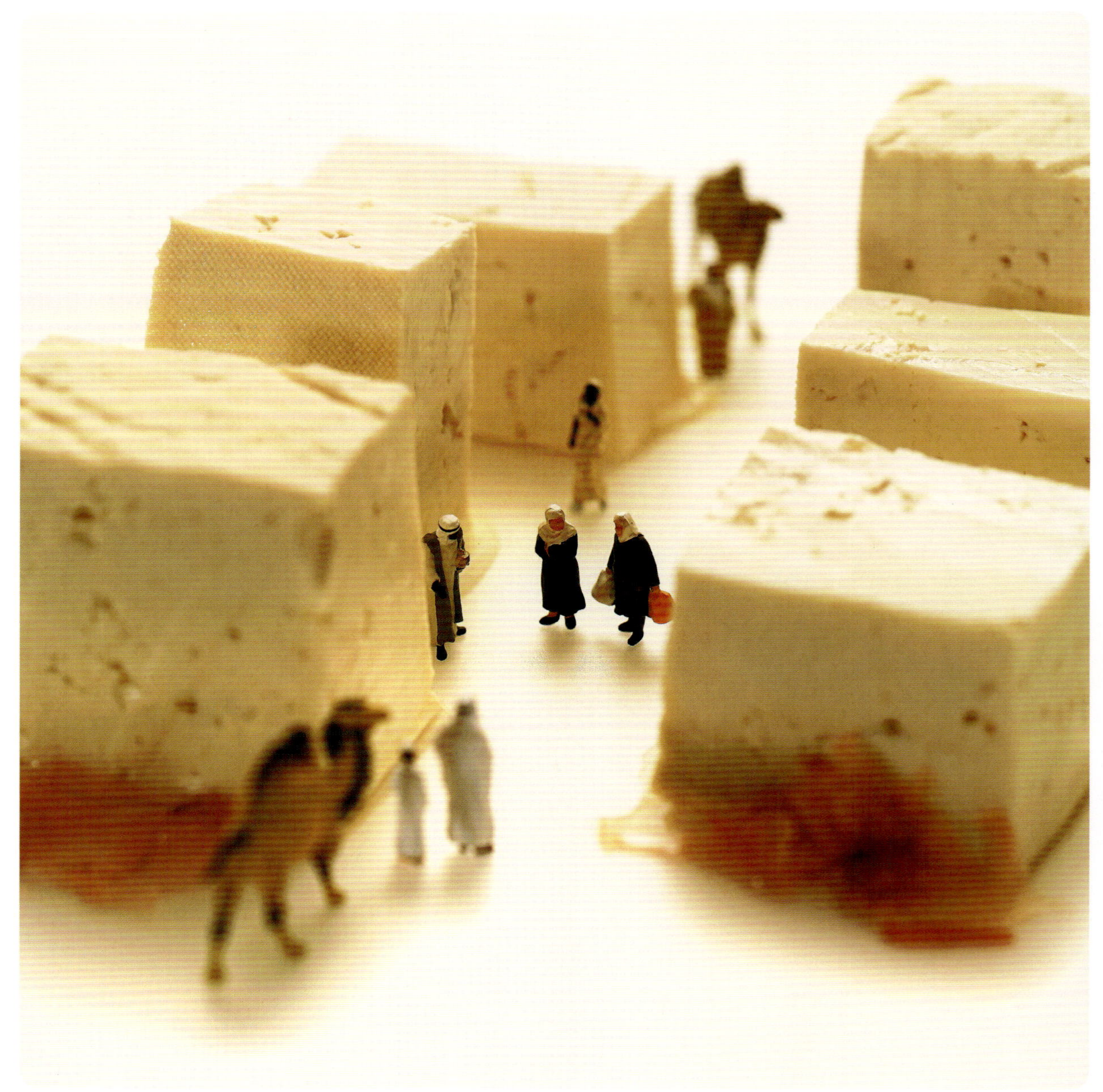

Tofu Town

TUNISIA

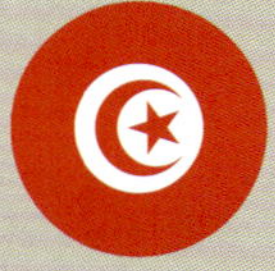

KSAR HADADA

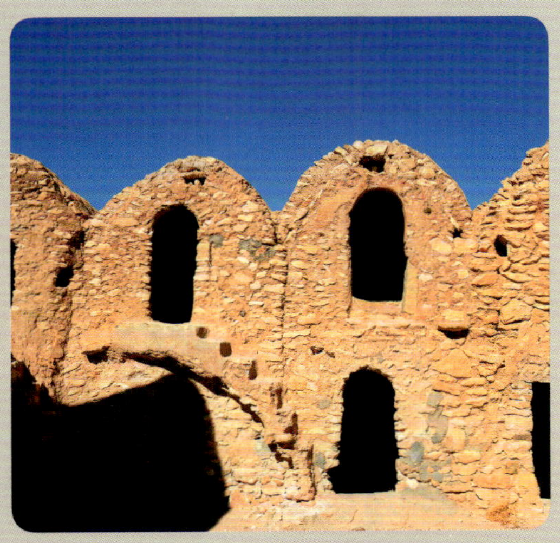

With its hot, windy, sandy scenery, rural Tunisia was a convincing location to depict life on another planet and it was for this reason that George Lucas chose Ksar Hadada as the birthplace of Anakin Skywalker in Star Wars: Episode I – The Phantom Menace. This village, population 1100, is located in southeastern Tunisia and its current residents rely on tourism, olive cultivation and goat and sheep farming for their livelihood. Tunisians express thanks with a simple, elegant gesture, placing their right hand on their chest close to their heart.

FIRM TOFU

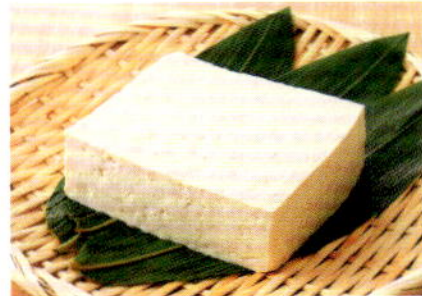

Some of the more organically shaped homes in this area share a texture and coloration reminiscent of firm momen tofu. Bonito flakes, a tasty and salty companion to tofu, suggest foliage that has been scorched by the hot sun.

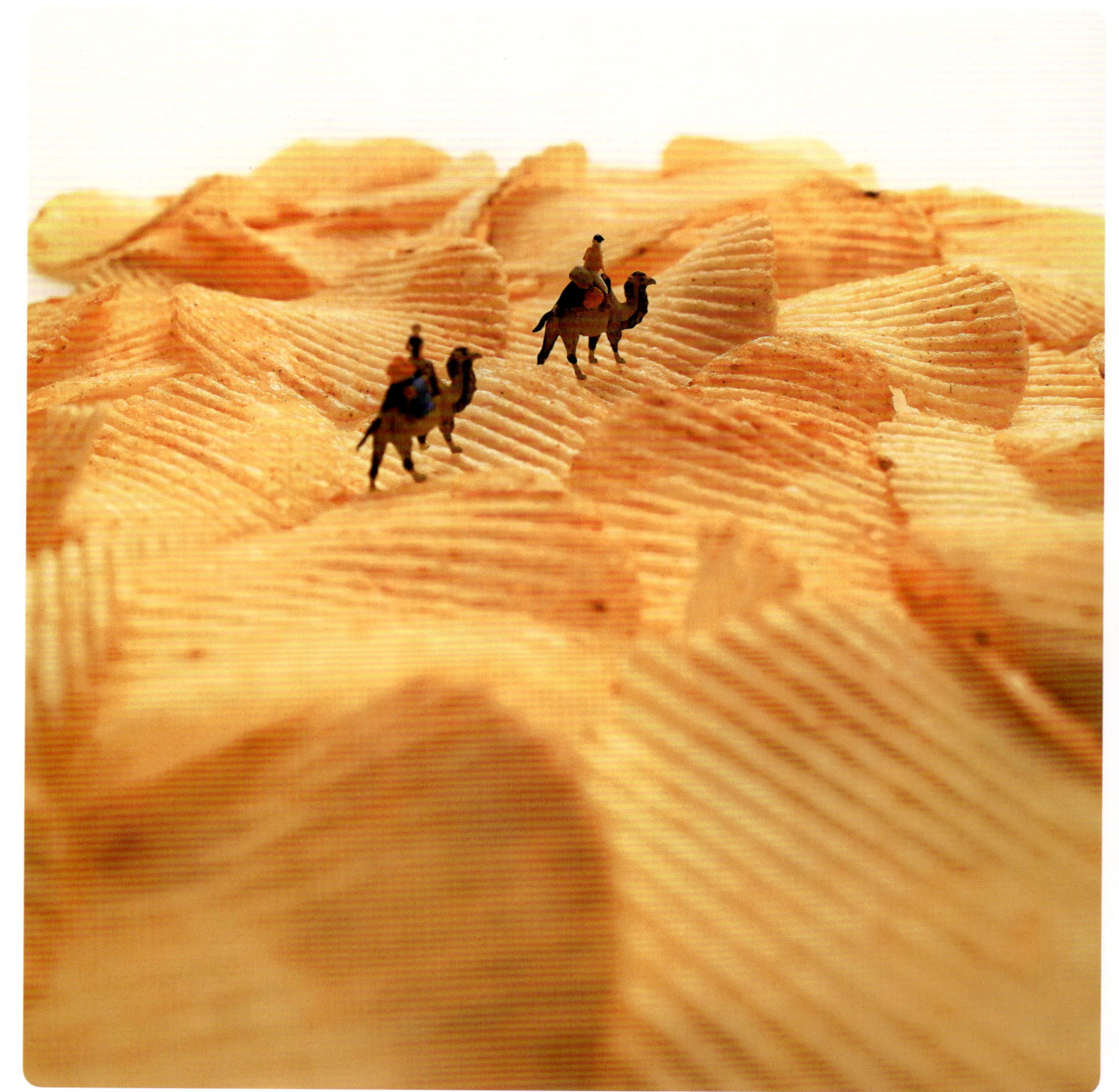

Potato Desert

MOROCCO

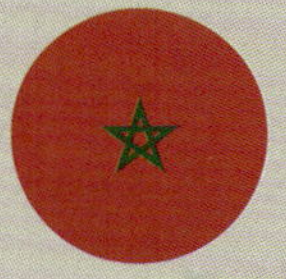

THE SAHARA

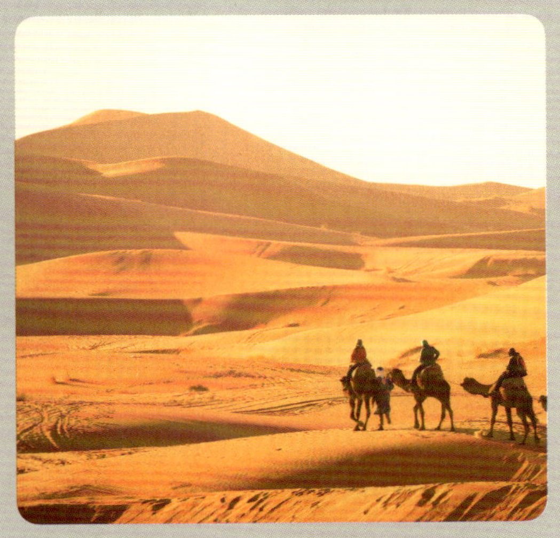

The Sahara stretches across 11 countries and accounts for almost one third of Africa. Its name comes from the Arabic word "sahra" which means "desert." Sand dunes account for about 25% of the Sahara, some reaching over 180 meters in height. About 2.5 million people live in the Sahara. Some live in settlements near water. Others live a nomadic life, traveling with their herds of sheep, goats or camels. While the Sahara is the world's largest and most famous hot desert, the Arctic and Antarctica are even larger, but they are defined as "cold deserts."

POTATO CHIPS

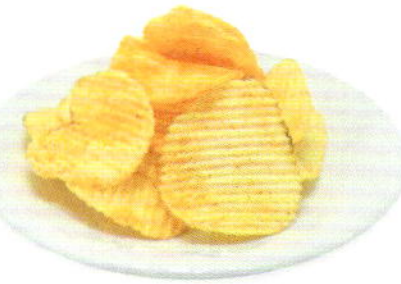

Tanaka-san makes use of plain, salt, ridged potato chips here in an effort to replicate the redundant, monotonal rise and fall of a sand dune landscape. In Japan, potato chips come in a huge variety of flavors and shapes so he must resist temptation.

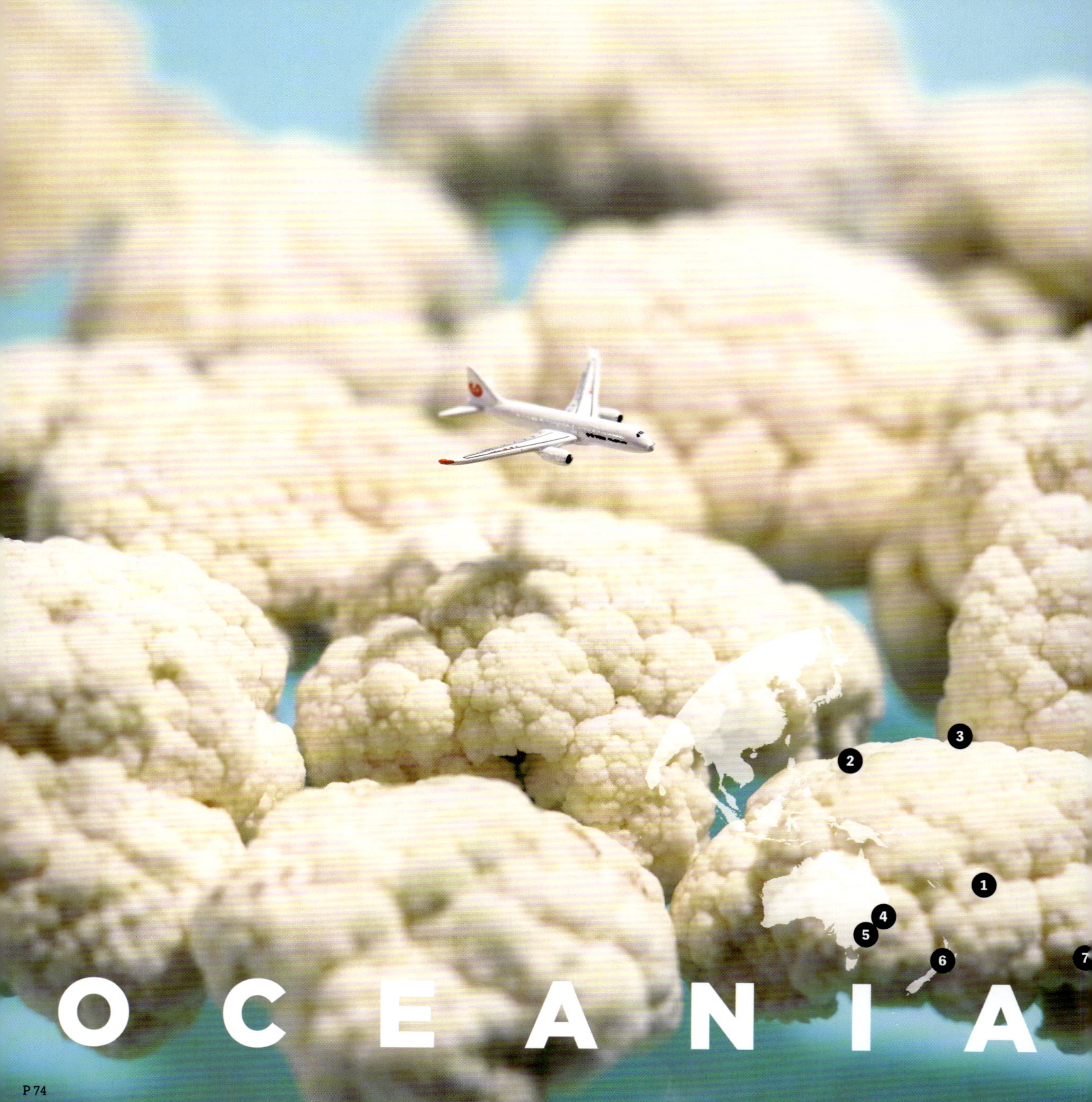

OCEANIA

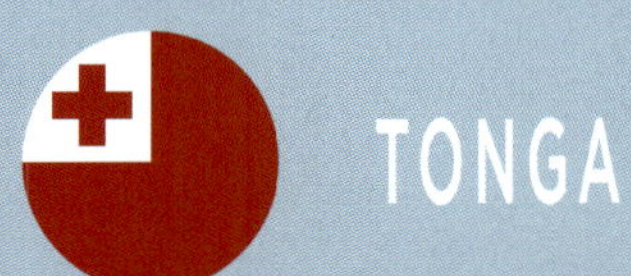

TONGA

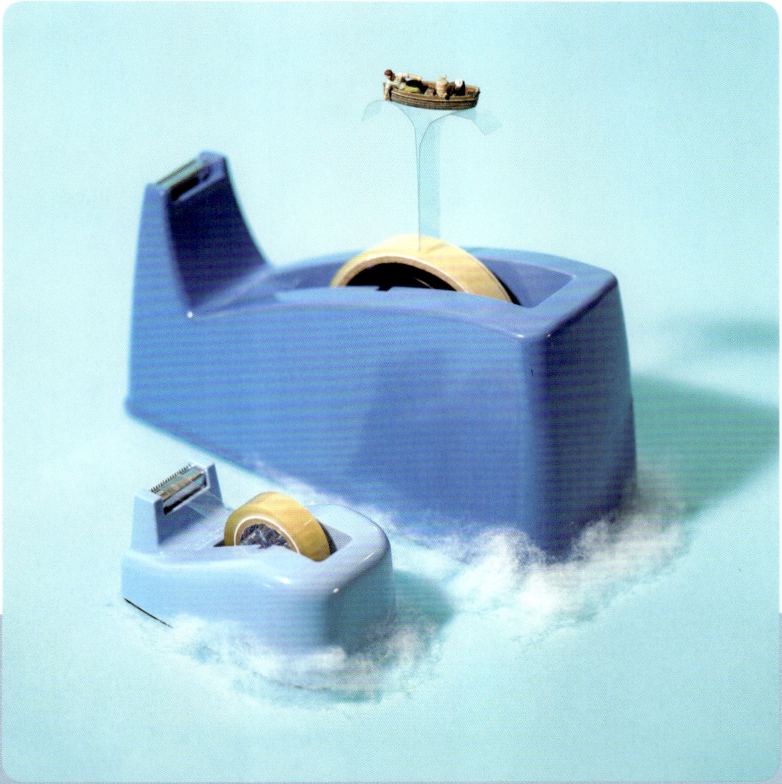

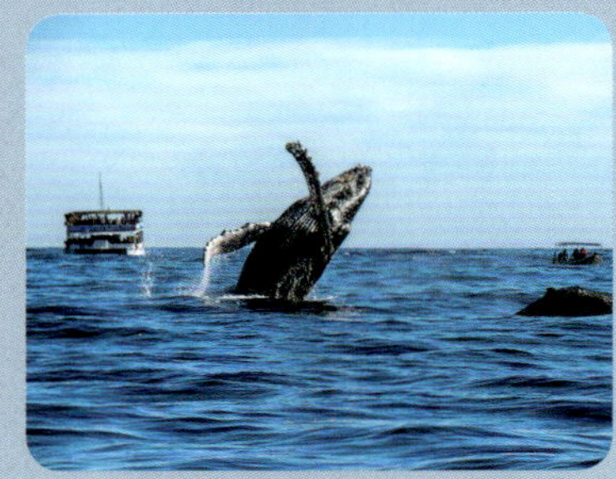

Tape Whale

VAVA'U ISLAND

This island is said to have been created by the god Maui who pulled it up out of the sea with a magic hook. Here Tanaka-san uses office supplies to depict stately marine life.

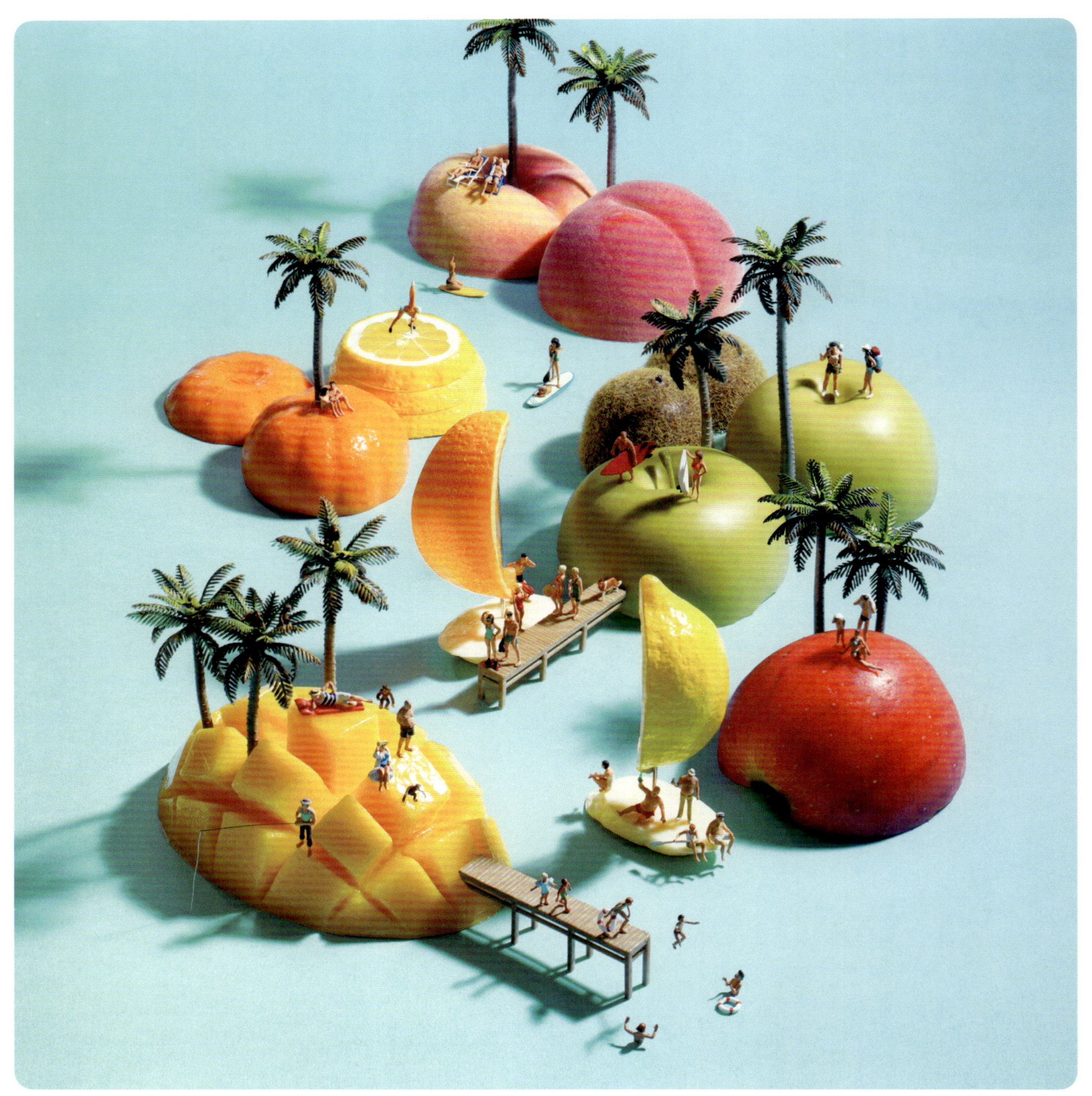

Juisea

PALAU

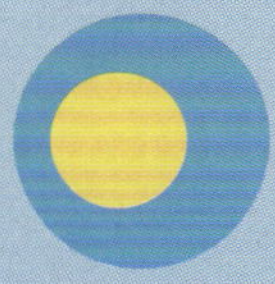

ROCK ISLANDS

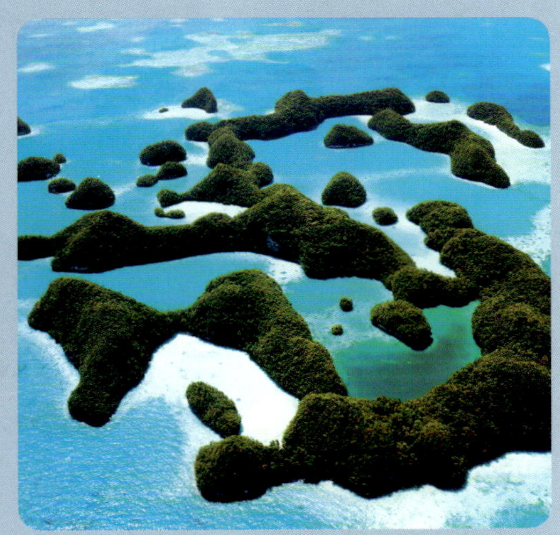

The Rock Islands of Palau, which were settled until the 18th century, are a cultural and natural heritage site. Depending on who is counting, there are anywhere from 250 to 300 islands, most of them small, uninhabited and made out of limestone or coral. The islands are popular among divers who enjoy marine lakes, shallow lagoons and decorated caves just to name a few attractions. Many of the islands have an unusual umbrella-like shape and the surrounding ocean is home to a reef system that sustains a wide variety of plants, birds and marine life.

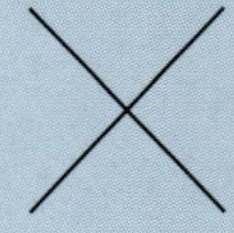

TROPICAL FRUIT

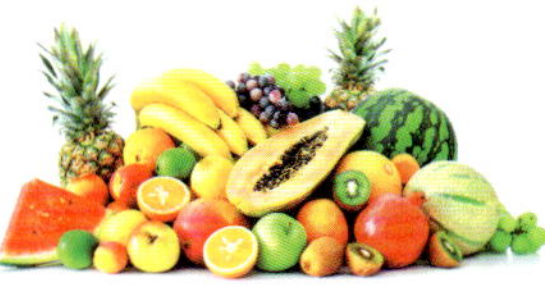

Any fruit, when cut in half, becomes an island. And the presence of a few palm trees makes even non-tropical fruit look tropical. Here, the boats are made from slices of a banana. Which island would you like to eat first?

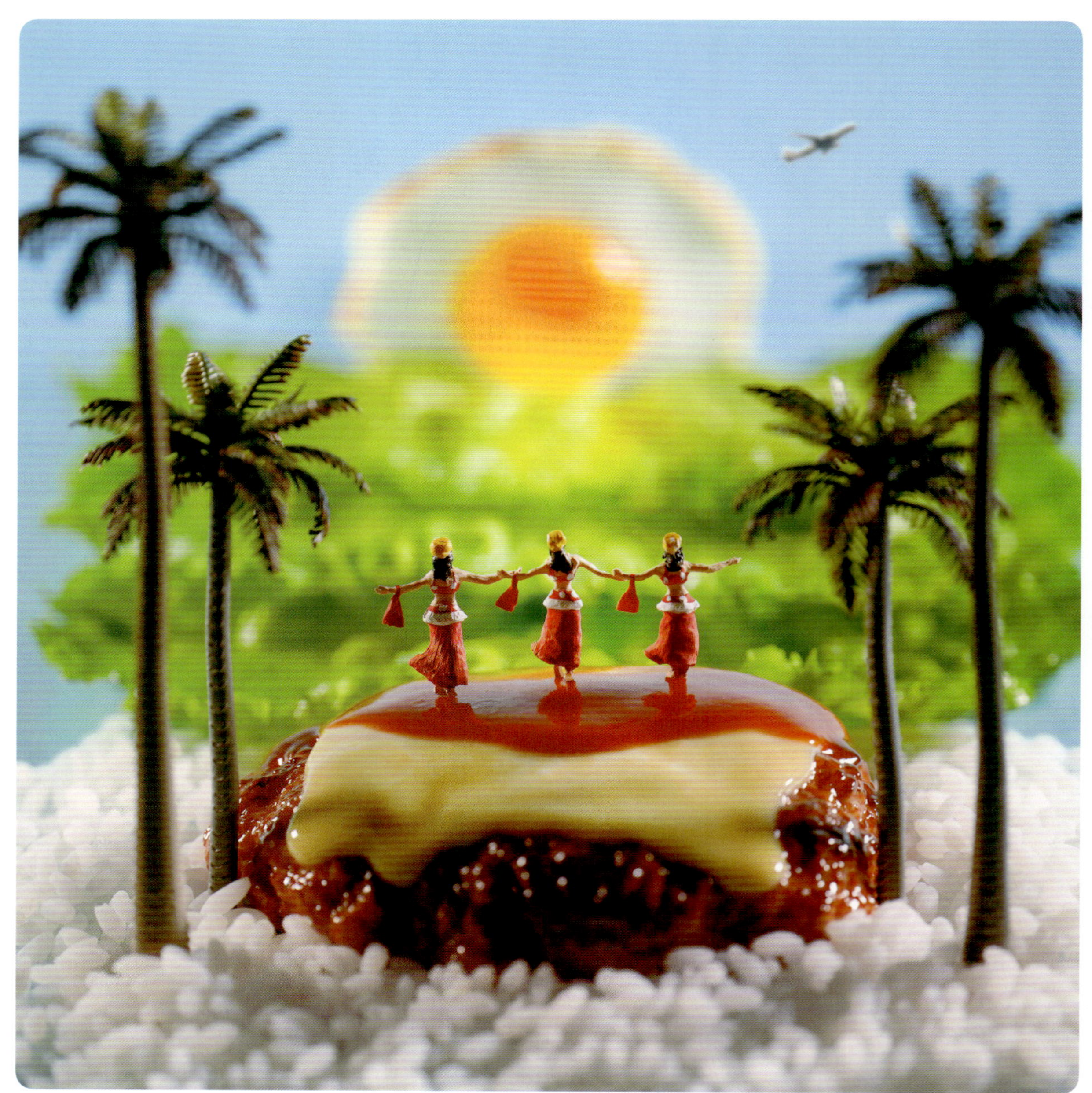

Loco Moco Beach

UNITED STATES OF AMERICA

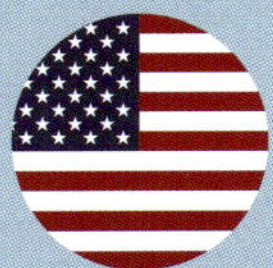

HAWAI'I

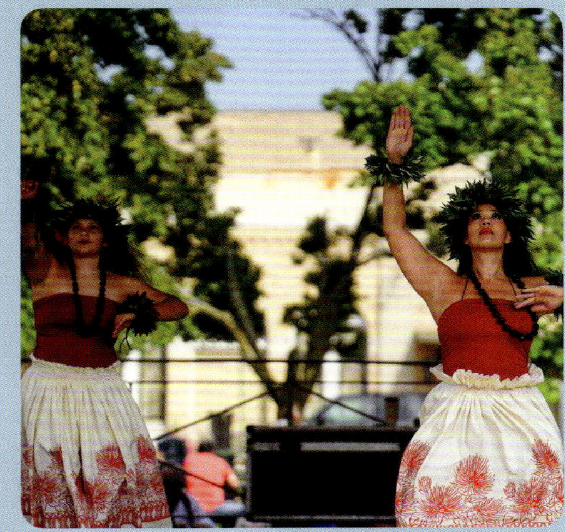

Hawai'i enjoys a rich and unique history and culture. Hula is an important part of that. Before Hawaiians had written language, they used hula chanting and dancing to tell and pass down stories of their past. Hawaiian culture is a culture of place, of humans tied to the land as responsible participants in the natural environment. Distinctively Hawaiian, hula also emphasizes this relationship. Hula has many schools, from the ancient to the modern. While loco moco is a Hawaiian soul food, hula is of and for the soul at a very deep and personal level.

LOCO MOCO

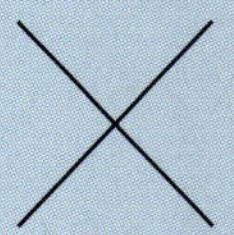

Way back in 1949, some high school athletes in Hilo, Hawaii were looking for a simple, filling and reasonably priced meal. They asked the owners of a local grill to fill a bowl with white rice and put a hamburger patty and gravy on top. The egg came later!

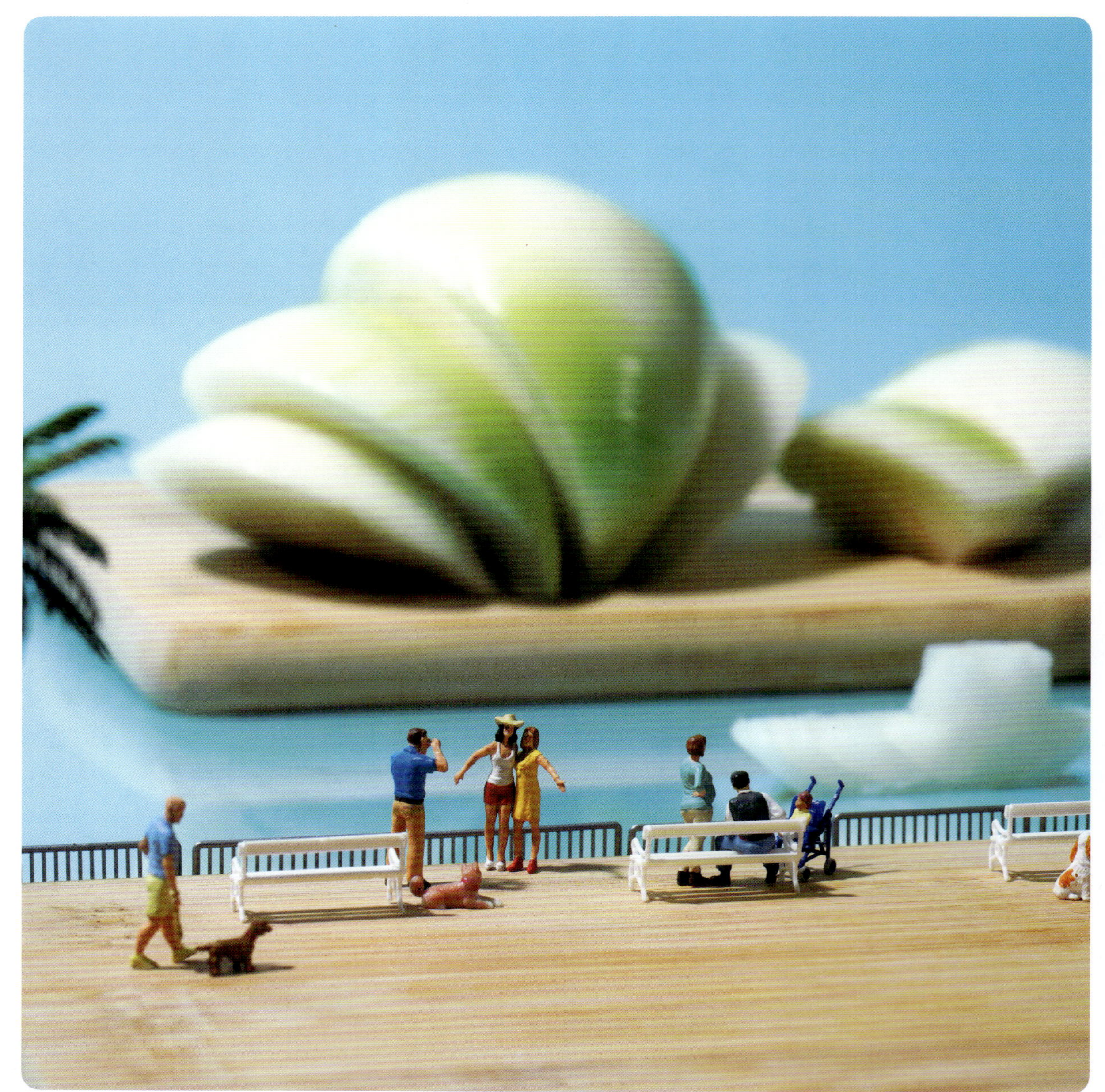

Sydney Onion House

AUSTRALIA

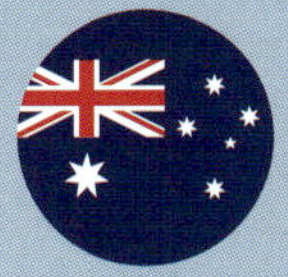

SYDNEY OPERA HOUSE

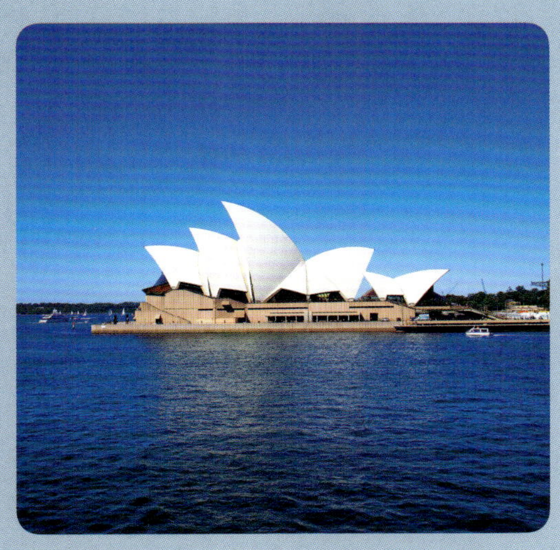

The original cost estimated to build the opera house was $7 million but it ended up costing $102, most of which was paid for by a State Lottery. It was also supposed to take 4 years to build but ended up taking 14 years which is no surprise given that the building has 1 million roof tiles that were made in Sweden. The opera house was designed by a Danish architect, Jørn Utzon, who may have come up with the unusual roof design while peeling an orange. Apparently he also got ideas from snails, palm fronds and Mayan temples. So onions are a Tanaka original!

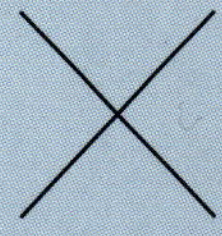

ONION

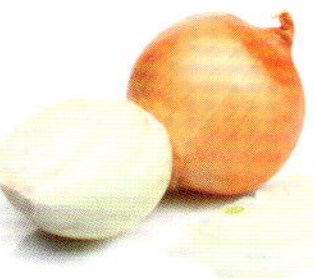

Tanaka-san likes the versatility of onions, originally for their expression of round, white objects. At some point he discovered their potential when sliced as well. Here they are balanced on a cutting board with an onion boat in the foreground.

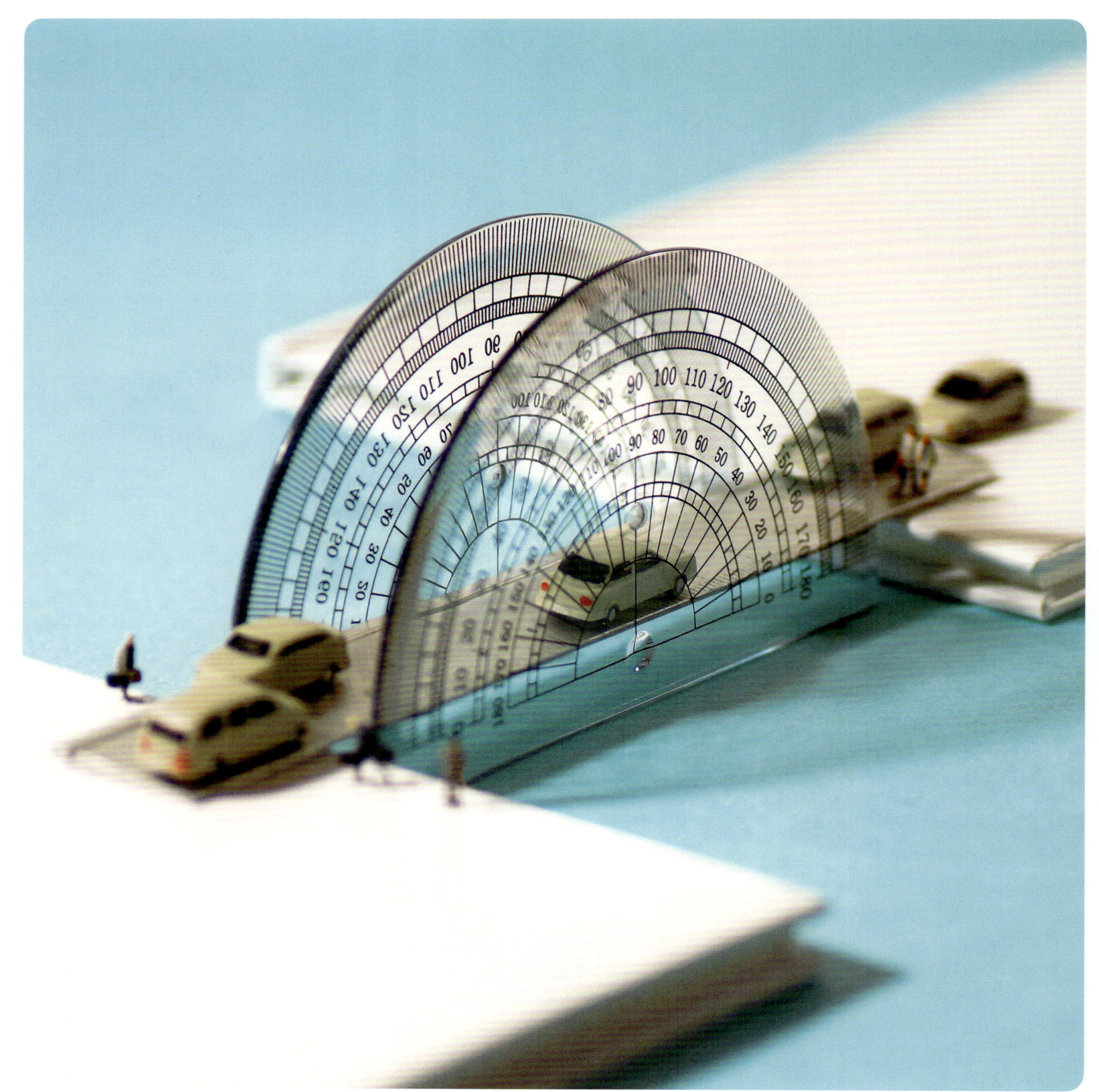

Protracted Bridge

AUSTRALIA

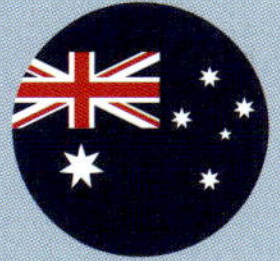

SYDNEY HARBOUR BRIDGE

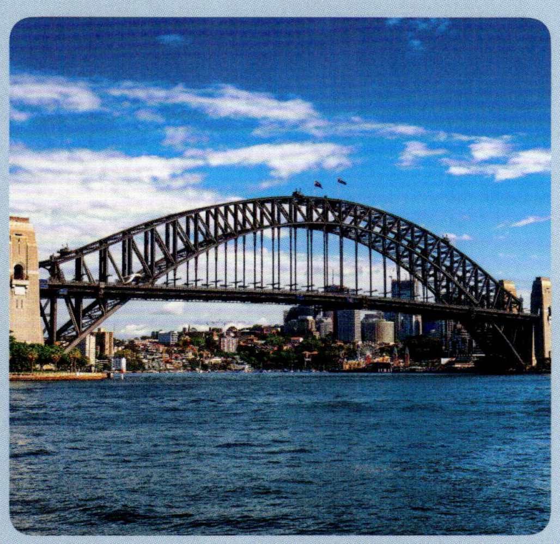

Another big bridge? This is the world's largest steel arch bridge. It took 8 years to build and made use of a lot of steel that was shipped in from the United Kingdom. It's actually possible to climb up to the peak of the bridge's arch and a lot of people who like high places and good views do just that. It's interesting to note that the four large concrete pylons – two at either end of the bridge – are just there for decorative purposes. That's probably why Tanaka-san left them out of his more pragmatic design. Sydney residents affectionately call it the "Coat Hanger."

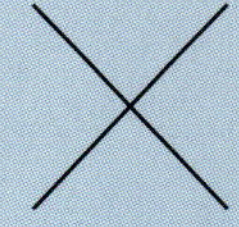

PROTRACTOR

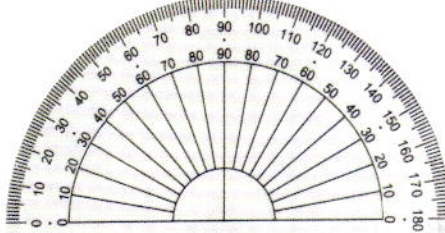

Here, the Sydney Harbour Bridge has been made with a protactor as the steel arch and a ruler as the roadway. The choice of these items reflects the number of careful calculations made when designing and building a bridge of this size.

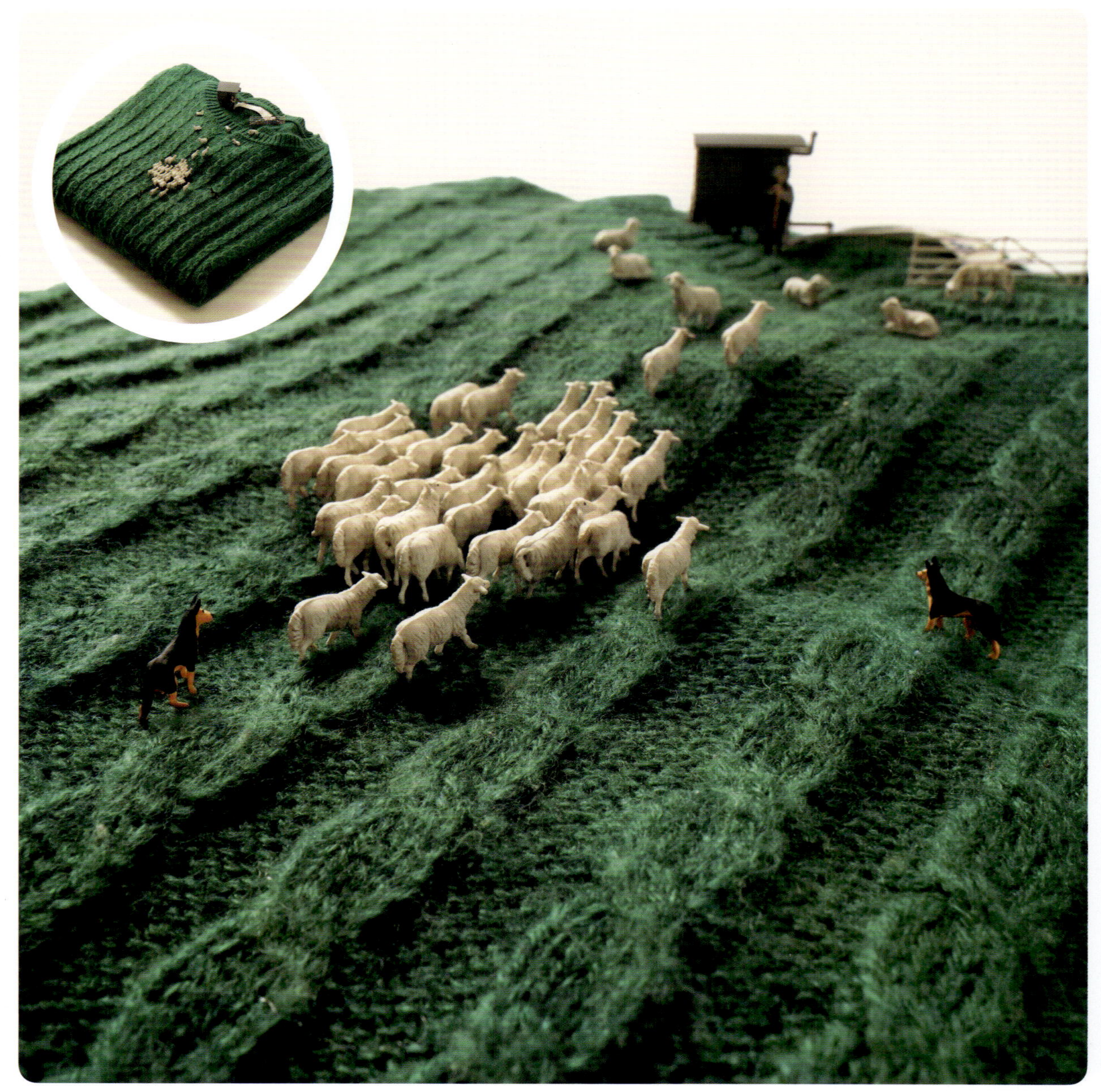

Warm Pasture

NEW ZEALAND

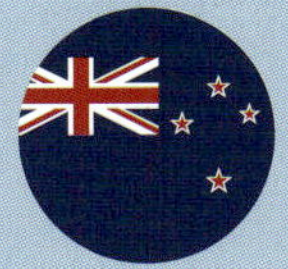

CORNWALL PARK

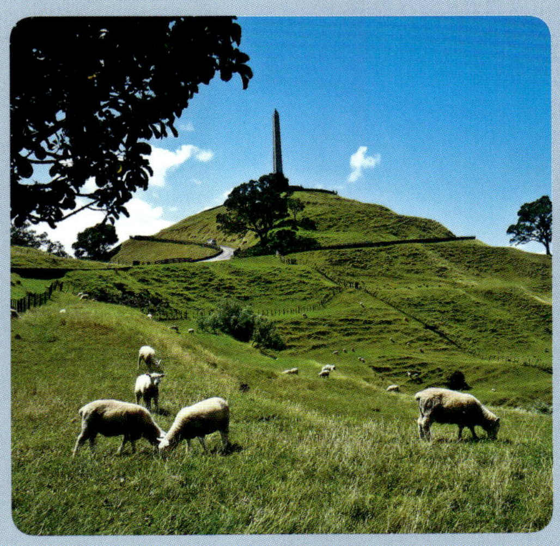

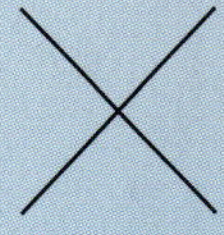

This 172-hectare park is located in the middle of Auckland. It was a gift of Sir John Logan Campbell back in 1901 with the hope that all New Zealanders could enjoy it for free. It is maintained by a trust and remains free to the public. A lot of the open space found in Cornwall Park is maintained by grazing sheep and cattle which is certainly an unusual approach to the management of public land. The park is also a place to celebrate Maori and Pakeha culture and is Sir John Logan Campbell's monument to the friendship between these two groups.

SWEATER

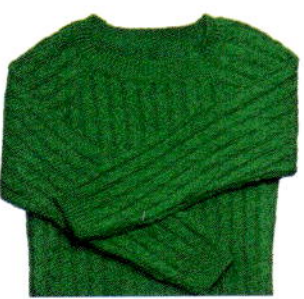

Tanaka-san has placed sheep on a warm sweater that was woven using sheep's wool. The sweater's braiding indicates grass of different lengths. Perhaps the shorter grass was mowed by the shepherd or the sheep like to graze in straight rows.

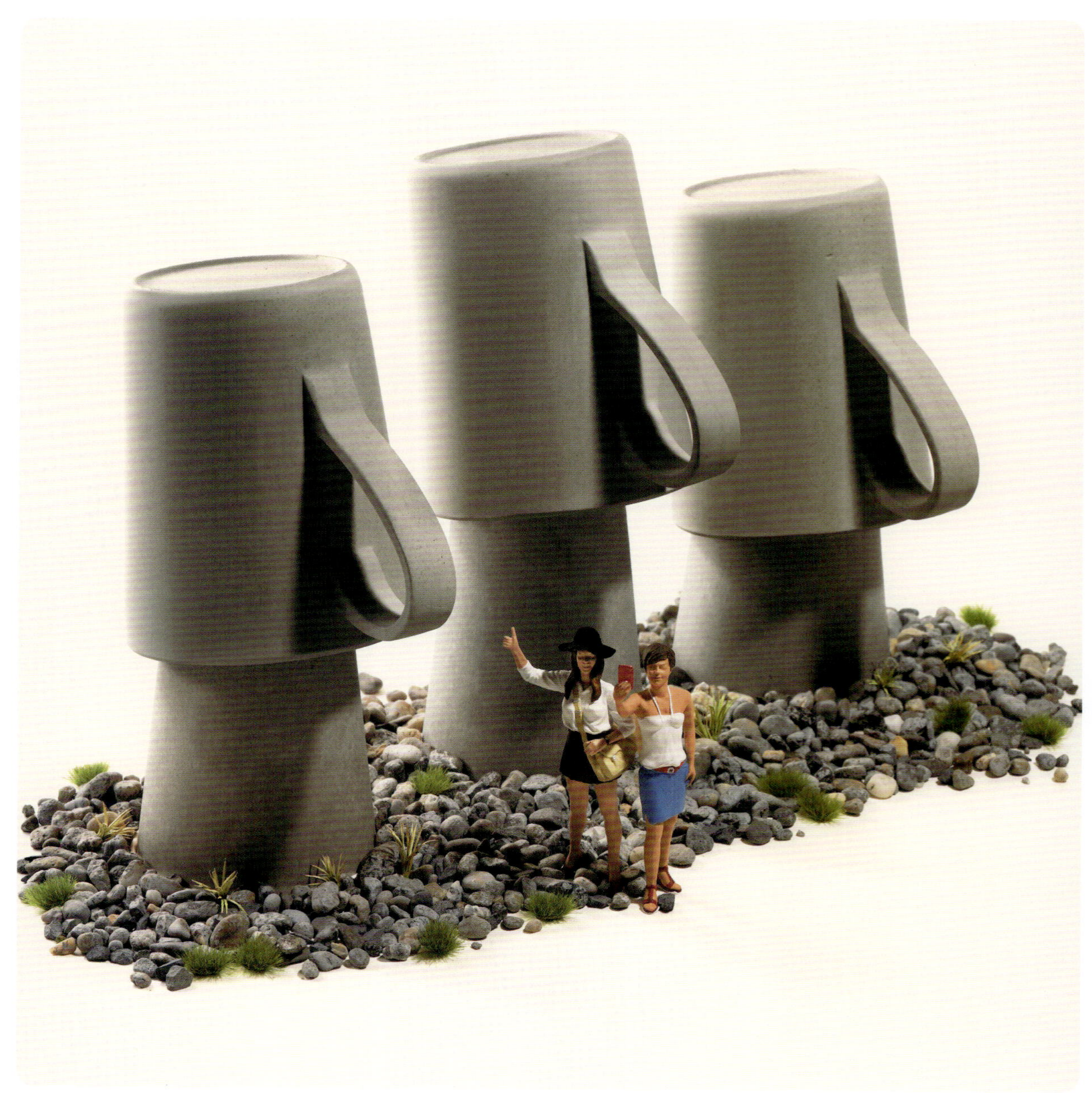

Moai Mugs

CHILE

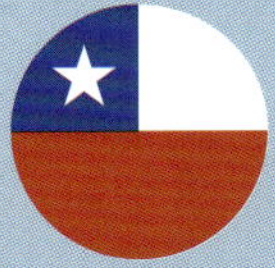

EASTER ISLAND

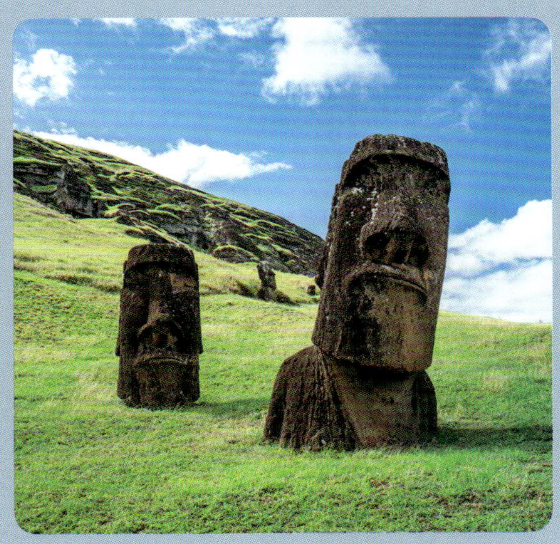

The original Polynesian inhabitants of this remote island sailed here on large canoes more than 1,000 years ago. When the island was "discovered" by a Dutch admiral on Easter Sunday, it came to be known as Easter Island by the outside world. Apparently the bodies of the massive moai statues are submerged in the ground and their heads were originally found lying down, only to be placed upright by archaeologists. Like all the other big rocks in this book, no one is entirely sure how these volcanic blocks were moved to their current locations. Most likely, a lot of very swarthy islanders pitched in.

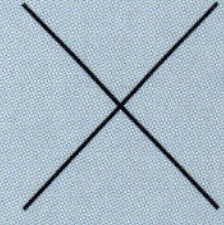

MUG

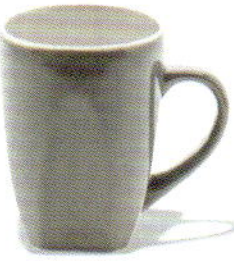

5,000 years ago, mugs were made out of wood and animal skulls. Care to join me in my cave for a cup of Joe? The English word "mug" also means "face," lending added, but purely serendipitous depth to Tanaka-san's use of mugs to convey mugs.

FRANCE

BALLERINA

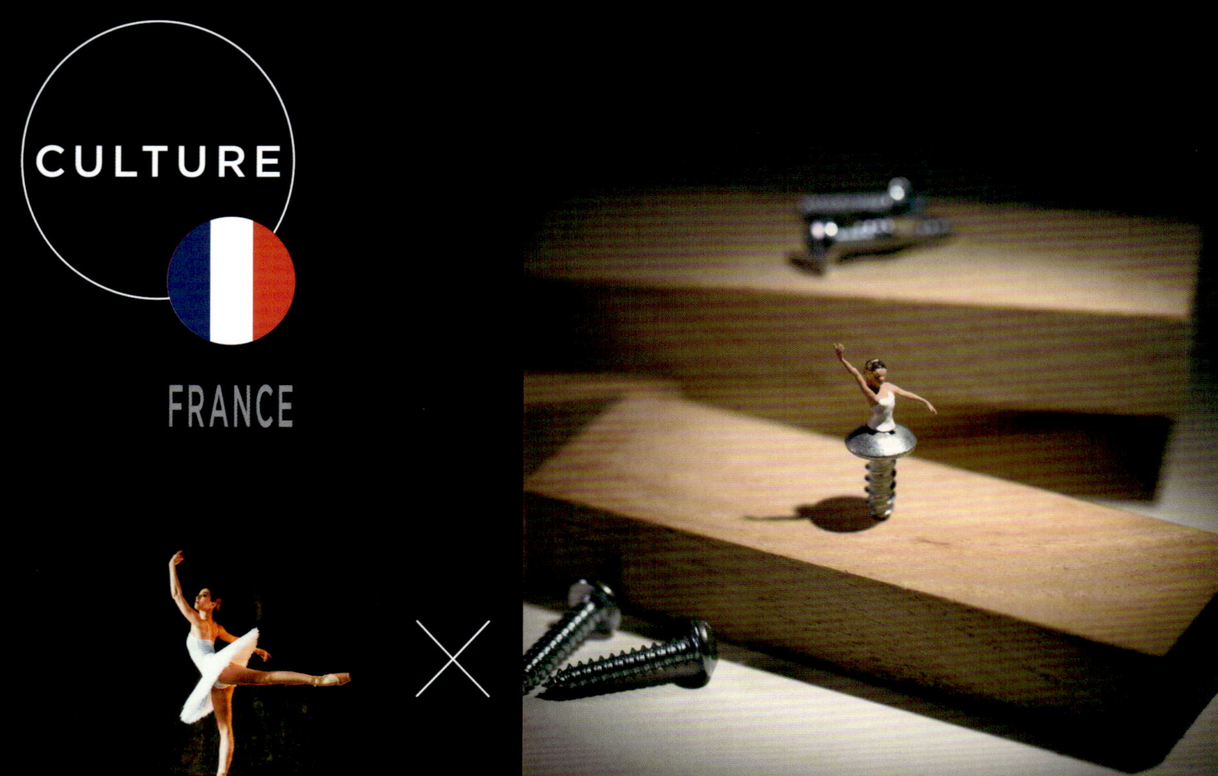

Ballerina

SCREW

Her toes pointed sharply, "en pointe," the ballerina pirouettes, around and around, screwing a hole into the stage's wood floor. If she's not careful, she may not be able to make the next move.

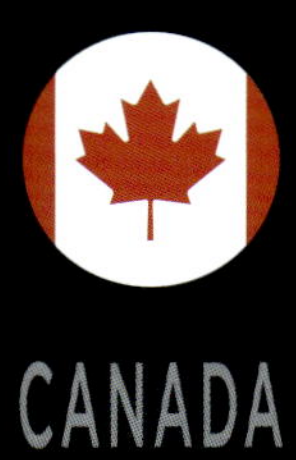

CANADA

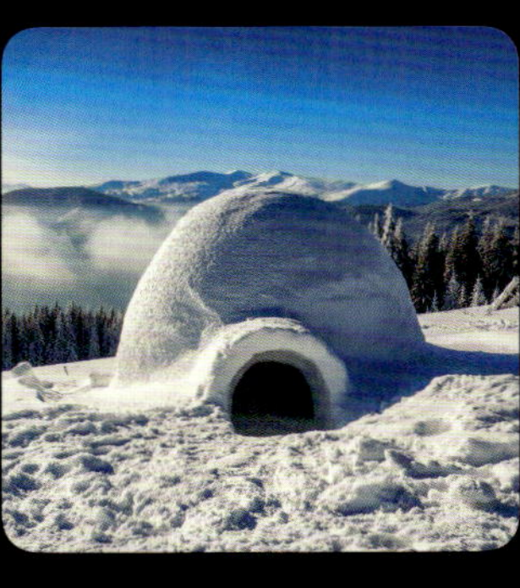

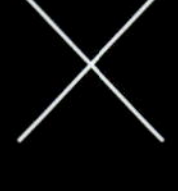

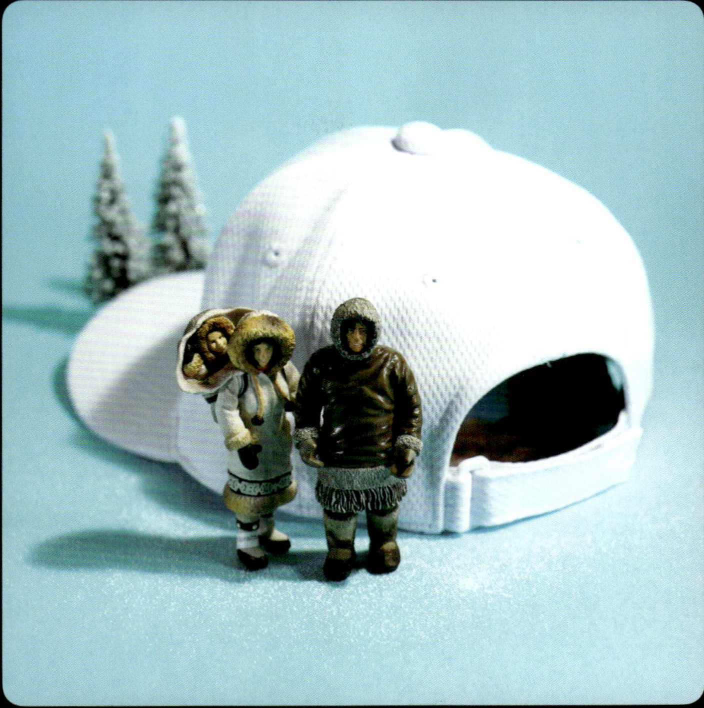

IGLOO

Igloo

CAP

A white hat may look like an igloo and, like an igloo, it can help to keep your head – and the rest of your body – warm. And the band in the back can be removed for easy entrance and exit.

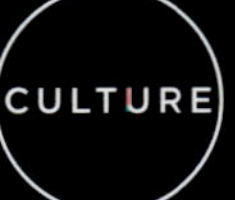

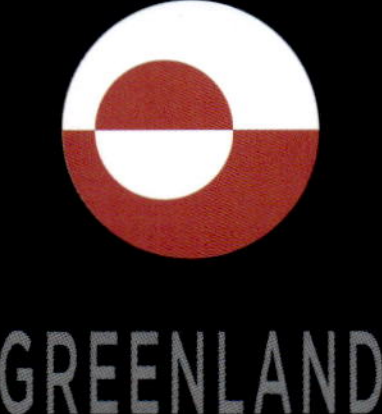

GREENLAND

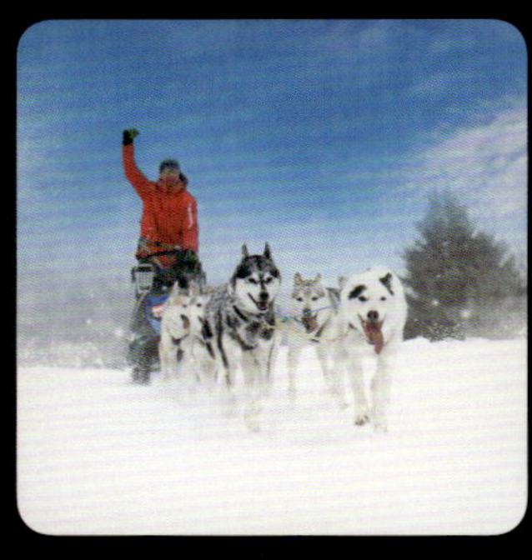
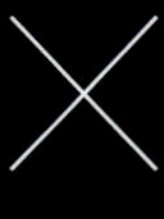

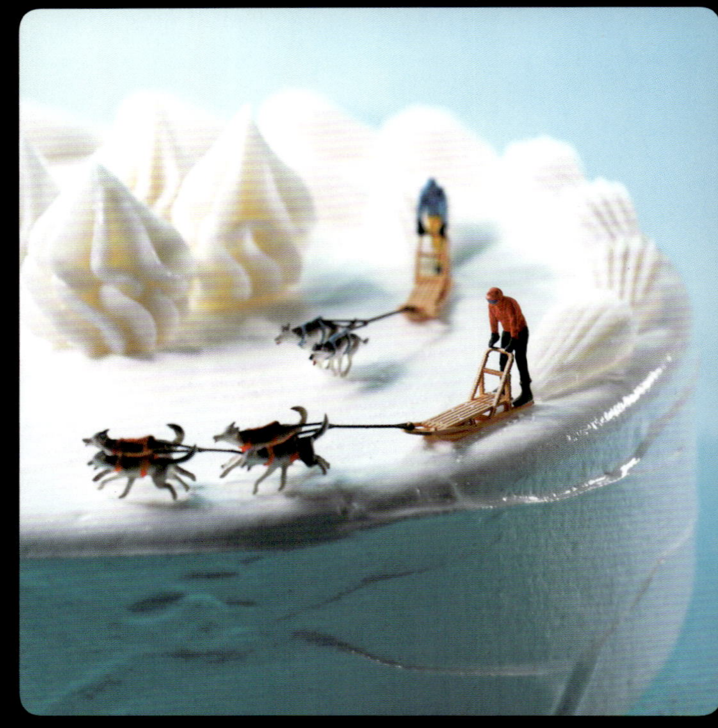

Dog Sledding

DOG SLEDDING

CAKE

A cake's white icing resembles freshly fallen snow and its decorations the snow spray kicked up by dog sled racers. How many revolutions does it take to create an entire cake?

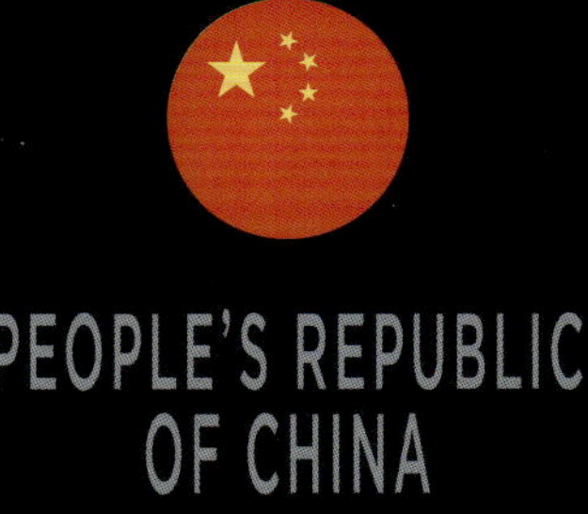

PEOPLE'S REPUBLIC OF CHINA

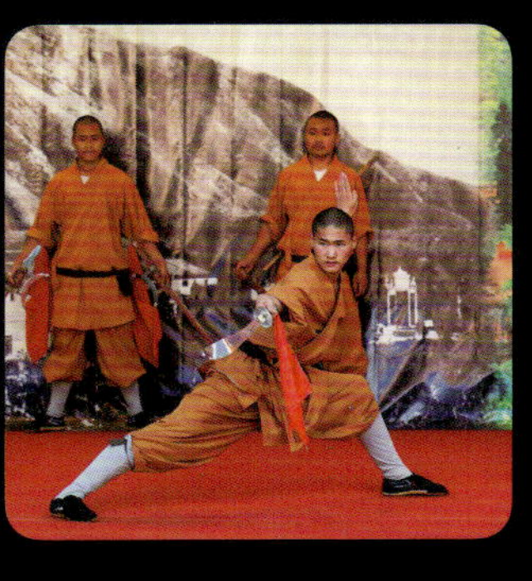

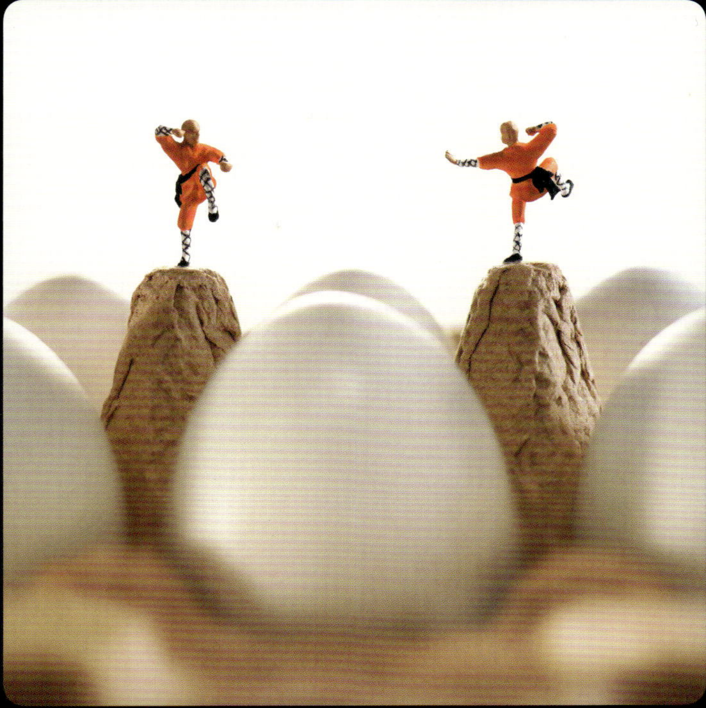

KUNG FU

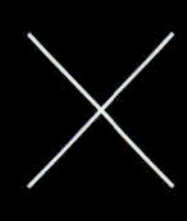

Hungry Spirit

EGG PACK

In Japanese, The word "tamago" for "egg" describes someone who is still in training. Here two young kung fu students practice their art on mountain peaks that jut from the clouds.

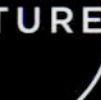

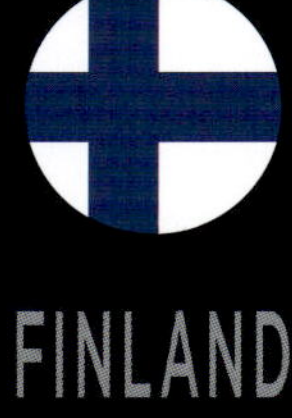

FINLAND

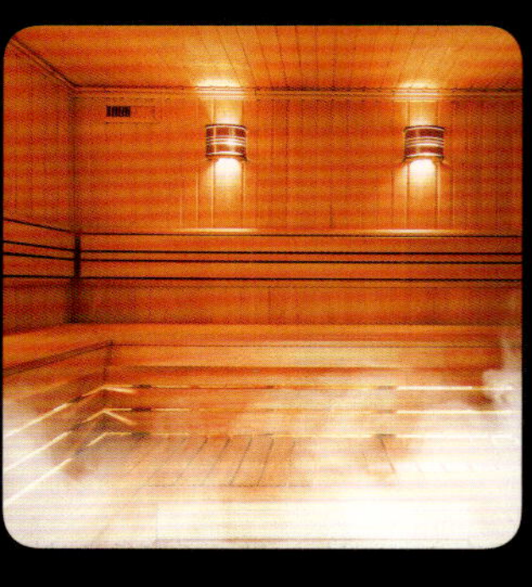

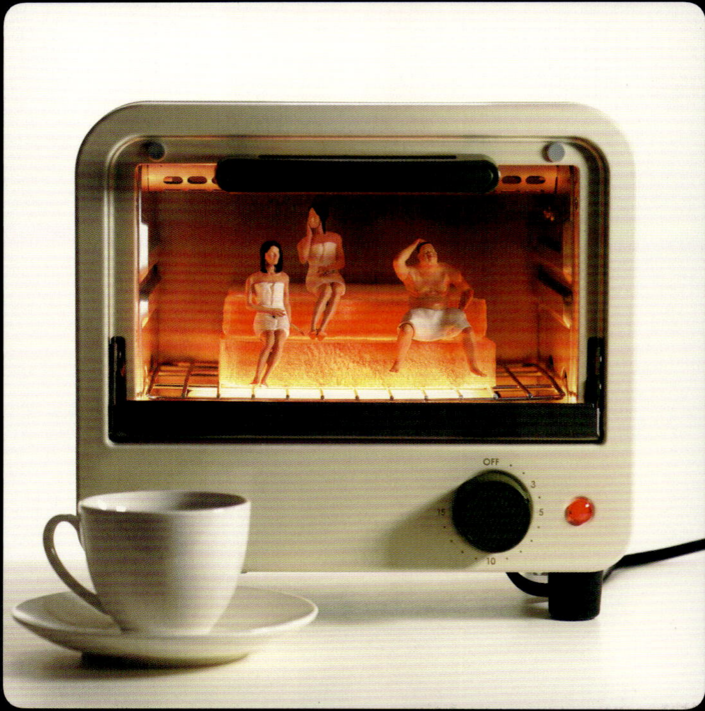

SAUNA

×

Toasty Sauna

TOASTER OVEN

Two pieces of toast make a comfortable wooden bench in your toaster oven. A good sweat in the morning might be just what you need to jump-start your day. You'll never know until you try.

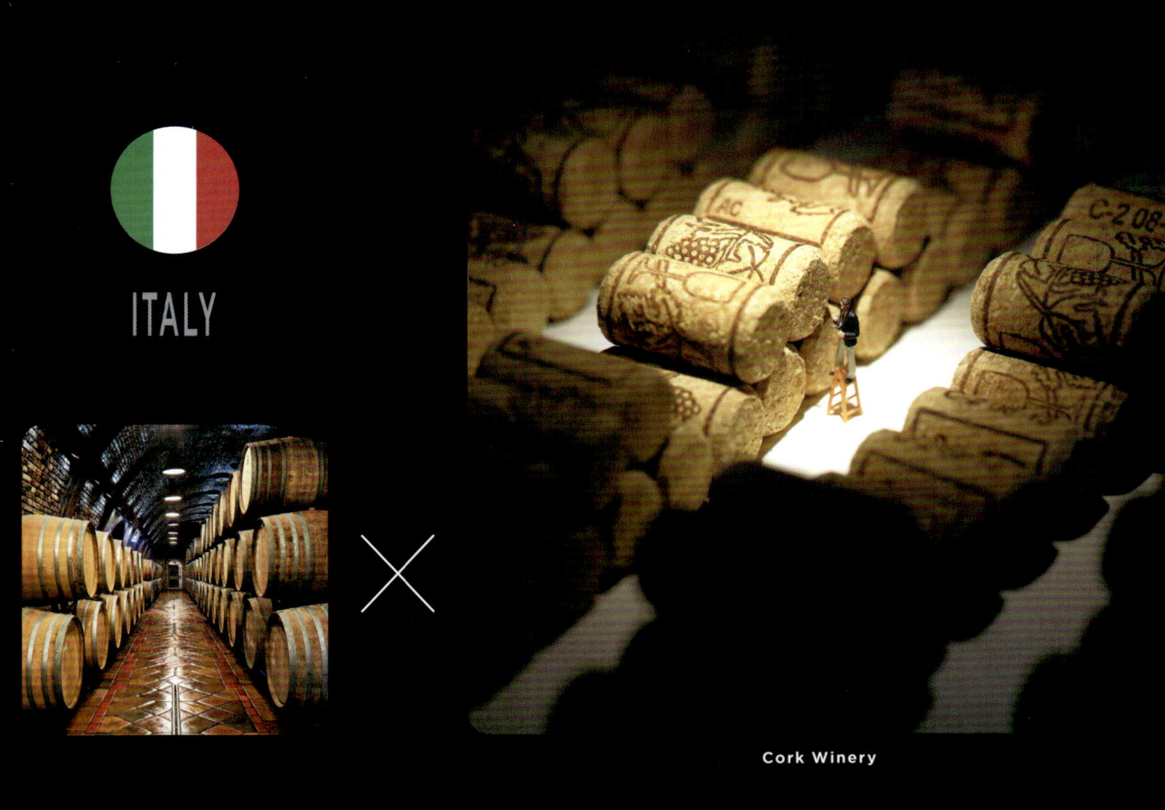

ITALY

WINE CELLAR × CORK

Cork Winery

A small amount of wine often soaks into the cork. In a miniature world, corks might become casks in a wine-cork winery. There we might fill our glasses with cork-aged wine.

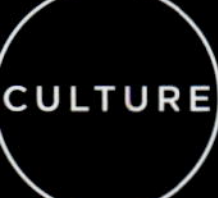

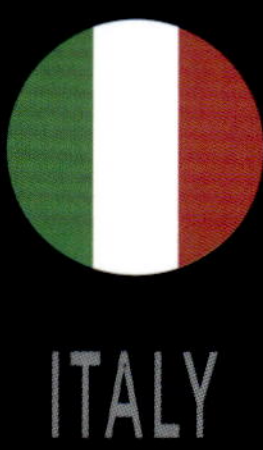

ITALY

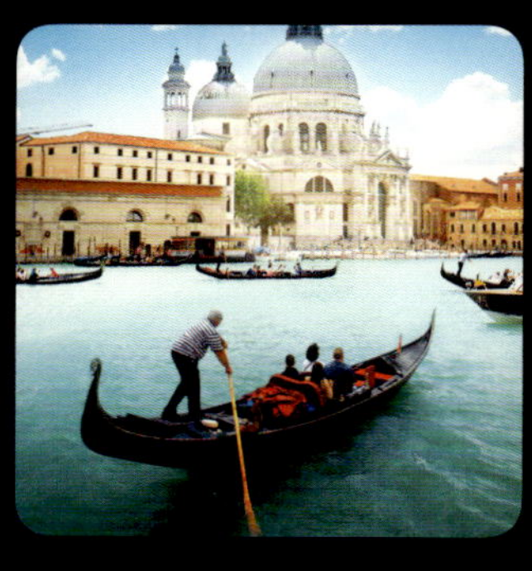

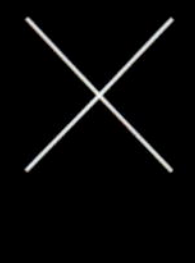

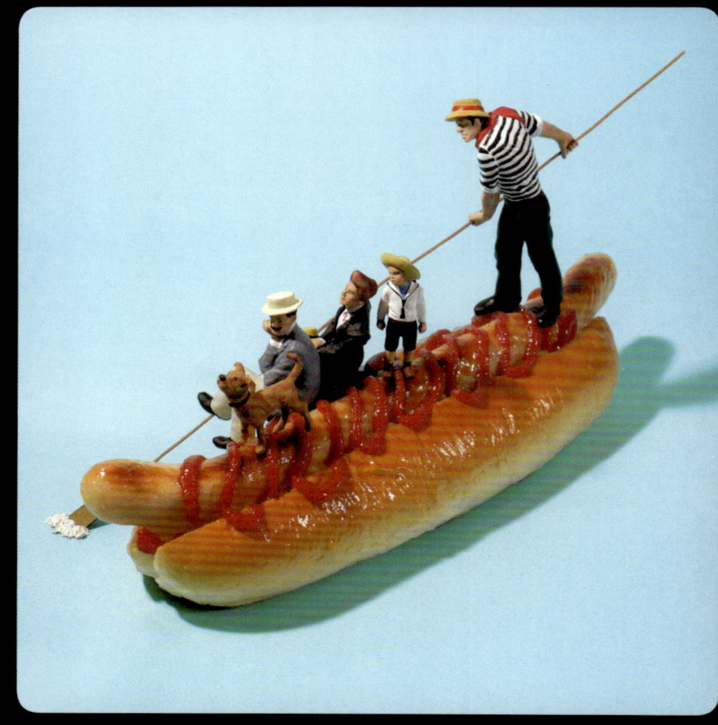

Gondola Ride

GONDOLA

HOT DOG

In waterlogged Venice, gondolas have been used to transport just about everything you – and Tanaka-san – can imagine for a thousand years! In the 18th century there were some 10000 boats.

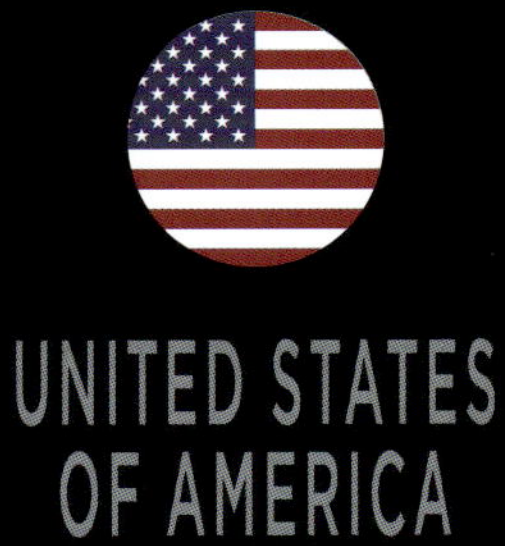

UNITED STATES OF AMERICA

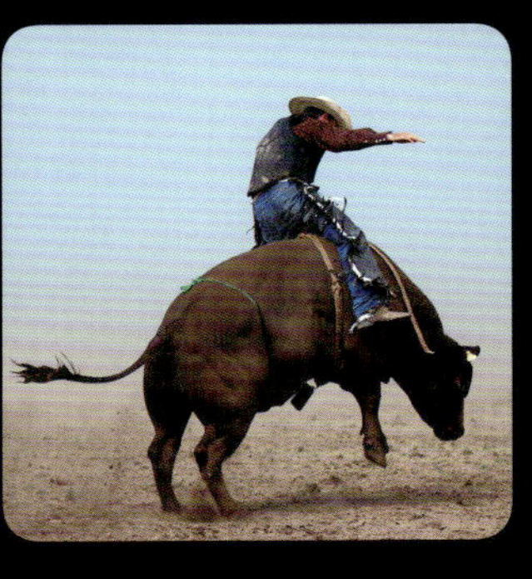

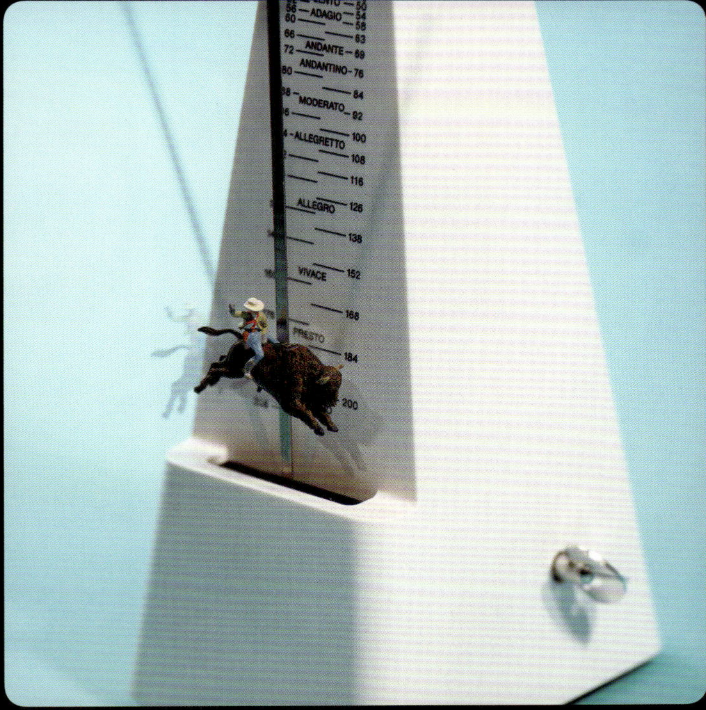

RODEO

×

METRONOME

Rodeo-nome

On its fastest setting, a metronome rocks frantically back and forth, much like a crazed bull in a rodeo, ultimately throwing its brave and well-shaken rider – or musician - to the ground.

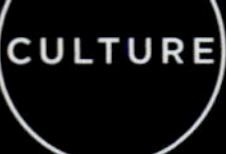

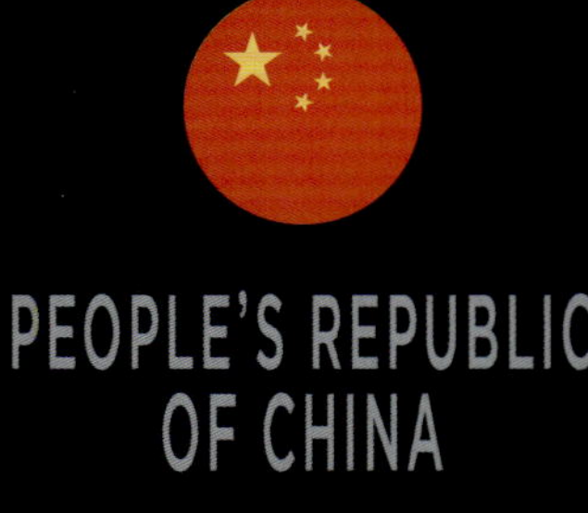

PEOPLE'S REPUBLIC OF CHINA

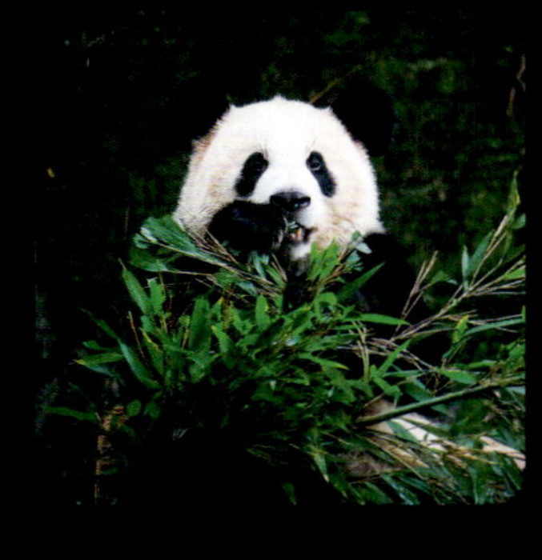

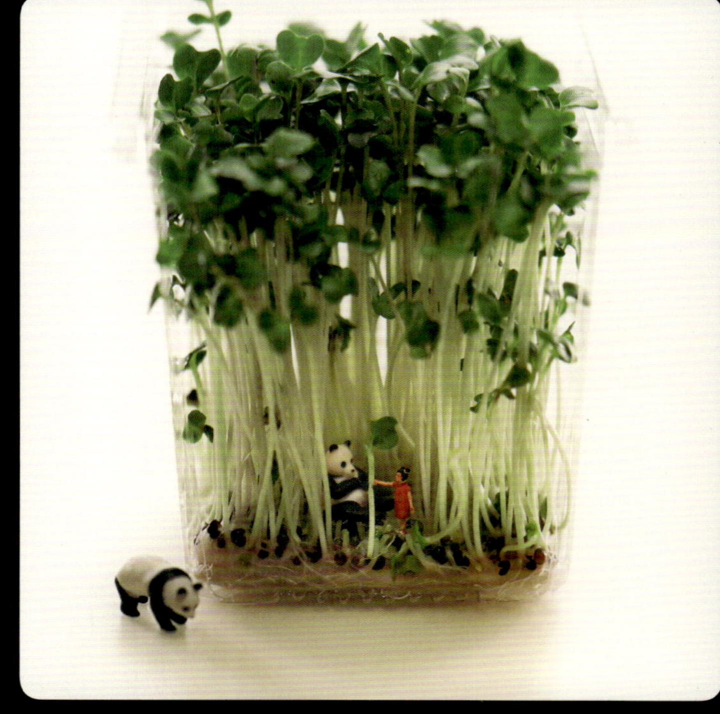

Microgreens

PANDA ✕ WHITE RADISH SPROUTS

A package of white radish sprouts becomes a bamboo grove and home to a panda until the panda consumes it. In the wild, 99% of the giant panda's diet is bamboo shoots and leaves.

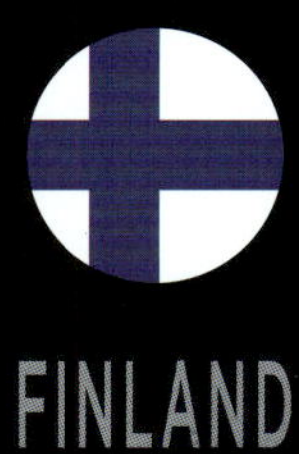

FINLAND

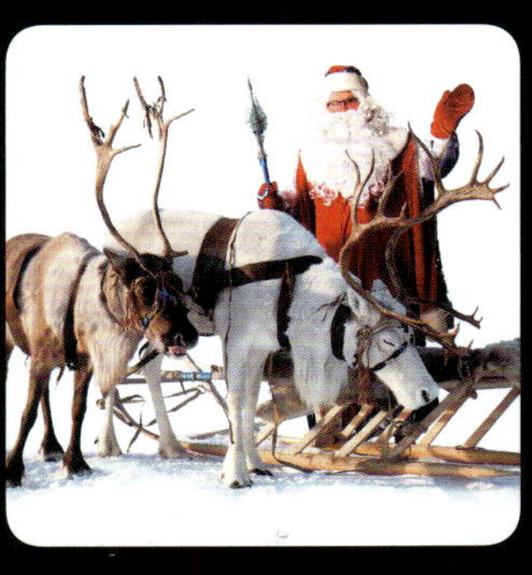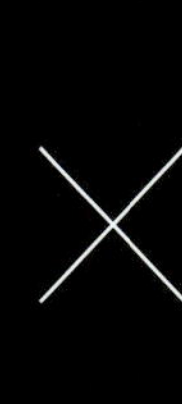

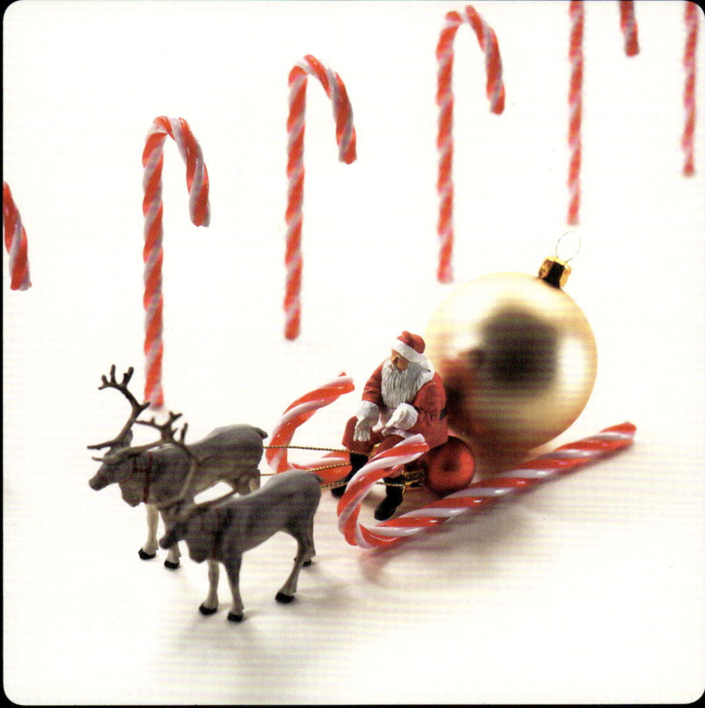

SANTA CLAUS

×

CANDY CANE

Candy Cane Sled

Making use of something from Christmas to depict Christmas, candy canes become streetlights and sled runners. Meanwhile, a tree decoration becomes a bulging bag of presents.

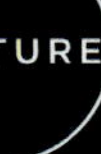

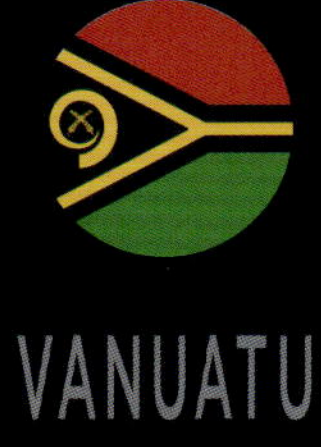

VANUATU

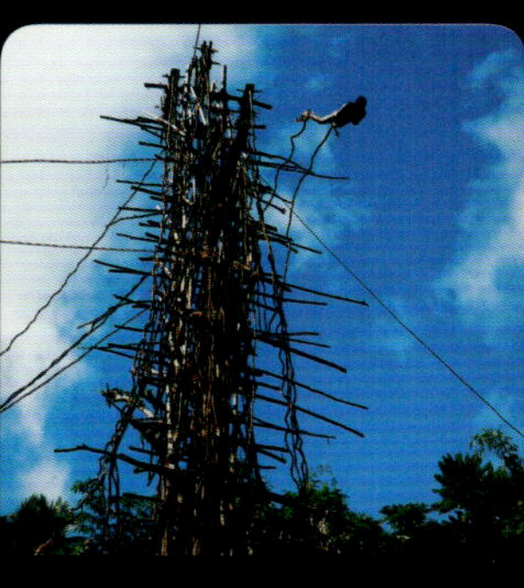

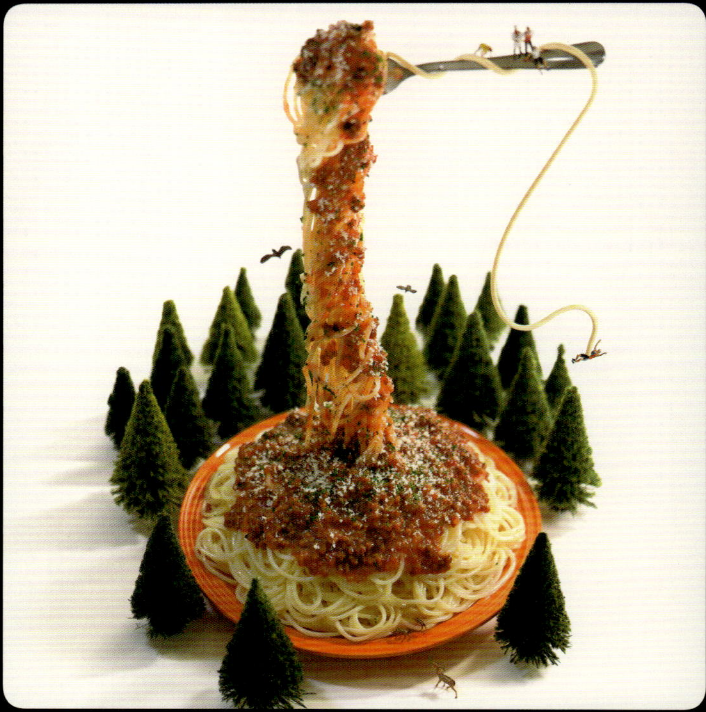

BUNGEE JUMP

×

PASTA

Making use of a restaurant window pasta display, Tanaka-san has added a pasta bungee cord and some jumpers. How did they get up there? An elevator? Stairs? Bolognese bouldering?

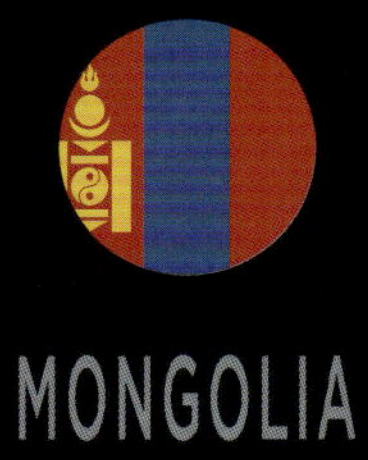

MONGOLIA

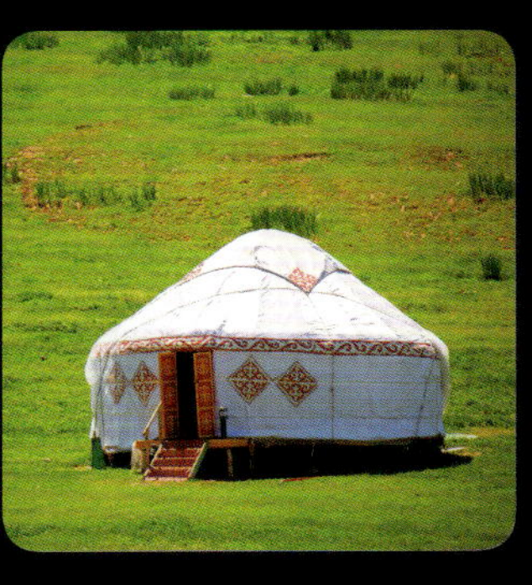

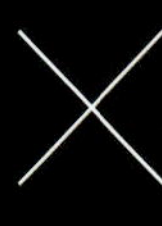

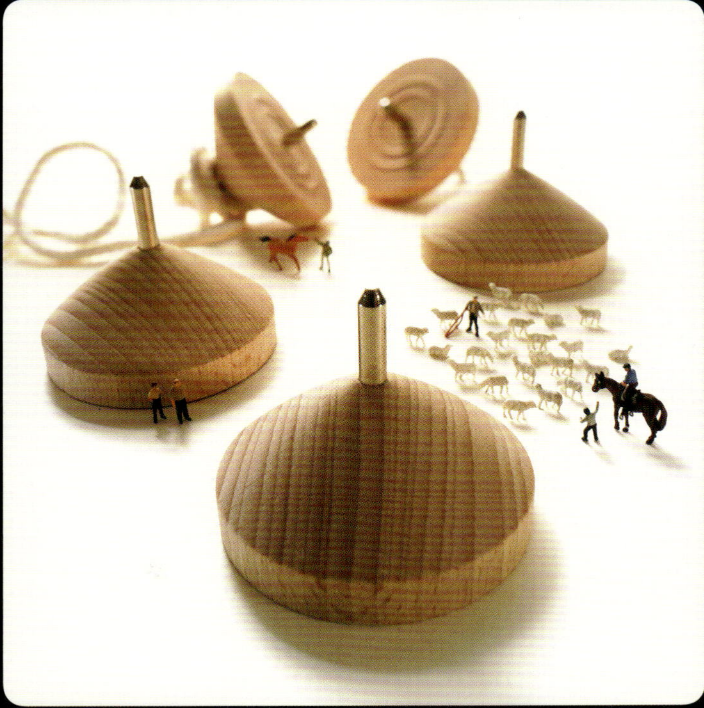

Ger Gathering

MONGOLIAN GER

TOP

In Mongolian, the word "ger" means "home." The number 9 is auspicious in Mongolian culture so gers are often made with 81 poles that converge to make their domed roof.

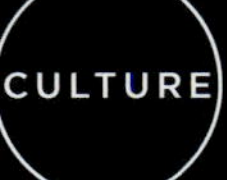

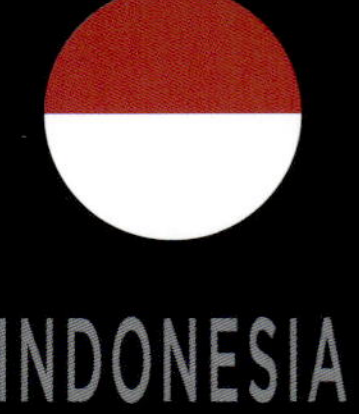

INDONESIA

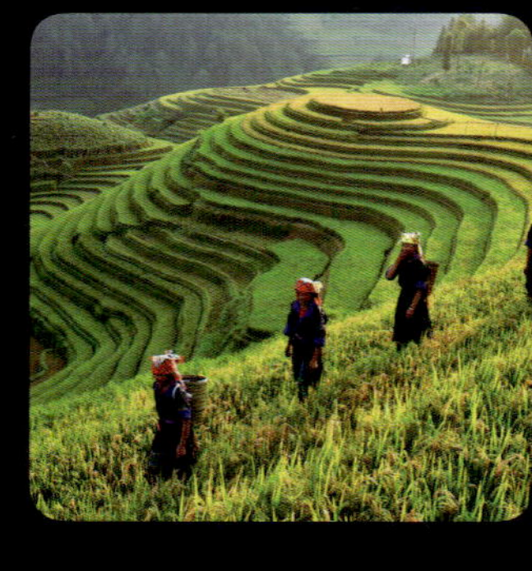

TERRACED FIELDS

×

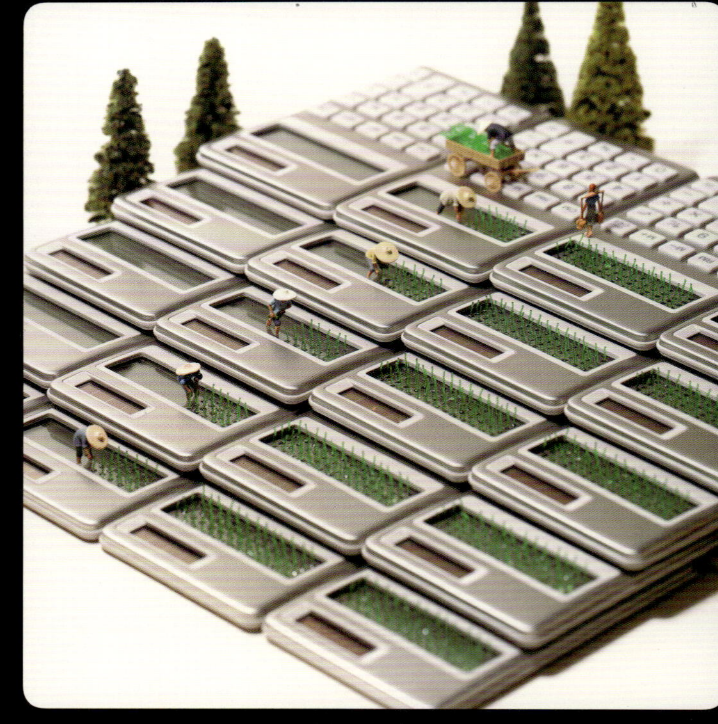

Rice Planting

CALCULATOR

LCD panels look a bit like water and make for ideal stepped paddies. And farming involves a lot of calculation. When to plant, how much to plant, the ideal amount of water used...

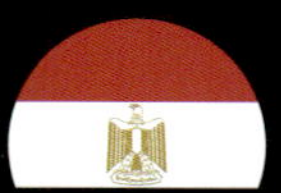

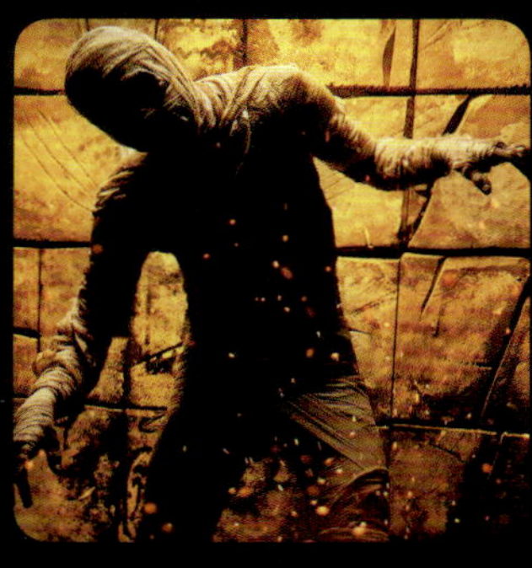

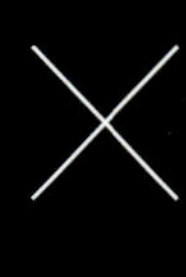

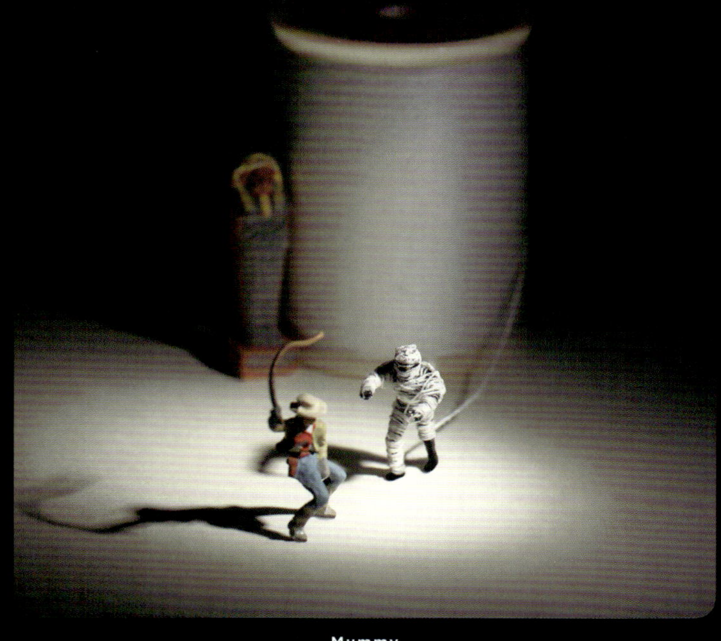

Mummy

THREAD

A narrow thread takes on the width of a bandage in the miniature world. Here, a pyramid explorer – or a treasure hunter? – encounters a mummy at the entrance to a tomb.

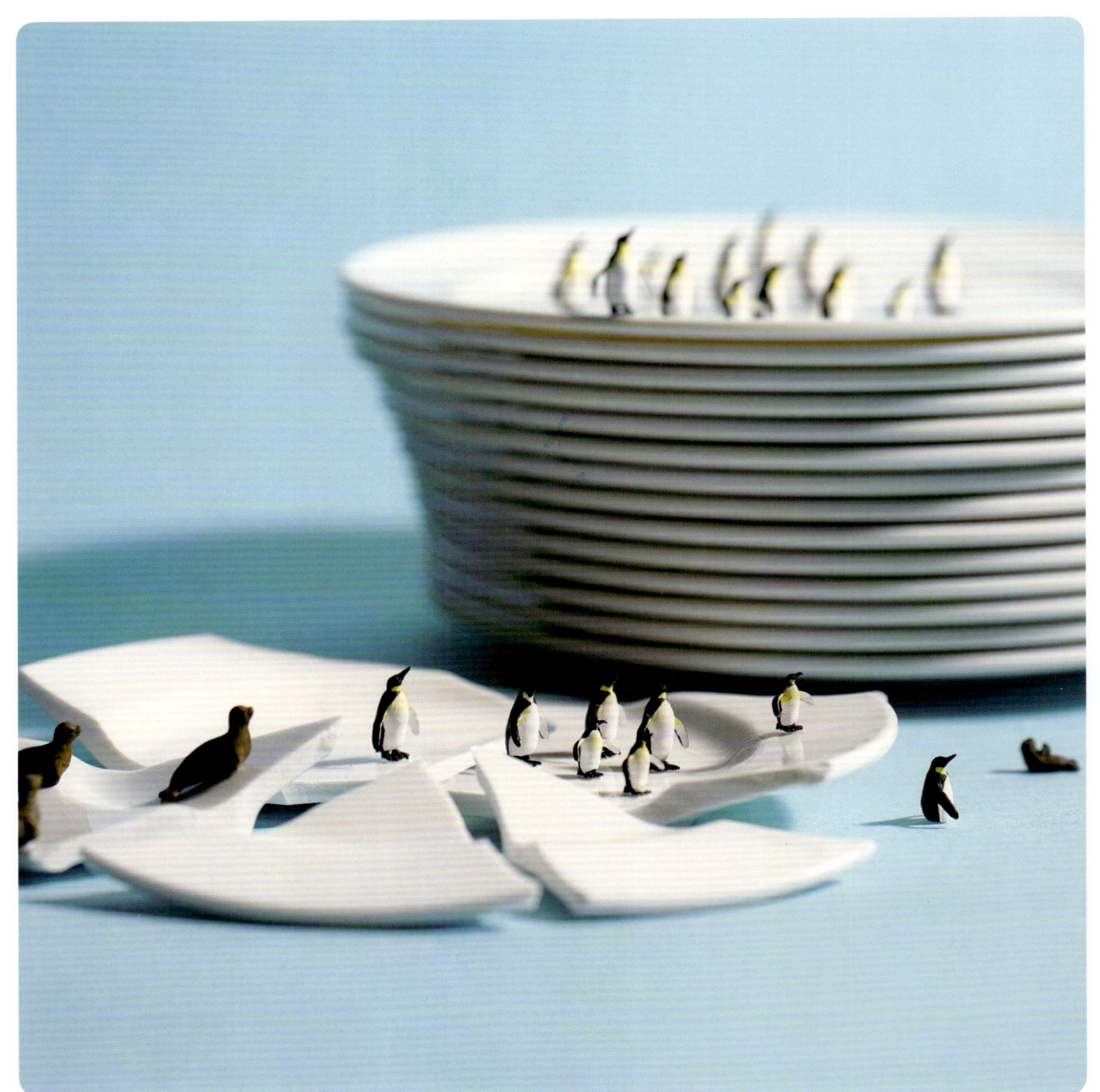

ANTARCTICA

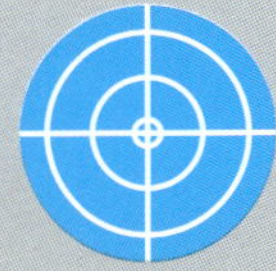

WEDDELL SEA COAST

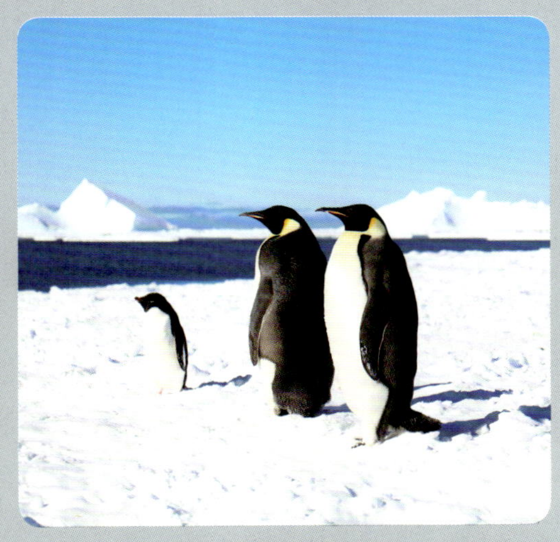

The Weddell Sea is said to have the clearest water of any ocean in the world and is home to whales, seals and the Adélie penguin, which a French explorer named after his wife. Adélie penguins are good swimmers and will travel great distances for a meal of shrimp, krill or squid. Many of these penguins live on ice shelves that border the Weddell Sea and the males build nests with rocks in an effort to attract a mate. The Weddell Sea is the focus of many scientific studies because it has an unusual layer of deep water that is relatively warm and salty.

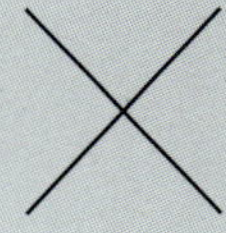

WHITE PLATE

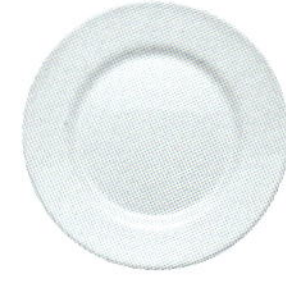

Porcelain plates were first made in China about 1000 years ago using kaolin and pentose. Ice in Antarctica has been around a lot longer but may now - thanks to dramatic warming - be more vulnerable than the plates on your dinner table.

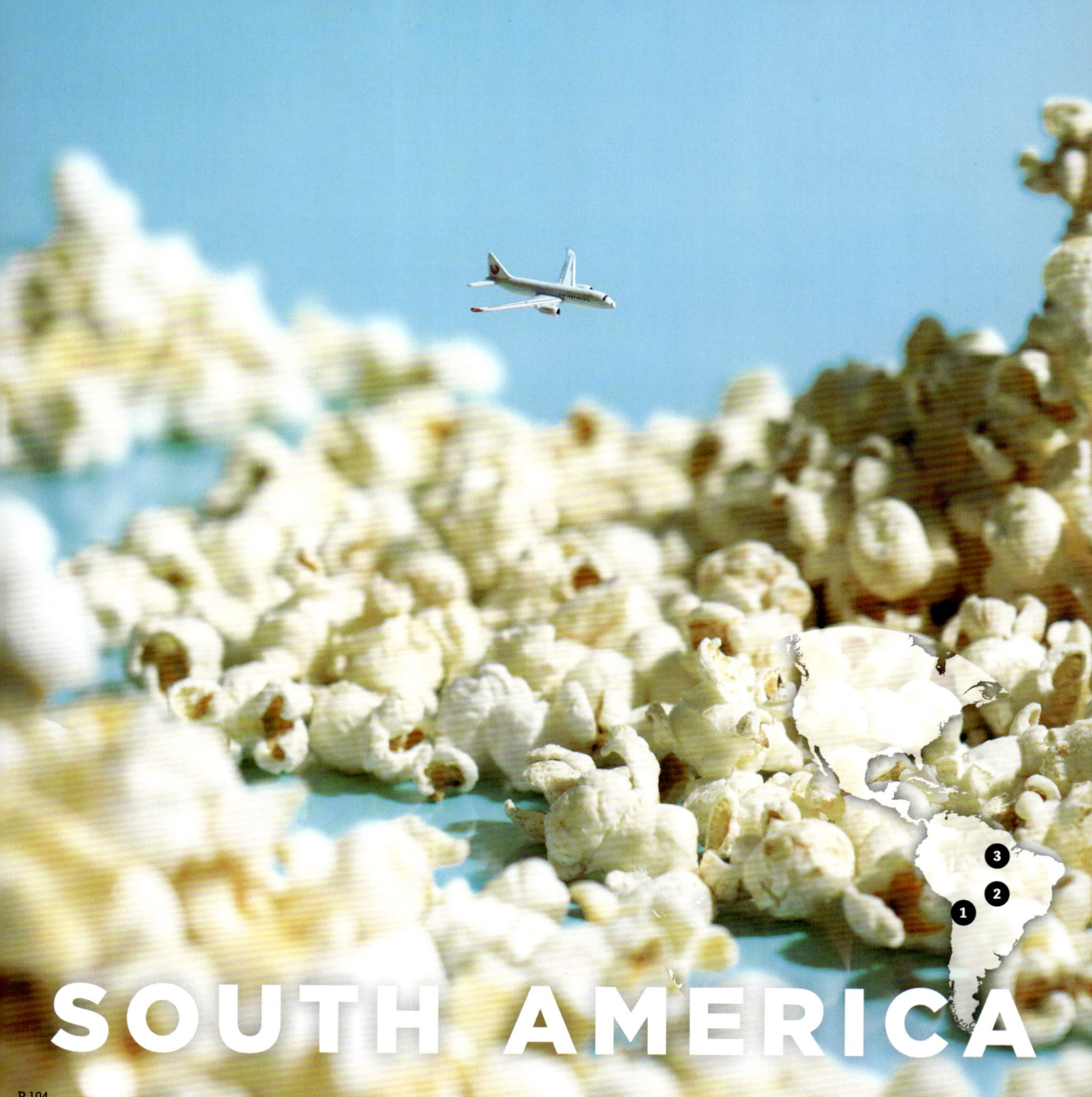

SOUTH AMERICA
1
2
3

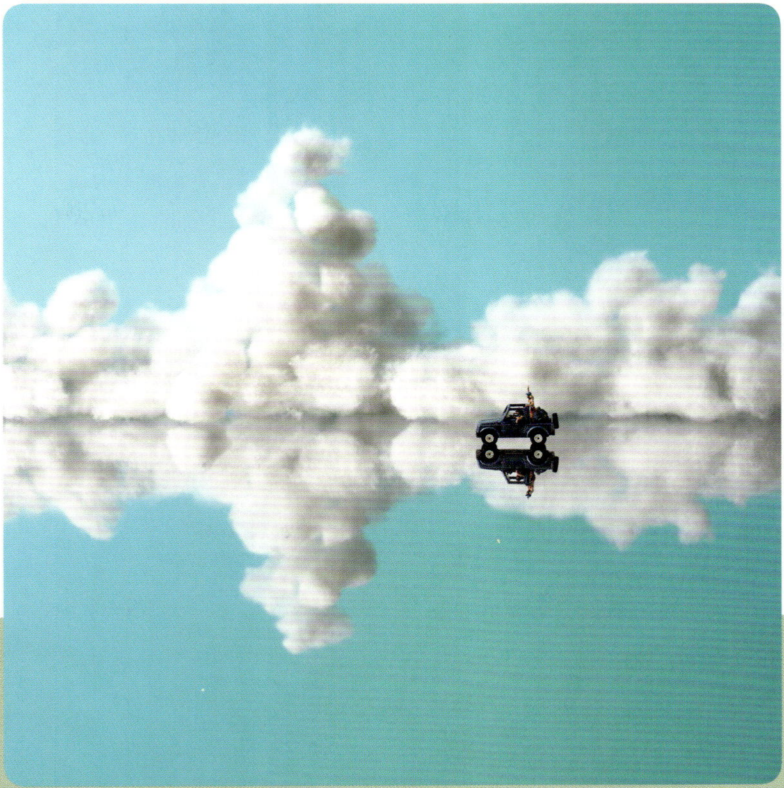

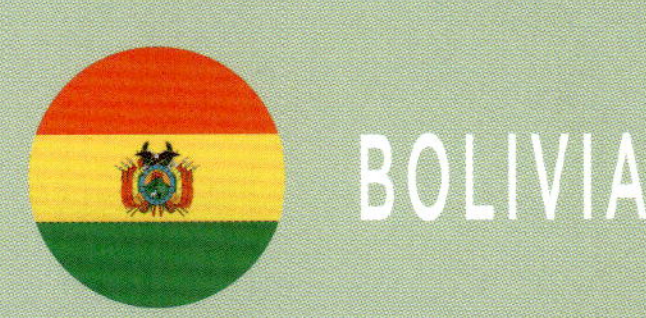

BOLIVIA

Salar de Uyuni

UYUNI SALT LAKE

With an area of 10,000 square meters, after a rain this salt flat becomes the world's largest mirror. It's surprising to find a place with this much salt 3,656 meters above sea level.

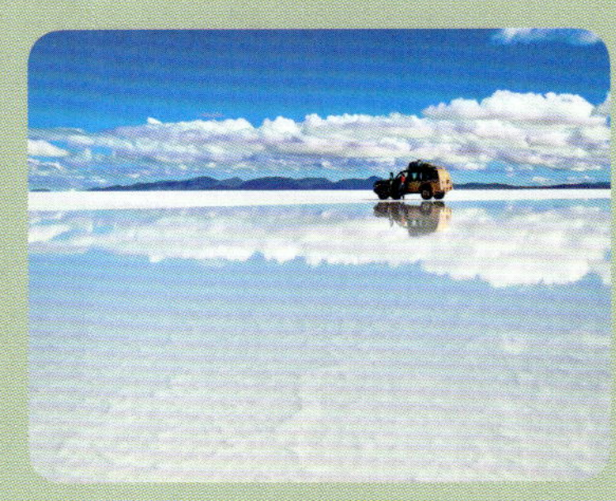

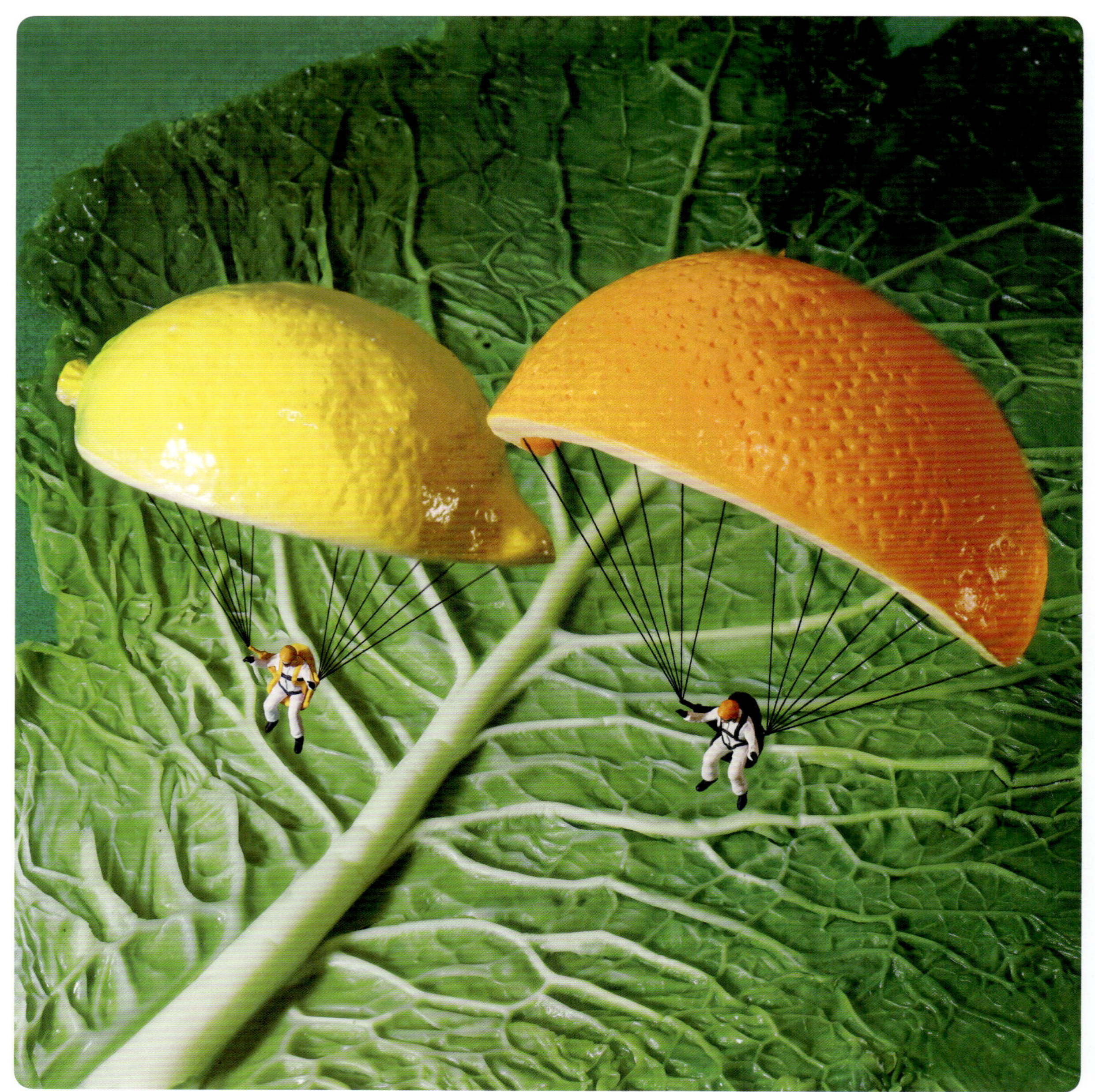

Landing on the Leaf of Life

BRAZIL

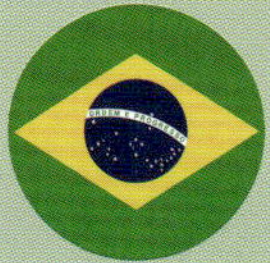

THE AMAZON RIVER

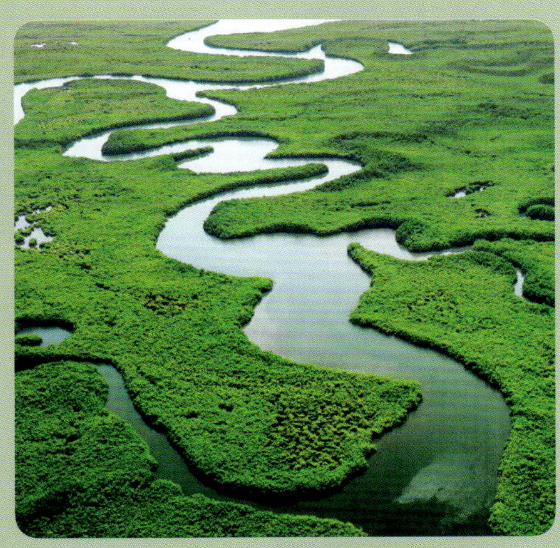

Originating in Peru, the Amazon River passes through nine South American countries before flowing into the Atlantic Ocean. At its widest the river delta there is thought to be 320 kilometers across. The Amazon River is responsible for 20% of the total river water discharged into the world's oceans. The Amazon is between 6000 and 7000 kilometers long and its only competitor for length is the Nile. Much like the veins in a leaf, the Amazon is fed by numerous, often large tributaries, approximately 1,100 in all. Can you imagine finding such a river on another planet?

LEAF VEIN

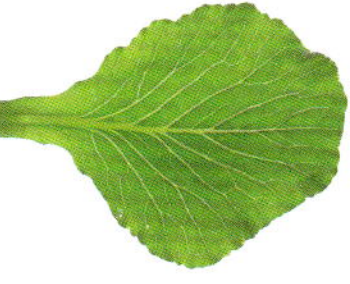

Nature on a macro scale often resembles nature on a micro scale. The mechanisms are the same, only the scale changes. In this way the vast network of rivers that feed into the Amazon River resemble the veins in a single leaf.

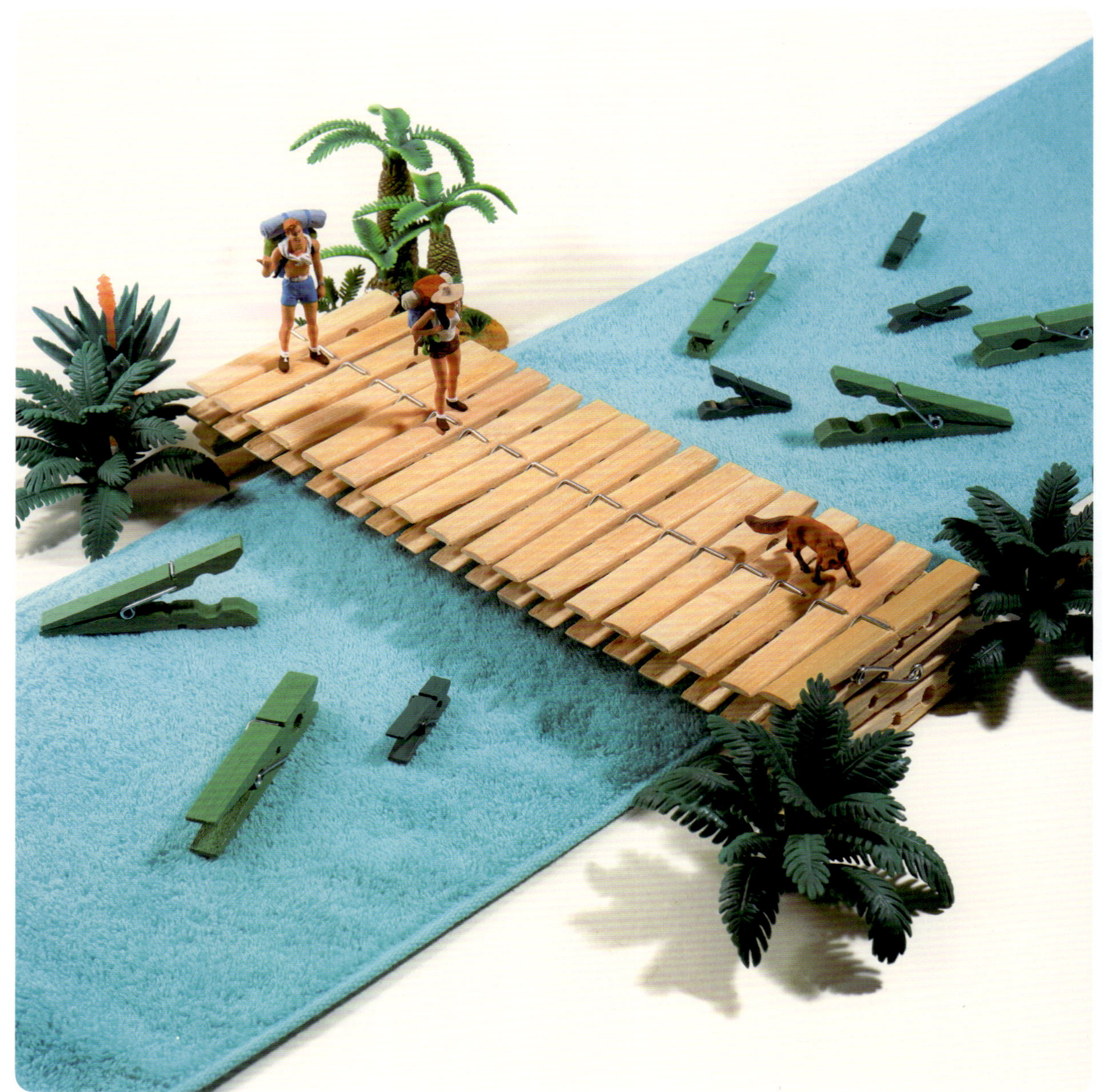

They're Looking at Us!

BRAZIL/PARAGUAY/BOLIVIA

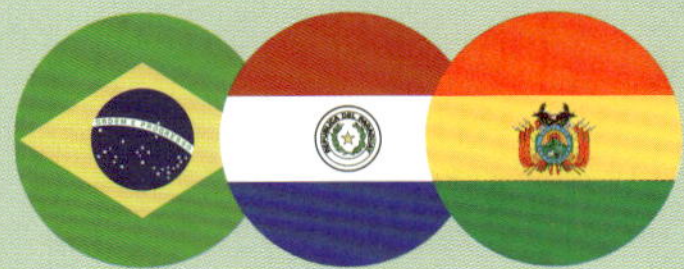

PANTANAL

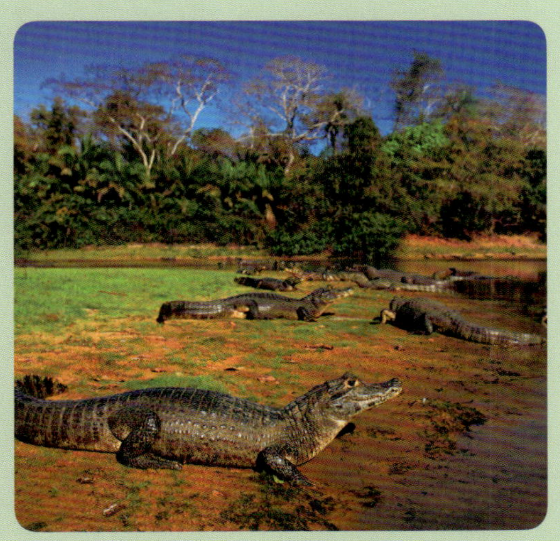

The largest tropical wetland and the largest flooded grassland in the world, the Pantanal spreads across Brazil, Bolivia and Paraguay. The environment here changes radically from season to season, submerged part of the year and dry the rest. There are large populations of birds, fish and the greatest concentration of crocodiles in the world with an estimated 10 million. With an average length of 2 meters, if we were to line them up tail to head, they would extend for 20,000 kilometers. That's half the circumference of the earth.

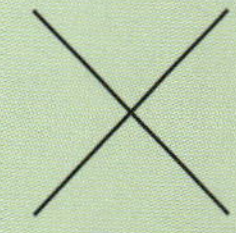

CLOTHESPINS

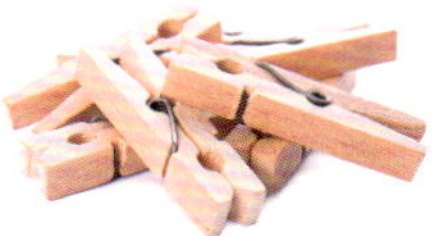

While white clothespins form a bridge, green ones have become hungry crocodiles. Although it hurts to be pinched by a clothespin it would be far more painful to be bit by a crocodile. Here, a towel that would normally be hung out to dry is a river.

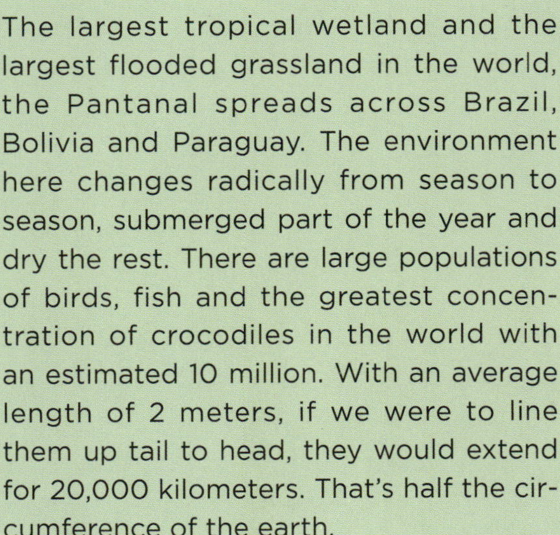

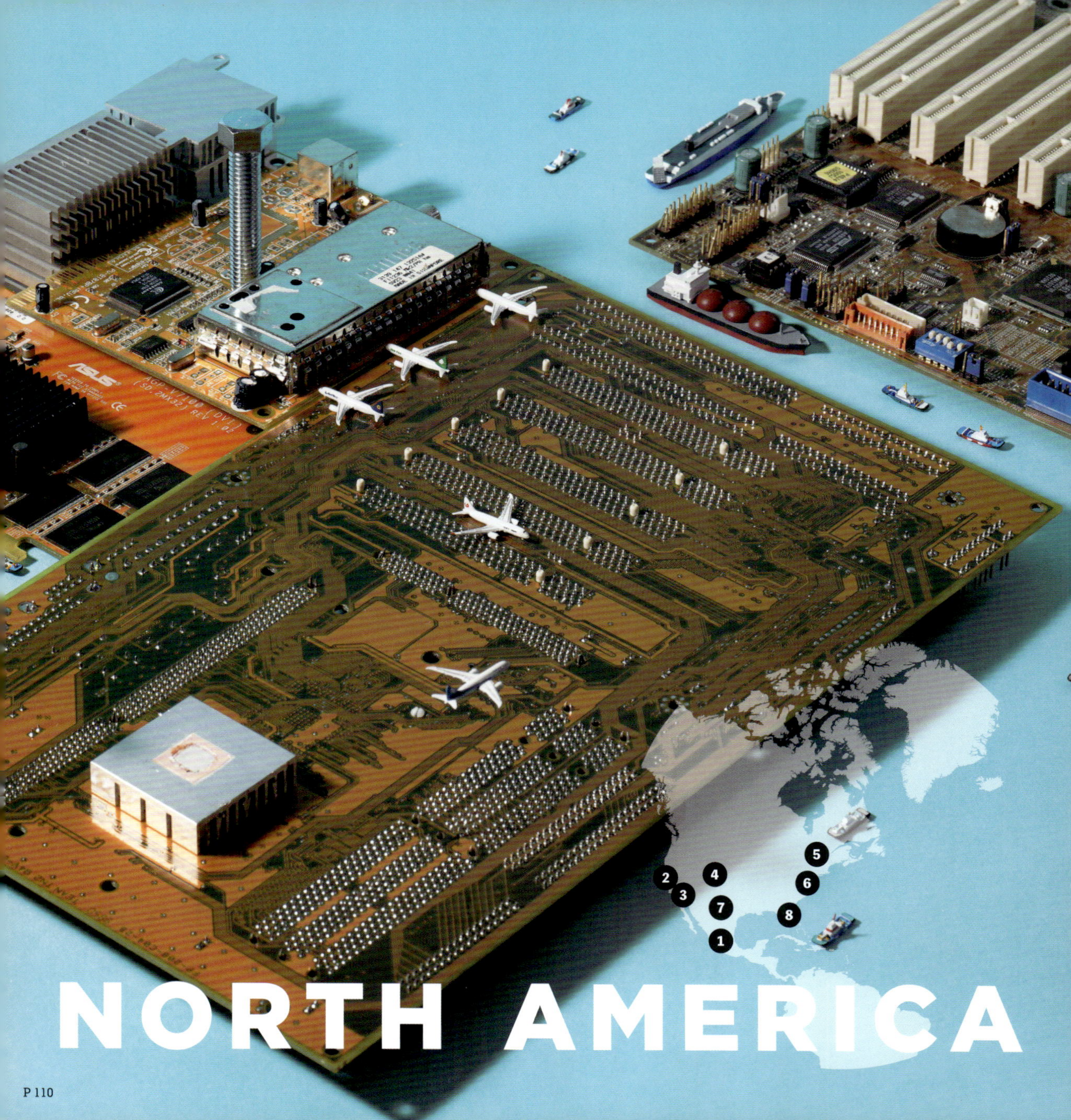

NORTH AMERICA

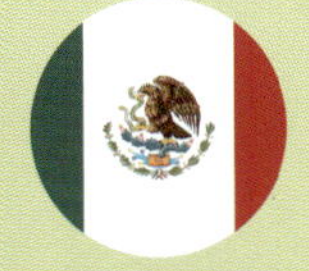

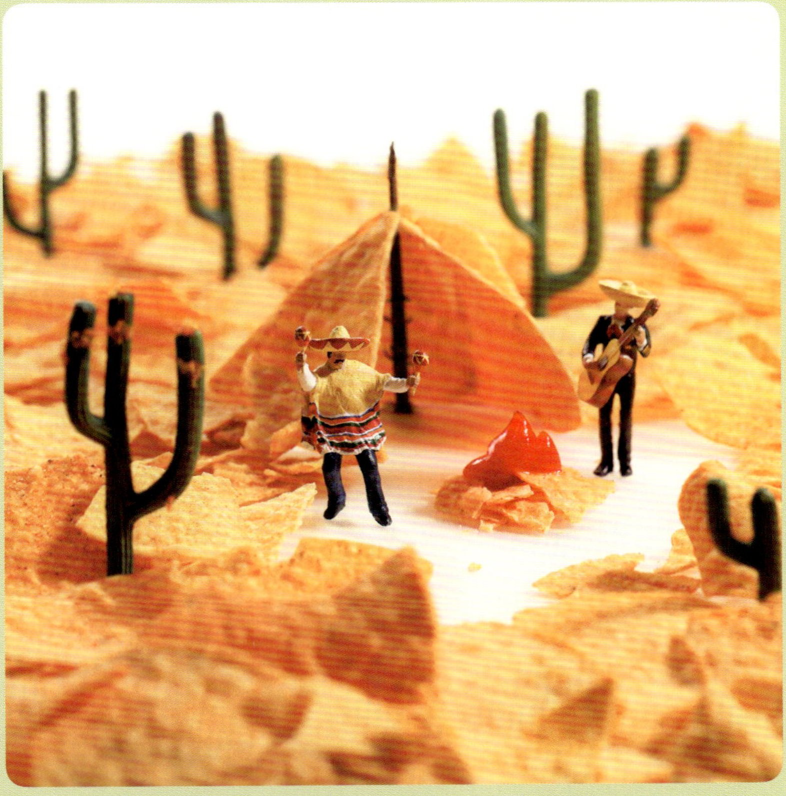

MEXICO

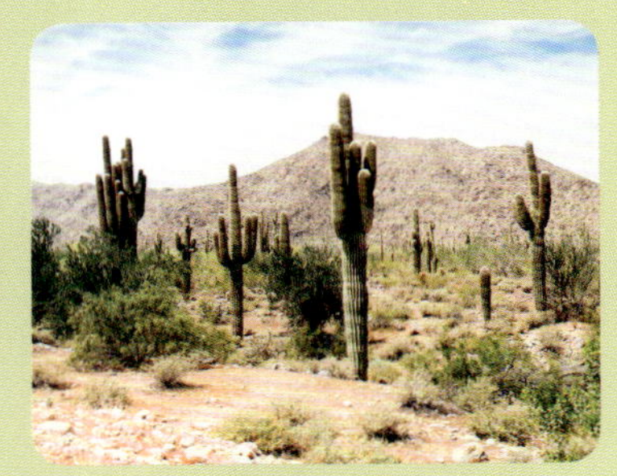
Mexican Camp

SONORAN DESERT

Imagine a desert that stretches from Northern Mexico into the United States. Then imagine an evening of dancing and music warmed by a hot salsa fire. What more could you ask for?

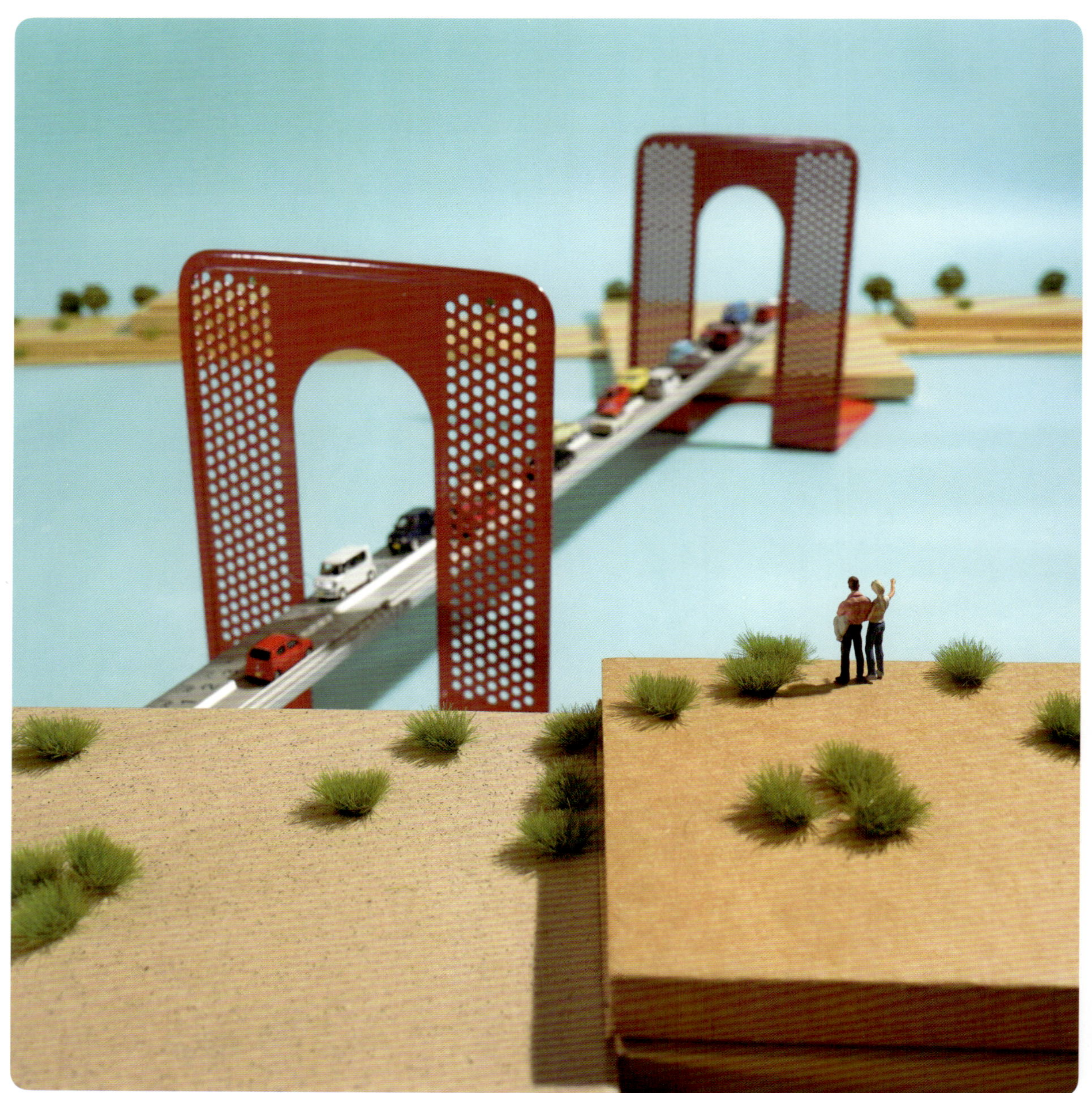

Golden Bookend Bridge

UNITED STATES OF AMERICA

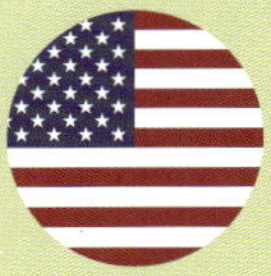

GOLDEN GATE BRIDGE

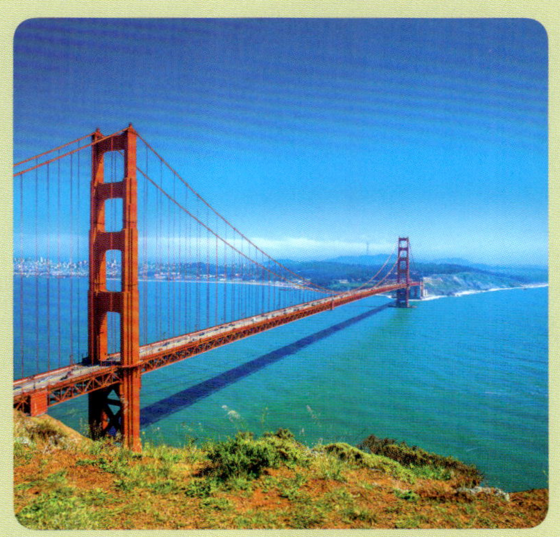

The Golden Gate Bridge was completed in 1935 and although it is only 2.7 kilometers long it was the longest and tallest suspension bridge in the world at the time. Now it is among the most famous – and photographed - bridges in the world. Given the height of the bridge, anyone who falls or jumps will most likely die upon impact with the ocean below. With this in mind, safety nets were strung just beneath the bridge when it was under construction and they saved the lives of 19 workers who became members of the "Half Way to Hell Club."

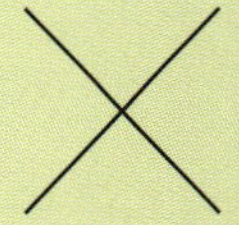

BOOKENDS

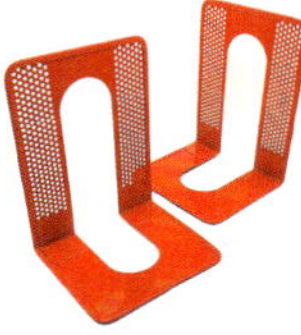

Bookends form the bridge's tall and elegant steel towers and books act as cantilever trusses. Back before the computer, the Golden Gate was designed using a slide rule, a variation on the metal ruler we find here.

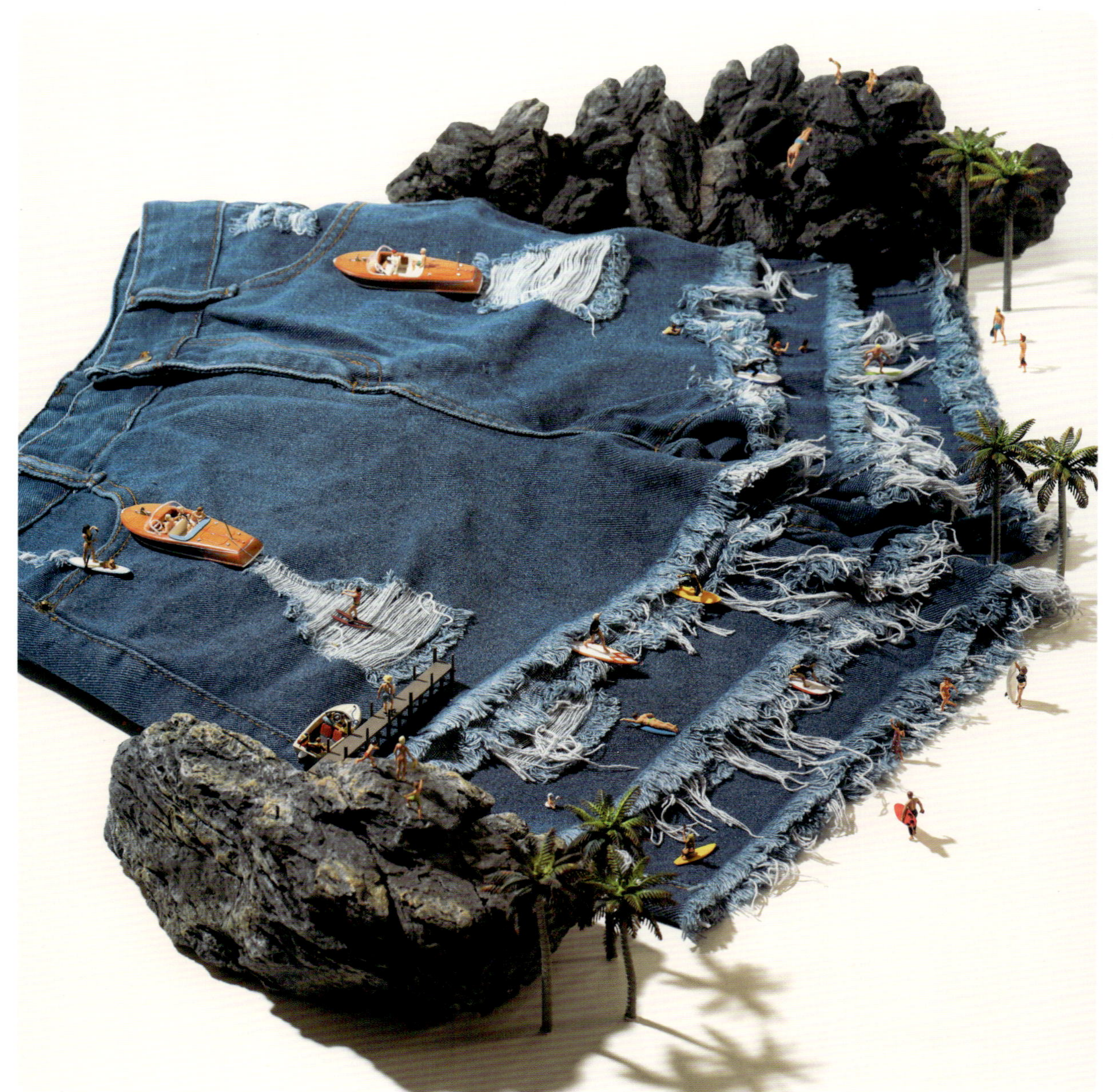

Waist Coast

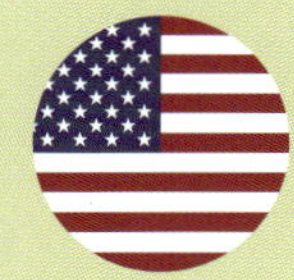

SANTA MONICA

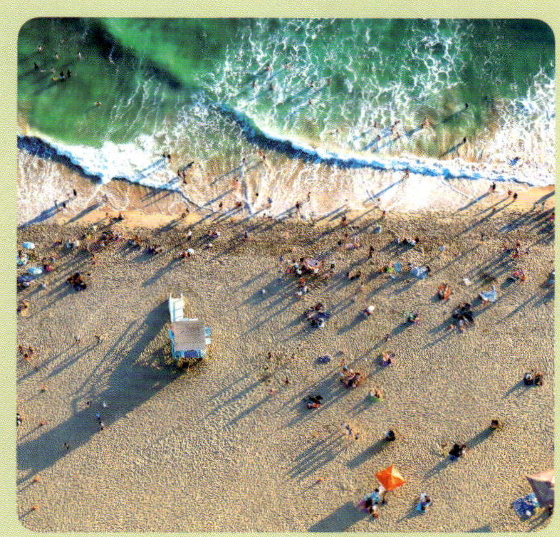

Among bikers there's probably no road more famous than Route 66 which extends from Chicago to Los Angeles and comes to an end at the Santa Monica Pier. The Pier, which opened in 1909 and appeared in Forrest Gump and about 1000 other movies, is a popular place to fish but also home to the first solar-powered Ferris wheel. If you want a little extra exercise, you can also walk or take a 15-minute bicycle ride from Santa Monica down to Venice Beach, another place where all manner of jeans and swim suits are on display.

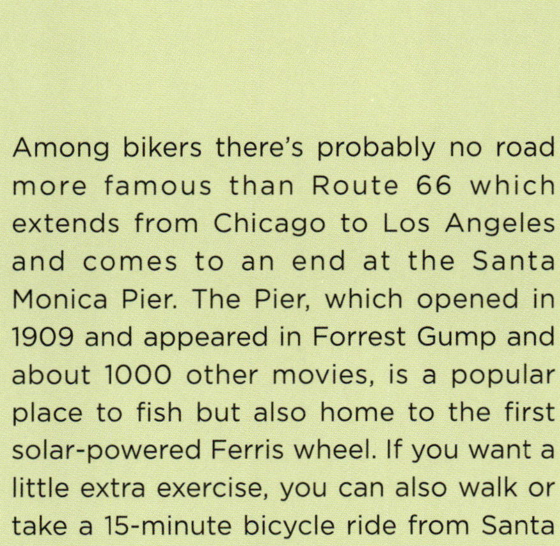

JEANS

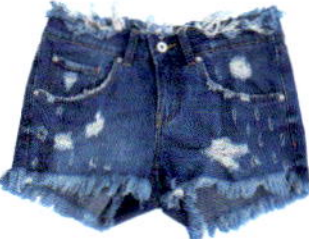

A popular west coast fashion, the loose and frayed threads in distressed jeans can also be seen as a rugged surf or the wake of a motorboat. This fashion finds its origins a continent and an ocean away, with British punk musicians in the 1970s.

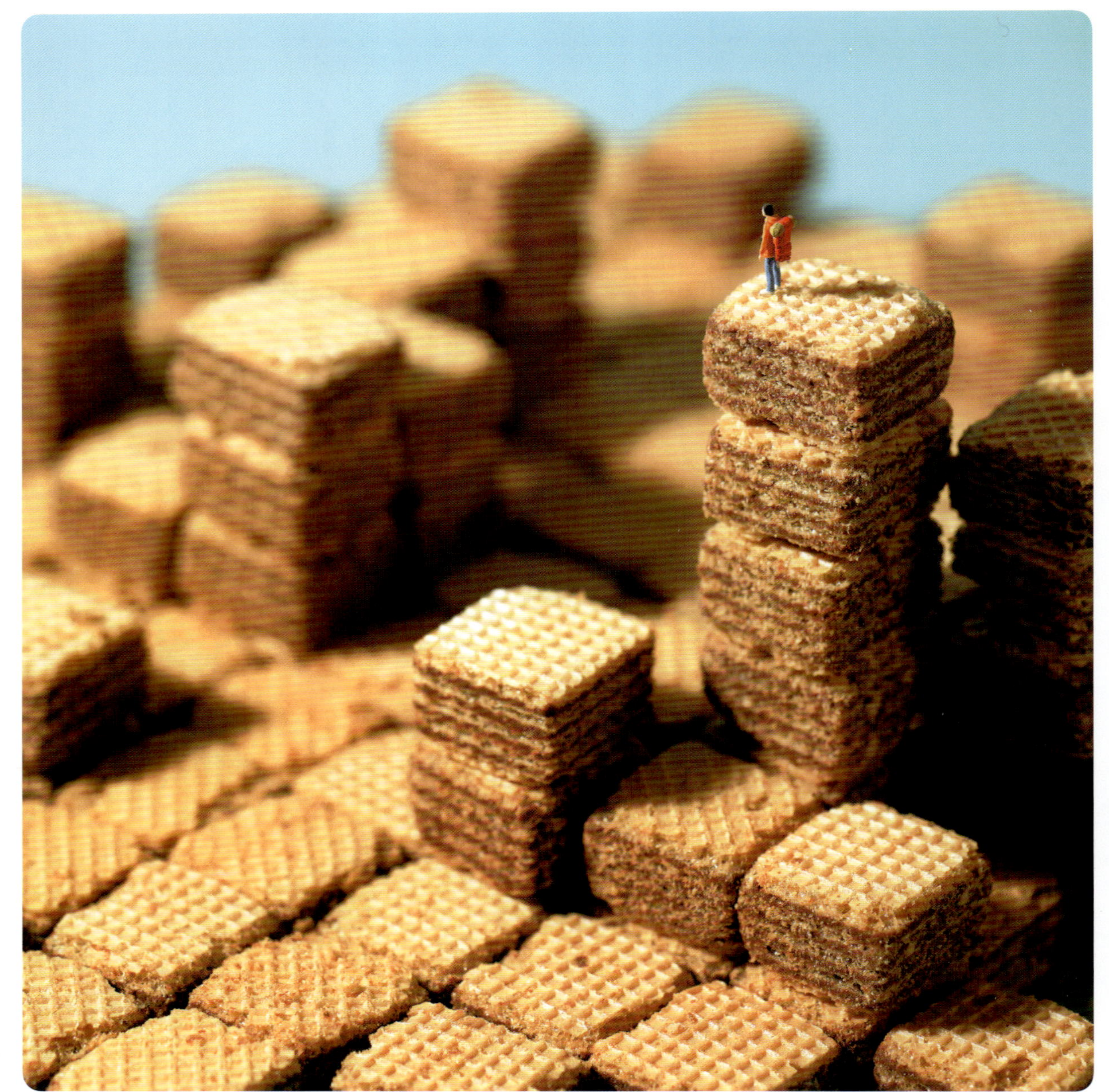

Wafer Canyon

UNITED STATES OF AMERICA

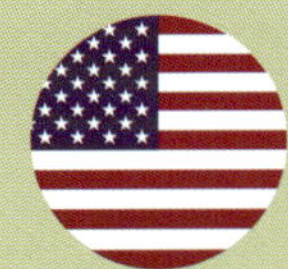

GRAND CANYON

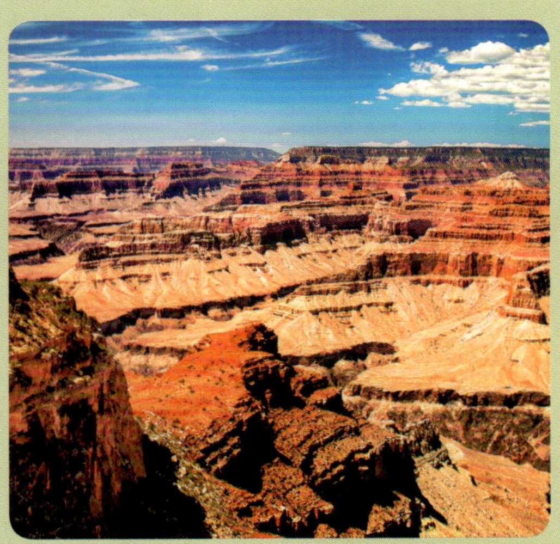

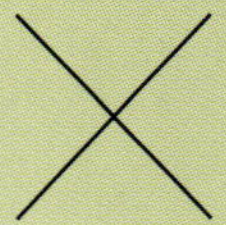

Viewed from a distance, the Grand Canyon exists on a scale that is quite difficult to fathom. Its scale surprises you even if you've seen it before and know what to expect. It would have been amazing to have "found" it. Up close, the canyon walls provide a rare showcase that will give you an idea what the world is made of, reminding you just how many layers of history and earth exist beneath your feet. It has taken 5 or 6 million years and a lot of water for the Colorado River to expose almost 2 billion years of geological history. That's a lot of wafers.

WAFERS

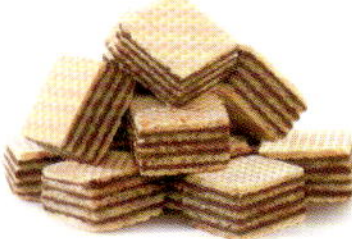

Wafers can be very light with layers of cream of various flavors sandwiched between thin waffle bisquits. In Japan they are sometimes made with soybean cream and are not to be confused with the also popular semiconductor silicon wafers.

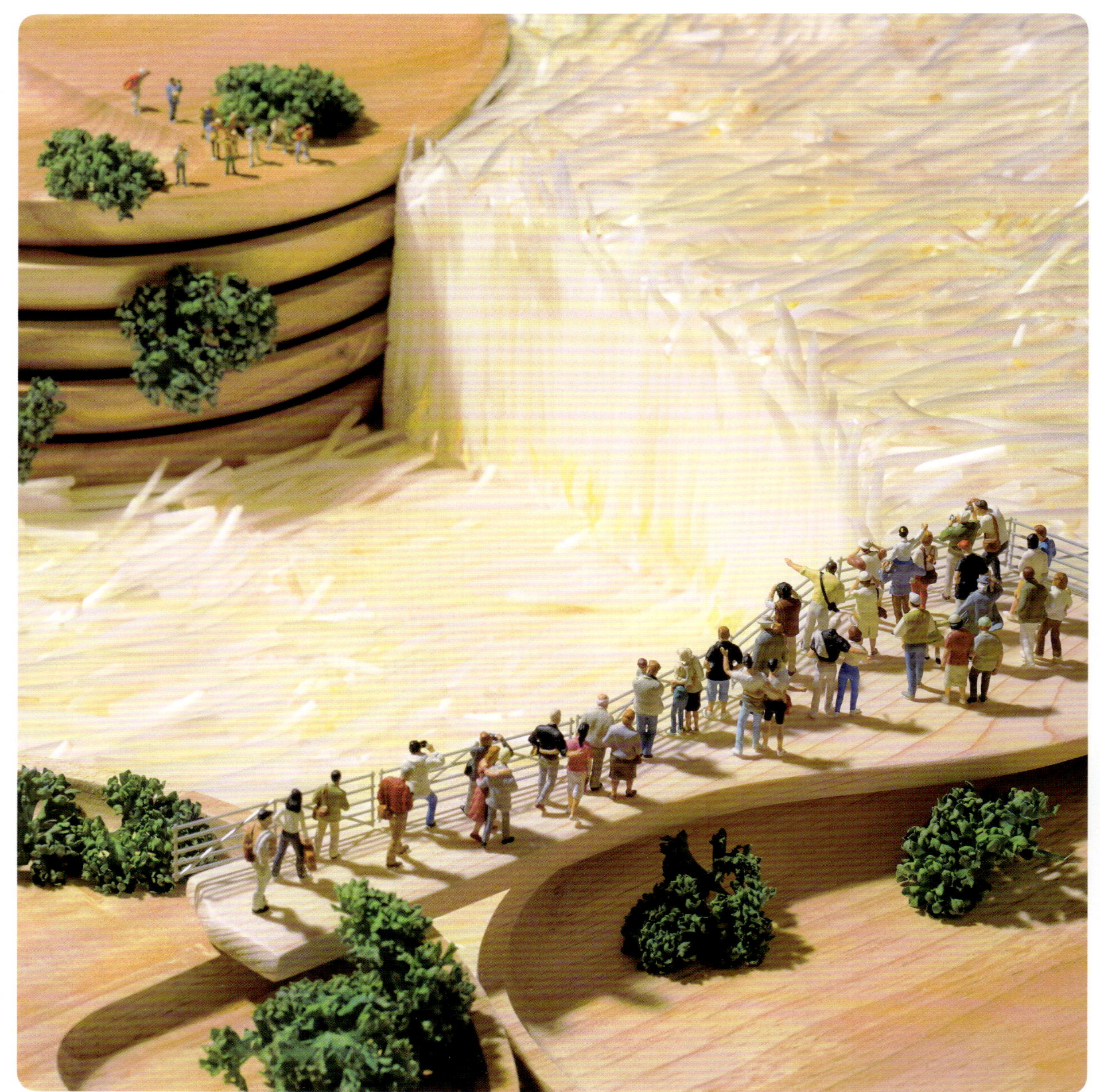

Niagara Sprouts

NIAGARA FALLS

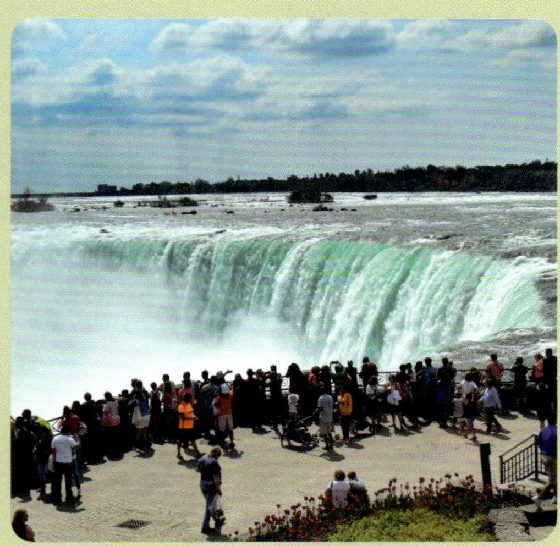

Tanaka-san has a thing for bean sprouts. Back in his student days he often sauteed them in sesame oil for a quick snack to stave off hunger. Standing alone they are weak, but in large numbers they are mighty powerful as in this rendering of Niagara Falls which makes use of stacks of wooden plates, a "shamoji" rice spoon, some parsley and a lot of bean sprouts carefully lined up to form the face of the falls. A friend who happened to stop by during this creative process was put to work as well and when it was all over Tanaka-san apparently ate the sprouts. I forgot to describe the falls!

BEAN SPROUTS

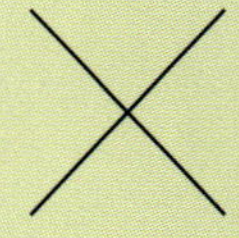

Bean sprouts are usually the young sprouts of mung or soy beans. In Japan, "moyashi" are usually mung bean sprouts. They are full of proteins and vitamins and are often used in stir fry and soups like ramen. They're also good in spring rolls.

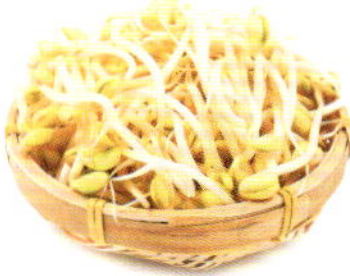

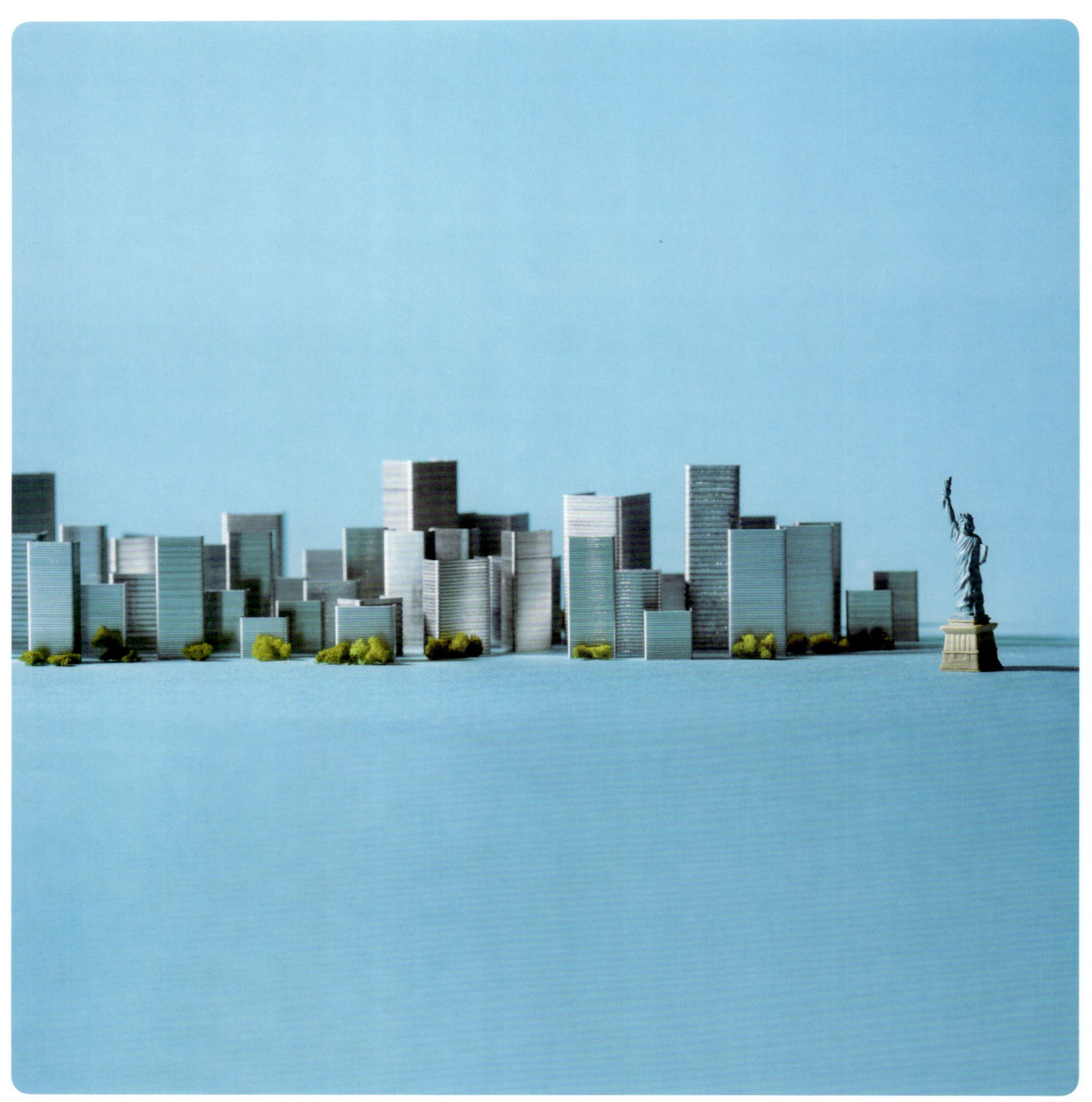

Staple Skyline

UNITED STATES OF AMERICA

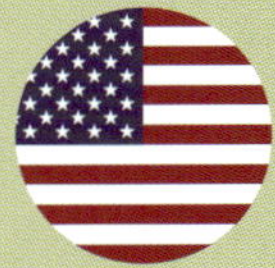

NEW YORK CITY

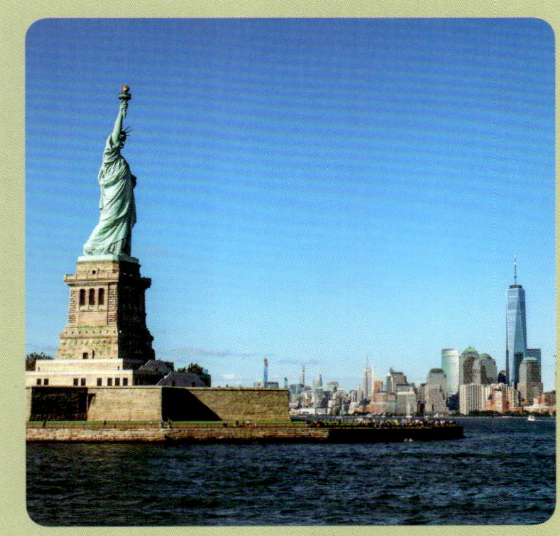

With more than 6,000 high-rise buildings and 274 skyscrapers that exceed 150 meters, New York City is a concrete and steel forest. Even the rights to air above the buildings are bought and sold. A person with a building that is shorter than zoning laws allow, can sell the unused space to an adjacent building owner who can then make their own building taller. In 1961, zoning regulations were drastically revised to keep structures from getting too tall and blocking out sunlight. The only city in the world with more tall buildings is Hong Kong, another city that rises up out of the sea.

STAPLES

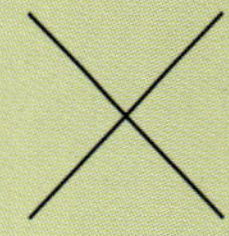

Staples have long competed with paper clips although now their livelihood is threatened by the universal clear file. Apparently the first stapler was designed for King Louis XV of France back in the 18th century to hold important documents together.

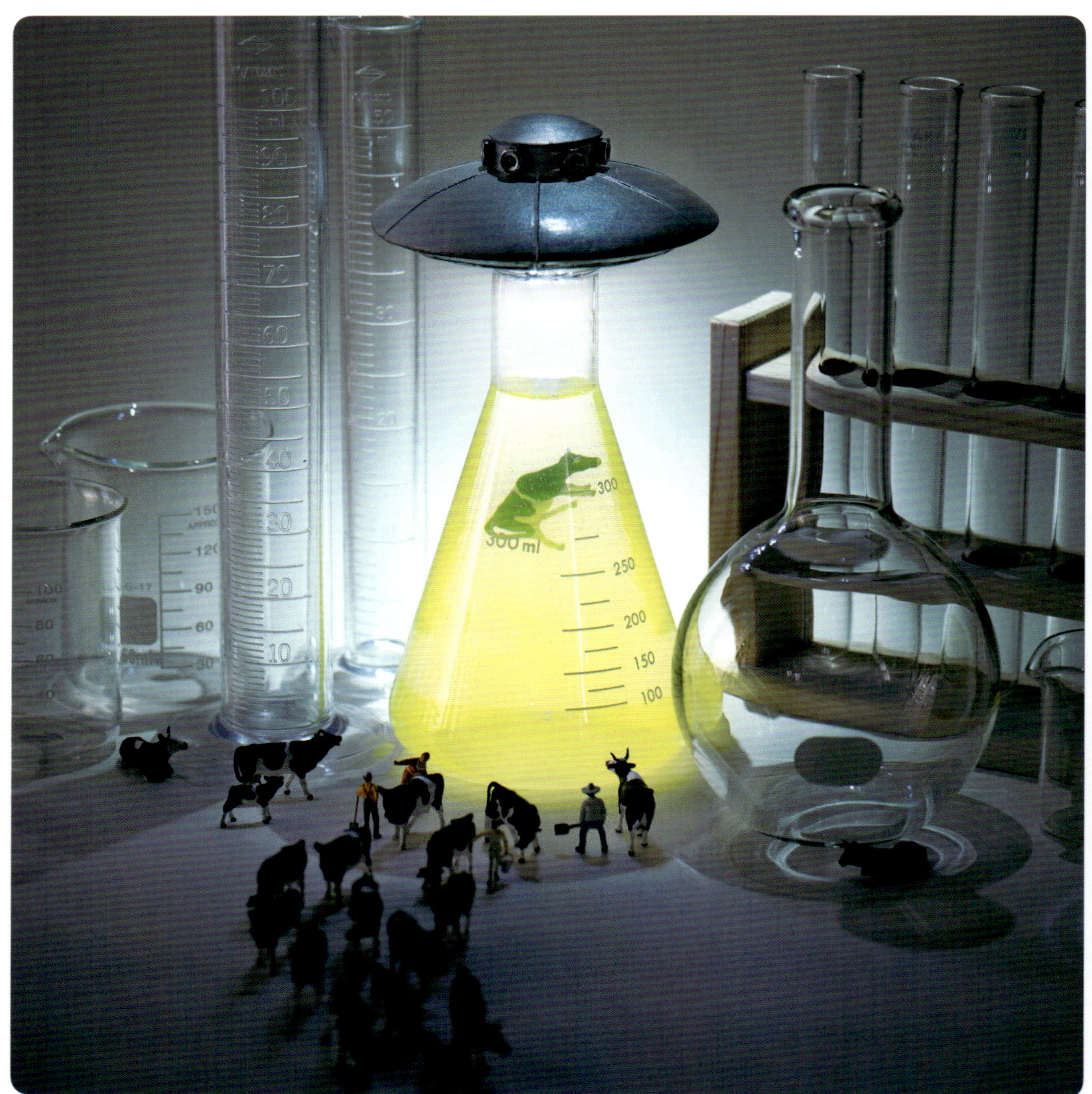

Beaming Her Up

UNITED STATES OF AMERICA

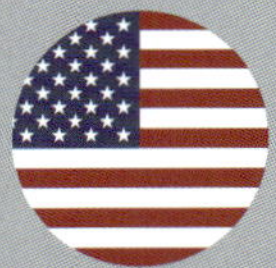

ROSWELL

Roswell, New Mexico enjoys a fair amount of tourism related to aerospace engineering and ufology. An incident in the vicinity in 1947 that supposedly involved the recovery of an alien aircraft and of alien bodies has made it a popular destination. Some people have come to believe that cows have been abducted and, in some cases, mutilated before being returned to the earth and that the government has covered up this and other revelations involving activities by aliens. A science fiction TV series called "Roswell" also aired for three seasons in the United States.

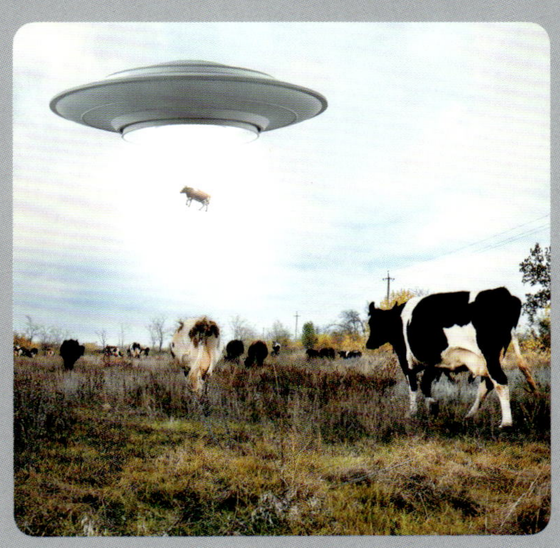

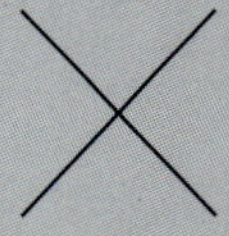

THE ERLENMEYER FLASK

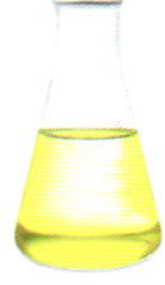

Here flasks are used to suggest that we are witnessing scientific experimentation. And it may not be a coincidence that "The Erlenmeyer Flask" is also the name of the first season finale of The X Files, a popular science fiction TV series.

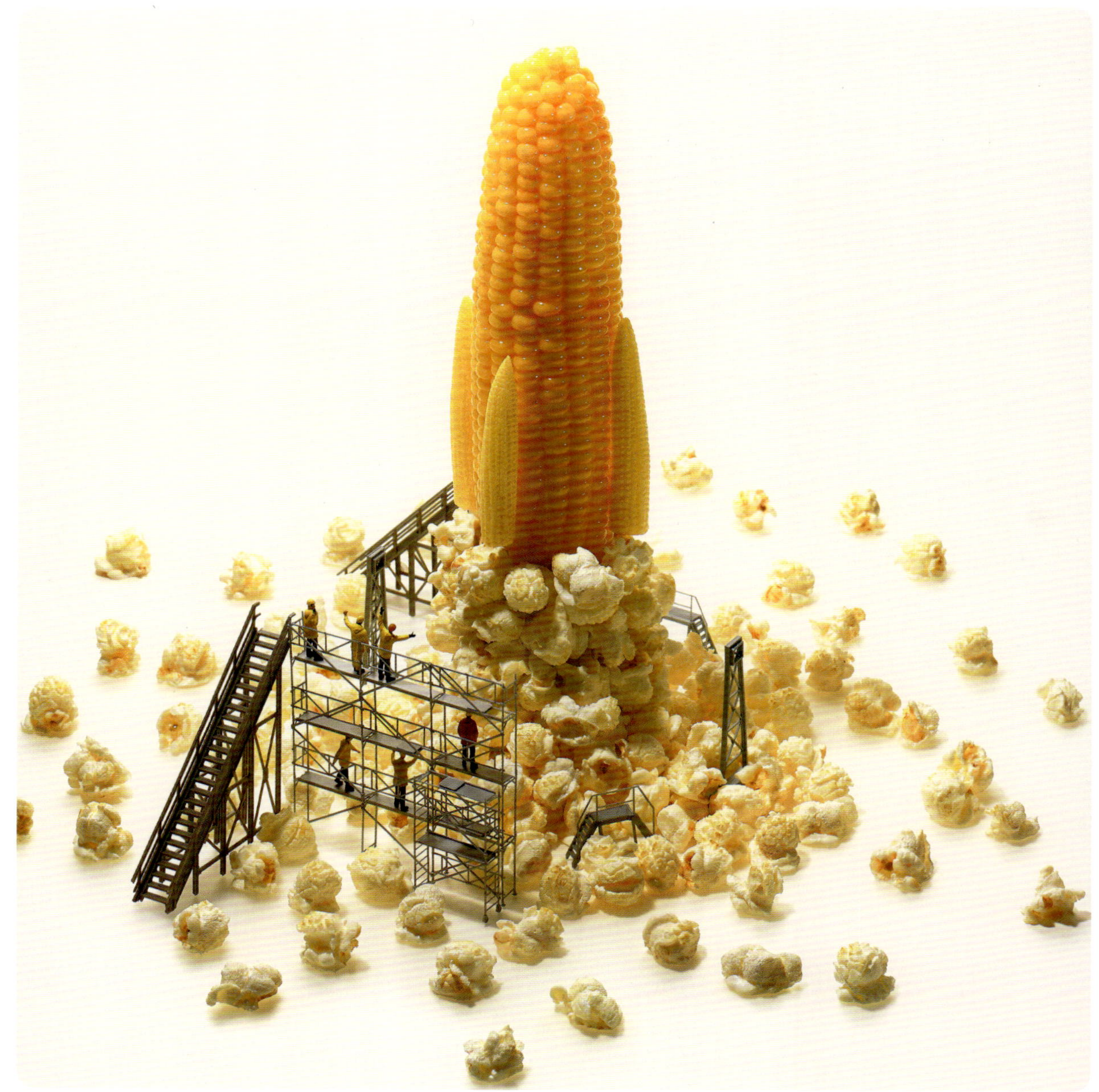

Corn Launch

UNITED STATES OF AMERICA

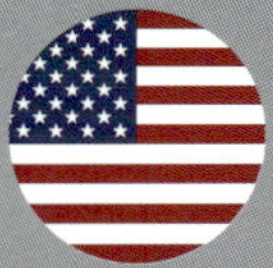

KENNEDY SPACE CENTER

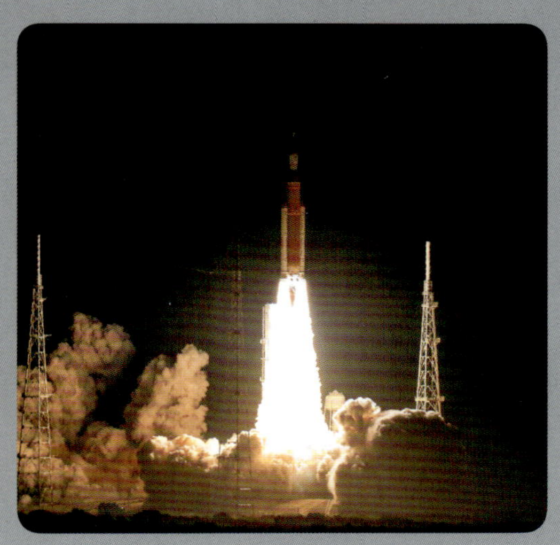

Baby corn straddles a full ear of corn, and the spaceship lifts off making use of the energy generated by popping popcorn. Here corn is being used, not just as food, but as a renewable energy source. Named after John F. Kennedy, the Kennedy Space Center is located on Merritt Island, off the east coast of Florida. It is 6 miles wide and 34 miles long, which is bigger than big US cities like Denver and New Orleans. NASA's manned and unmanned launches have all been managed by this center, handing off mission control to Houston after liftoff.

POPCORN

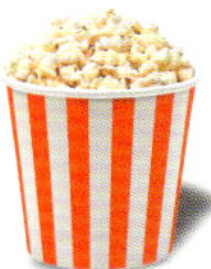

When popcorn was first sold in movie theaters in the U.S. back in the 1930s, theater owners made more money selling popcorn than theater tickets. During World War II, when sugar and candy were rationed, Americans ate a lot of popcorn instead.

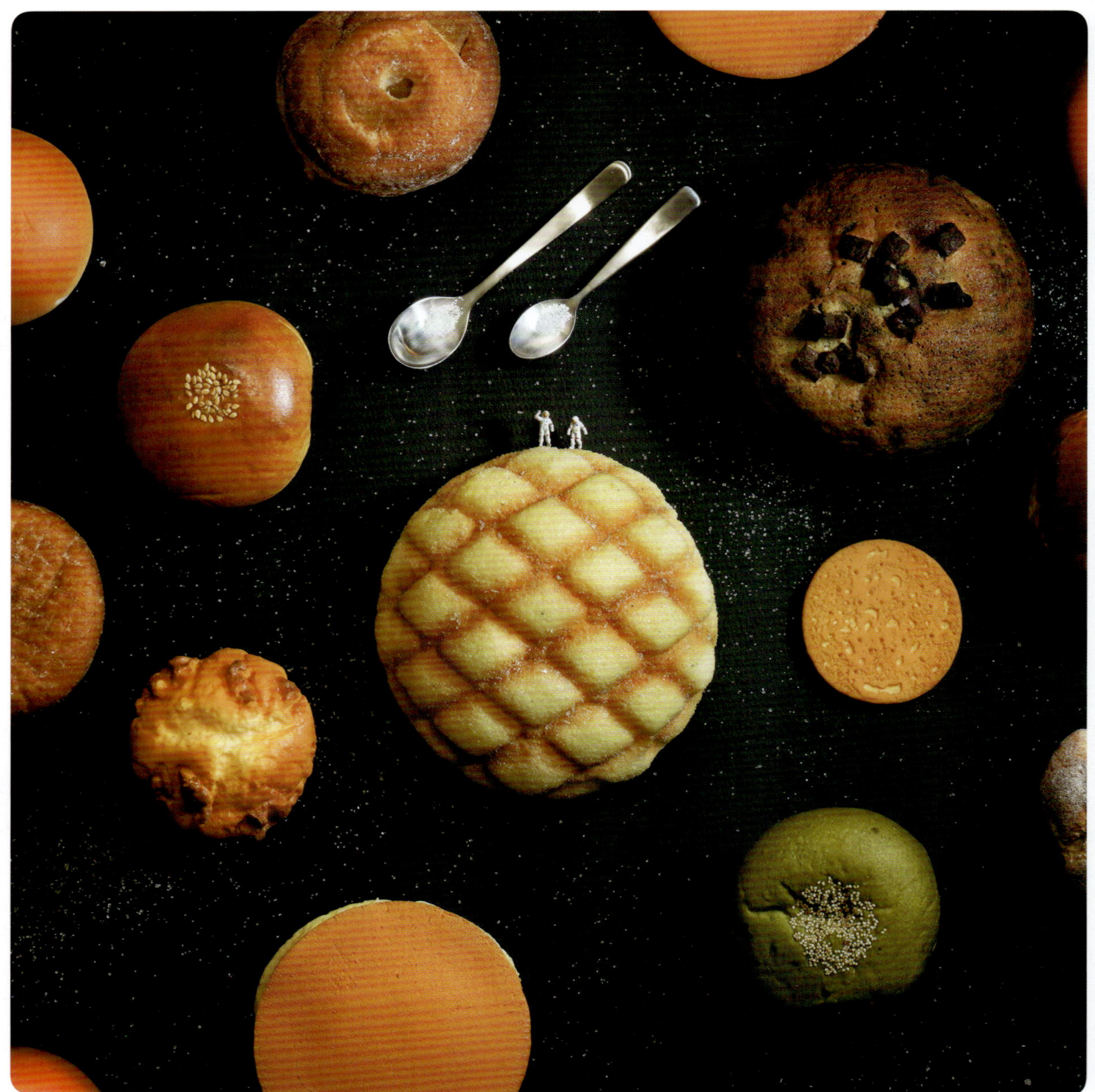

Big Bun Theory

SPACE

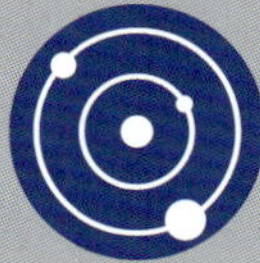

SPACE TRAVEL

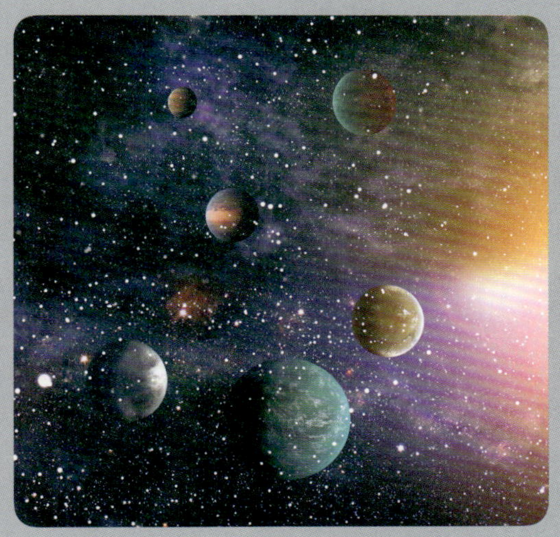

When Tanaka-san visited his neighborhood bakery he was struck by the number of round, planet-shaped options there were. He was inspired by baked goods of all colors and shapes and placed them on a black, iron plate the color of deep space. He added spoons as shooting stars and sugar for distant galaxies. Currently all of Japan's rockets and satellites are launched from Tanegashima and Uchinoura, two sites located in Kagoshima Prefecture where Tanaka-san lives. For this reason, space may feel a bit closer to home than it would if he lived elsewhere in Japan.

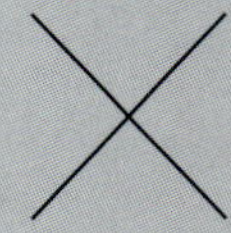

BREAD ROLLS

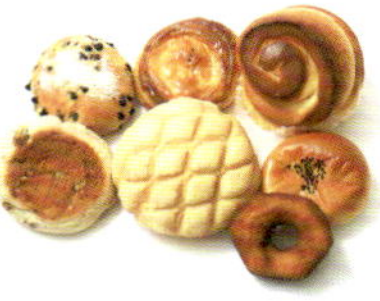

Melon bread – which looks but usually doesn't taste like a cantaloupe melon – is quite popular in Japan. Here it is joined by milk bread rolls, rolls with chocolate chips, adzuki bean-filled rolls and simple, old-fashioned donuts. Are you getting hungry?

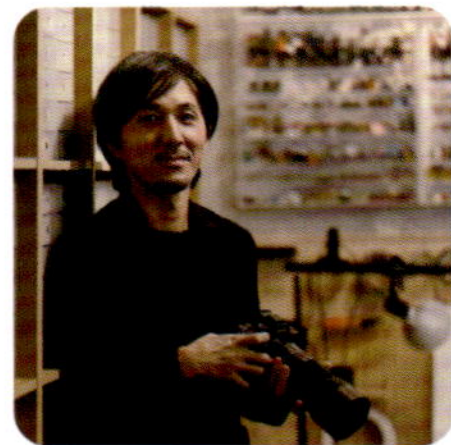

Miniatures Artist and Re-Imagining Author

TATSUYA TANAKA

Tatsuya Tanaka was born in 1981 in Kumamoto. In 2011, he launched his "MINIATURE LIFE" project that re-imagines familiar objects, situations and locations from a miniatures perspective. As of January, 2023, he has more than 3.6 million followers on Instagram. Tanaka's publications include MINIATURE TRIP IN JAPAN from Shogakukan, MINIATURE LIFE and MINIATURE LIFE 2 from Suiyosha and SMALL WONDERS from NIPPAN IPS CO., Ltd. Tanaka travels extensively for exhibits of his work, and continues to explore the world in his mind, in his studio at home.

TATSUYA TANAKA

MINIATURE TRIP AROUND THE WORLD

MINIATURE TRIP AROUND THE WORLD
By Tatsuya Tanaka

Published in 2025 by: NIPPAN IPS Co., Ltd.
4-3 Kanda-Surugadai, Chiyoda-ku,
Tokyo 101-0062, Japan

ISBN 978-4-86505-550-4

English Text by Jeffrey S. Irish
Original Design by Atsushi Miyasaka (snowfall)
Photography by Ami Kuroishi (pages 15, 23, 37, 127)
Production Assistance by MINIATURE LIFE Co.,Ltd. Mitsuhiro Kodama, Ikumi Watanabe, Saori Tanaka
Editing and Original Text by Koji Terada

Cooperation by KAIYODO Co.,Ltd., Shibainu Maru, DAISEY Co.,Ltd., Minaminihon Broadcasting Co.,Ltd., Ryohin Keikaku Co.,Ltd., MPX Gallery, Harbour City Estates Limited, Preiser, ©NASA, ©Shutterstock

Original Title:
MINIATURE TRIP AROUND THE WORLD by Tatsuya TANAKA
©2025 Tatsuya TANAKA
All rights reserved.
Original Japanese edition published by SHOGAKUKAN.
English translation rights arranged with SHOGAKUKAN.

Layout & Design of English Edition: Xiucui Ke
Printed in China